Arthur I. Blaustein is presently Associate Director of the National Economic Development Law Project at the University of California. He was a Director of Inter-Agency Coordination at the U.S. Office of Economic Opportunity and also a founder and board member of Capital Formation. Co-author of *Man Against Poverty: World War III*, his articles have appeared in *Harper's, Urban Review Quarterly*, and *New Generations*.

Geoffrey Faux was former Director of Economic Development for the U.S. Office of Economic Opportunity in Washington, D.C. An economist and author of *CDC's: New Hope for the Inner City*, he is presently co-director of the Center for Community Economic Development in Cambridge, Massachusetts.

THE STAR-SPANGLED HUSTLE

The Star-Spangled Hustle

ARTHUR I. BLAUSTEIN AND
GEOFFREY FAUX

Foreword by Ronald V. Dellums

Doubleday & Company, Inc.

1972 | GARDEN CITY, NEW YORK

The authors wish to acknowledge the personal support of the staffs of the National Economic Development Law Project in Berkeley, California, and the Center for Community Economic Development in Cambridge, Massachusetts, and in particular David Madway and Stewart Perry. We are also thankful to Peter Sussman for his help in editing parts of the manuscript and for his thoughtful suggestions.

Grateful acknowledgment is made for permission to use extracts from the following:

"The Political Legacy of Reconstruction" by C. Vann Woodward which first appeared in the *Journal of Negro Education*, Vol. XXVI, Winter 1957, pages 231–40.

"The Southern Roots of Urban Crisis" by Roger Beardwood which first appeared in *Fortune* magazine, August 1968. Copyright © 1968 by *Fortune*, reprinted courtesy of *Fortune*.

Article by Whitney Young, Jr., from the New York *Times* of March 14, 1971. © 1971 by The New York Times Company. Reprinted by permission.

CONTENTS

FOREWORD

I often feel that books attempting total analysis of the politics of America have been useless efforts—except as academic exercises or as training tools for student political scientists. For the masses, such books have been meaningless because they do not force readers to identify the importance of understanding and learning from the analyses. And since readers fail to relate to the analyses, these books remain totally alienated from their actual needs and lives.

The Star-Spangled Hustle is different, not only because it effectively puts recent events into a general framework, but also because it specifically addresses itself to and for the victims within our society.

To me, this thrust is crucial. We must move past the rhetoric, beyond the dangers of being oversimplistic about what is going on and face the realities of what politics in today's America is all about. Until that kind of understanding is achieved, it is impossible to develop any strategies at all. Only when it is possible to show the absurdities and exploitations that have become the normal response of the Nixon Administration to the rising cries of desperation can something be done.

This Administration has been effective only at perpetuating and extending the myths that divide people; myths that pit black against white against brown against poor against blue-collar workers against women against young against old against environmentalists and so on.

When the myths are exposed, people are forced to deal with the reality that other people are like themselves in many ways and that they all must deal with basic human problems. And while people find that their needs may be seen in different ways, commonalities are enough to bridge the various gaps.

Today you do not have to be black to be a nigger in America. The people who are struggling to bring about real human change in this country suddenly have found themselves all niggers.

You do not have to be black to live in misery. You can be any color. You can have long hair. You can oppose the war. You can say that we ought to put corporate presidents in jail for polluting the air and water.

Ask the students on the campus of Jackson State. Ask at Kent State. Ask the young people who get harassed simply because of their hair, the people who march in peace demonstrations, the women who ask for freedom and equality for themselves and other people. Ask Lieutenant Calley.

The key is self-interest, and the reality is that self-interests are tangential more than they are competing. When a person loses his own sense of self-interest, he also loses his hope and motivation—and it is impossible to mobilize people out of pessimism and guilt. This the Nixon Administration understands and exploits.

For example, Richard Nixon has consistently appealed to the hard-hats for support, yet his appeal was based on issues such as "the flag" and "patriotism," not on the real issues at hand in which they had a stake. The whole time Nixon was appealing to them for support, the hard-hats were paying the price for his economic policies. Employment figures indicated that they were the ones losing jobs. One of their true self-interests, keeping themselves financially secure through their jobs, was diverted to Nixon's idea of what their self-interest should be, and they were conned into thinking they should be supporting the war in Vietnam.

Millions of people in America today live desperate lives controlled by too few leading affluent ones. When groups such as the hard-hats raise questions concerning the quality of their lives, they are given only myths as answers. When the hard-hat says, "I am overworked, underpaid, and overtaxed," and yells for help, the Administration answers with "Black Panthers, Angela Davis, United Farm Workers, radical women's liberation, student revolutionaries, campus unrest, welfare recipients, law and order."

And, tragically, it works. Suddenly the hard-hats perceive the symbols in a direct causal relationship. "Oh, so *those* are the people that make me overworked, underpaid, and overtaxed. *They're* the ones who stand in the way of improving the quality of my life."

This Administration seems to operate on the thesis that when conflict arises between government and the people, it is the people who have to change. Yet the democratic process was meant to function in exactly the opposite way: to be responsive to the *people*.

People tend to be concerned with the issues that affect them daily—issues they see as real. The politics practiced by the Nixon Administration keeps groups separated. Administration rhetoric says that the economics of black people are dealt with in one specific way, those of Mexican-American people in another, and those of the working class in yet another way. But different people cannot be dealt with in different ways on a scale as large as our economic system, which addresses itself to every person in this country. That system cannot be altered to deal with the problems of blacks differently from those of poor whites, or those of any other oppressed group.

Before coming into the Presidency, Nixon promised minority entrepreneurs a "piece of the action" in the economic system. Some programs were started to ensure this would take place. Yet this turned out to be another of the myths—for even if blacks fought for the lion's share of the programs' action as the larger minority, and got all the benefits of the Administration's programs, it would still serve less than 10 percent of the total needs of black people alone. What it amounts to is fighting over crumbs.

The Administration portions out money so that the resources devoted to a given program meet only 3 to 5 percent of the total needs of the program. We must now face the key question of the control and distribution of wealth in America and not just pass the expedient legislation that defines what small piece of the action people can have.

It makes no sense for blacks and chicanos and poor whites to fight over crumbs. That is not the issue. The issue is redefining the distribution of wealth on a broader scale. The system—and certainly not the Administration alone—has forced minorities and the poor to fight among themselves. And as long as there is fighting over minute shares, the broader perspective can never be seen —that all the resources do not get allocated to enhance the quality of life of all the people.

That is what our politics must be all about.

For me, the critical issues are:

How do we explode the myths, the fear symbols?

How do we find a way to communicate with the silent majority in such a way that they understand they are being manipulated, duped, and programmed?

How do we get through to them that their issues are very real, that their pain is real—but that it is no different from that of other groups?

How do we communicate to them that the people pointed to by the Administration as scapegoats have absolutely no control over their problems?

The Star-Spangled Hustle goes a long way to help us find those answers.

Ronald V. Dellums
U. S. Congress
June 1972

To Mary and Sharon

THE STAR-SPANGLED HUSTLE

1 | INTRODUCTION

This is a political book. It is about American leadership, political and corporate—those who have the power and the capacity to influence decisions relating to the inequities of distribution of wealth in the United States. We agree with Harold D. Lasswell's definition of politics as "the study of who gets what, when, and how."[1] And we try to raise questions about the desire and the will of the American political/economic establishment—to "open" that system so that it can provide a sufficient standard of living for the poor and the dispossessed. Although our central focus is on recent attempts by government and the private sector to bring minority groups into the "economic mainstream" of American life, it is important, initially, to provide some frame of reference.

The United States today is, in many ways, like one large hemophiliac waiting for a big scratch. Politicians and the media (as no doubt will the Nixon Administration during the election campaign) have made much of the fact that recently there have been no serious civil disorders and the campuses have remained relatively quiet. Kingman Brewster, the president of Yale, called it an "eerie tranquillity." However, it would be a grave miscalculation on the part of the Establishment to assume that the "natives are happy" or "the kids have given up." The mood is more one of frustration and hopelessness, of anxiety and despair; minority group leaders and student activists sense that for the time being, at least, the *system* is in control. But circumstances could change, overnight. Thus, the Establishment need not pat themselves on the back and behave like the problems which threaten us as a nation have been resolved. It is a delusion and all the corporate billions that go into advertising, marketing, and public relations and all the incantations and dutiful prayers of our President (or the Reverend Billy Graham) cannot make these problems go away. As Philip Slater has pointed out, their efforts are a desperate attempt to stop change, "—to convert the deep social unrest of the day into the blank torpor of suburban life—to translate Watts into *Julia,* Berkeley and Columbia into *Dobie Gillis,* Chicago into *Mayberry,* and Vietnam into *McHale's Navy.*"

A close analysis of President Nixon's administrative decisions and legislative requests reveal him to be the ultimate practitioner of political expedience and shows that even the appearance of his concern is misleading. His public pronouncements on every major issue, e.g. minority entrepreneurship, unemployment, hunger, school busing, welfare reform, tax reform, the Clement F. Haynsworth, Jr., and G. Harrold Carswell nominations to the Supreme Court, the drug problem, revenue sharing, the Lieutenant William L. Calley, Jr., case, Mylai, the plight of POW's, Vietnamization, the India-Pakistani war, etc. . . . are geared for the glamour of p.r. effect and are devoid of serious content. They do not even hint at a general understanding of our critical social problems nor do they offer any programs that will bring us closer to their solution. Nixon's sensitivity to human needs is quite vacuous. Instead he has chosen to lend his Presidency to the *consolidation of corporate power.* This policy was articulated by his chief political strategist Attorney General John N. Mitchell in a speech delivered on June 6, 1969. After pointing out that in 1948 the nation's two hundred largest industrial firms controlled 48 percent of the manufacturing assets he added, "Today these firms control 58 percent while the top five hundred firms controls 75 percent of the assets." And Mitchell left no doubt in the minds of his listeners that the policies of the Nixon Administration would be to accelerate this unprecedented and alarming trend, at the taxpayers' expense.

Since the day of the inauguration, Executive authority flowing from the White House to Federal departments, regulatory agencies, and the courts has been exerted and manipulated in every possible way, to protect and increase (or bail out) private-sector control and profits. The luckless leaders of the industrial tin-cup brigade (Lockheed, Penn Central, ITT, Boeing, et al.) are far more important to our President than minority groups, wage earners, or six million children suffering from malnutrition. The former make campaign contributions while the latter do not even vote! Nixon is a practical man and a shrewd politician. He borrows many of his ideas from the Democrats (family assistance, revenue-sharing, a full-employment budget) whenever necessary and discards them as quickly as suits his purpose. What is most important is that he wants to be re-elected and he knows which side his bread is buttered on; big money comes from the piggy banks of industrial leaders and Wall Street wheeler-dealers and the check-off dollars of working people go to the Democratic Party.

Joseph Pechman, the President of the American Finance Association, recently pointed out the simple arithmetic of income disparity. He divides the country into five quintiles, each fifth having the same number of families. Thus, the American income pie is divided into five portions. They are in order, from lowest to highest:

(1)	Below $3,000	3.2%
(2)	$3,000–$6,000	10.5%
(3)	$6,000–$8,600	17%
(4)	$8,600–$12,000	24%
(5)	above 12,000	46%

The top 20 percent therefore get *15 times* as much as the bottom 20 percent. It was also reported that the top 1 percent (those who receive $33,000 or more) get the healthiest slice, 6.8 percent of the total pie. In short, those 1 percent at the top of the income pyramid receive more than twice the total income of *all* those poor families in the lower 20 percent.

The graduated income tax was supposed to remedy these inequities. It obviously has not and this Administration has studiously devoted itself to guaranteeing those disparities by protecting old loopholes and drilling new ones in the tax structure, thereby insuring the income of the rich, while at the same time proposing every imaginable gimmick to give added tax bonanzas to corporations. Congressman Henry S. Reuss of Wisconsin estimates that at least 112 Americans earning $200,000 to $1 million paid no taxes at all in 1970. Meanwhile, the poor and middle-class working people carry the heaviest load by paying local sales taxes, social security, and other forms of regressive taxes.* In a recent study, "Wages, Prices and Profits" (Conference on Economic Progress), Dr. Leon H. Keyserling points out that the poorest people pay 50 percent of their income in taxes while those who earn $50,000 or over, pay less of a percentage (45 percent). (Ronald Reagan—the plastic cowboy-Governor—for example, has not paid state income tax at all but leads posses to round up welfare "chiselers" who are, ironically enough, taxpayers.) At times, it is difficult to tell the difference between the eleven o'clock news and the late night movie.

In late January of 1972 Senator William Proxmire held hearings on tax reform. At that time some of the best tax experts in the country demonstrated to the satisfaction of the Chairman of the Joint Economic Committee that there was at least $60–70 billion in Government subsidies going to the fiscal elite-rich individuals and large corporations—as a result of loopholes in the tax structure. The sum and substance of the testimony laid bare the intricacies of "welfare capitalism" for the rich. And these are the very same people who vociferously mouth the platitudes of self-reliance. Welfare applicants such as Mrs. Mary Smith or Jack Jones, they argue, should be forced to work lest they become too dependent and their initiative becomes dampened. Their righteous indignation is only overshadowed by their gross hypocrisy . . .

As Philip M. Stern, author of *The Great Treasury Raid,* said of the tax incentive rebates in his testimony before the Senate Committee, "Welfare payments averaging some $720,000 a year will go to the nation's wealthiest families. For the poorest families

---

* Nixon's latest bit of political magic is to substitute a "value-added" tax (VAT) for the property tax in order to subsidize education. The realities behind this intoxicating scheme are less than euphoric. In more simple terms it represents a new national sales tax which is designed to soak the poor and wage earners.

(under $3000) the welfare allowance will average $16 a year, or roughly 30 cents a week. The program, enacted by Congress in a series of laws over a period of years, would give America's most affluent families added weekly take-home pay of about $14,000. Total cost of the program—the most expensive welfare program ever voted—comes to $77.4 billion a year." A curious phenomena, indeed!

At the very same time the Nixon Administration was pushing for bargain-counter tax changes that were geared to make a bigger sieve of the structure, rather than reform the inequities. The candidate of mid-America proposed to transfer more taxes away *from* corporations *to* individuals—not to rich ones but to gouge *the "silent majority,"* a betrayal of his own constituency. This was a deliberate policy decision and the result of recommendations set out by the President's "Task Force of Business Taxation." The committee's back-stage deliberations were chaired by one John H. Alexander, who is a tax man from the Nixon-Mitchell New York law firm. At the risk of seeming repetitious it should be reiterated that the *paramount concern* of this Administration has been to use its political muscle in order to secure windfalls and advantages for the economically powerful (rich individuals and large corporations) at the expense of the poor and the *middle class*.

This policy is further underlined by the facts that the unemployment rate for adult men rose from 2.1 percent in 1969 to 4.4 percent in 1971; that the rate of long-term unemployment has tripled; that unemployment among nonwhites rose to 10 percent in 1971; that women and young people coming into the job market cannot find a decent job; that a "6 by 6" policy continues unabated (6 percent unemployment, 6 percent inflation) and that the figures for hard-core minority poor have become so frightening that the Administration is no longer giving out figures. All of this is happening at a time when the Administration has a $38.8 million deficit this year (1972) and is projecting a $26 million for next year (1973). Without the benefit of tea leaves we will bet our bottom dollar that the President is once again misleading the American people and that the deficit will be closer to twice that figure as a result of loss of revenue from wealthy individuals and corporations, because of the Administration's "swiss cheese" tax policies. Nixon's total three-year deficit is at present nearly $90 billion. Not bad for a recent convert to Keynes!

As Monroe W. Karmin observed in the *Wall Street Journal:* "President Nixon's 'new American revolution' is not only rakish new garb for his pin-striped administration but also a political blueprint for re-election in 1972." A close look at his twin revolutionary themes would lead one to think that "executive reorganization" and "revenue-sharing" will be to the "new American revolution" what the Cambodia and Laos invasions were to ending our involvement in Southeast Asia. This is an Administration that is first and foremost committed to nothing more than perpetuating the status quo with extra bonuses, wherever possible. And it is doing so at an enormous cost to both the public sector and social services while at the same time placing an inordinate and unnecessary burden on the vast majority of the American people.

It is no great secret that in the first year of the Nixon Administration, 70 percent of our Federal budget was used to pay for present and past wars and to support the military and its contractors. More money annually was spent by the Pentagon than went into housing, education, health, poverty programs, old-age assistance, and manpower training on the *Federal, state,* and *local* levels combined. Astounding but true. And the total Federal commitment to community economic development nationally was the same as the cost of *one* Cheyenne helicopter, that Lockheed couldn't even deliver in working order ($7 million). Such is the state of national priorities of the American political economy.

C. Wright Mills identifies three important elites in our country —the political leaders, corporation executives, and the military— and he suggests that the three groups form a power elite which influences the most important decisions affecting the American people. Implicit in this view is that the enormous size of economic, political, and military organizations has removed them from review or control by the ordinary citizen—including, at times, the United States Congress. The power that these three organizations have amassed is a result of concentration of wealth;[2] party affiliations (national, state, and local); and huge budgets, veterans groups, and a substantial number of industrial defense contractors.[3]

The Dr. Strangelove aspect of militarism will not be dealt with in this book. However, the connection between the military and corporate America and its impact on our national political economy are ever present and cannot be totally ignored. For example, on January 6, 1971, a survey compiled for Congress disclosed that in the previous three fiscal years 993 high-ranking military officials and 108 high-level Pentagon civilian employees moved into top executive positions with key defense contractors. During the same period 232 former industry executives accepted jobs with the Department of Defense. The system for reporting these "exchanges" was set up at the insistence of Senator William Proxmire after a spot check in early 1969 revealed that 2,122 former high military officials were employed by defense contractors. The leading employers were Lockheed, Boeing, McDonnell Douglas Corporation, General Dynamics, and North American Rockwell. President Eisenhower certainly was correct in his farewell address when he warned the nation about the perils and incestuousness of the military-industrial complex.†

Thirty years of arsenal diplomacy has kept us on war footing. And, if this Administration with its military-defense complex has its way there will be no end in sight for the American people.

† But the fears of Ike certainly never rubbed off on his Vice President. For, on January 5, 1972, Nixon ordered the Federal Government to proceed "at once" to develop another multibillion dollar boondoggle for the aerospace industry. Most Americans cannot get back and forth between their jobs and homes without an incredible hassle. Yet, the President thinks the country needs a space ship to shuttle easily from earth into earth orbit and back again. The White House said that this program, projected over a six-year period, would cost the American taxpayers $5,500,000,000. James Fletcher, Director of NASA, said that the prime contractors for the program had not yet been chosen but that leading candidates would be Lockheed, Boeing, General Dynamics, North American Rockwell, and McDonnell Douglas. There wasn't even a facsimile disclaimer. The only mystery is whether or not the Hughes Tool Company will become a subcontractor. If it seemed that the Army, the Air Force, and their corporate contractors were getting a disproportionate share of the action, the President in his 1972 State of the Union Address redressed this lopsidedness. Nixon, therefore, ordered the Defense Department to speed development of a $15 billion submarine system—which the President said would serve as a key element in the nation's nuclear deterrent from the 1980s into the twenty-first century. The President told Congress that he would ask for $900 million immediately

What is of greater significance, however, is that in a mass society, unrelated individuals and groups exercise very little influence over these elites (the Establishment); and the vast majority of middle Americans are manipulated by the political and economic power that the Establishment commands. Moreover, modern techniques of mass communications—the media, advertising, and public relations—are readily at their disposal. In addition to the media (television, radio, newspapers, and magazines), labor unions, academia, and bureaucracy have vast power to limit or to reinforce the power of the political/corporate axis. Two other crucial points should be made. They are (and Mills explicitly made this clear): that the power elite is not altogether clear on an agenda or a unified policy, nor is it entirely stable; which means that it often lacks direction and therefore can behave in a highly irresponsible fashion.

As if this weren't enough to contend with, the mighty governments, Federal, state, and local, and corporations have themselves unwittingly created bureaucratic behemoths over which individuals—even the elites—are gradually losing control. These "subsystems" have acquired lives of their own. Once events, policies, and programs are set in motion, not even individuals or corporations can stop them, no matter how dire the consequences. Human beings thus become victims of these Frankenstein-like monsters which owe their lives to the concentration of corporate-political-military power.

Whereas Mills's analyses and criticisms are cogent and precise, he is not very clear about the institutional mechanisms that should be established in order to redress or cure the ills he perceives. However, he does refer to the need for the creation of local organizations that can give individuals and groups a means to gain control over the policy decisions that affect their economic and political well-being. In Chapter 9 we shall discuss at length the kinds of institutional mechanisms—with appropriate organizational and legal tools—that, we believe, can fulfill this purpose. Given this background we can now move on.

---

for the new system called ULMS—for Undersea Long Range Missile System. One of the most venerable of American wards is the shipbuilding industry. In addition, the President asked for $838 million for defense research and demonstration.

Although the focus of this book is concentrated on blacks, it should be made crystal clear that most of the *problems and issues discussed concern chicanos, Indians, Puerto Ricans, and poor whites alike*—for they specifically affect the more than 25 million Americans for whom survival, under substandard conditions, is an everyday fact of life. To a slightly less extent, these complex issues also directly affect those 23 million Americans—the "near poor"—for whom existence is marginal. And, by implication, the political problems must indirectly relate to the larger middle-class majority; those who are, at least, more financially secure. Contrary to the popular notions of romanticists of the New Left and radical chic, the middle classes have very little political mobility, for that is the price that has been extracted for limited economic privilege. The "meatball"—as Madison Avenue depicts him—has paid very heavily for his home in the suburbs, his car, and his tube. Humiliation and resentment have been his history, and he is constantly manipulated by establishment forces who use him as a buffer against the exploited poor and minority groups of America. (In many respects the references to he and him could just as easily apply to she and her.)

At the outset, it should be noted that recent data released by the Census Bureau (May 7, 1971) indicated that poverty in the United States is now on the *increase*. This disturbing fact was confirmed and documented in a report which demonstrated that a startling change occurred between 1969 and 1970. The sudden increase in the poverty population reversed a decade of progress. Since 1959, the first year for which data on poverty is available, there had been an average annual decline of 4.9 percent in the number of persons living in poverty, according to the Census Bureau. This trend was reversed in 1970 when the ranks of the poor swelled by over 1.2 million or 5.1 percent. Moreover, most analysts seriously question the criteria that are used in establishing the so-called poverty index, which is presently set at $3,970‡ a year for a family of four. For example, the Department of Labor sets a figure of close to $8,000 as a mini-

‡ The figure is based on the assumption that food costs for a family of four are $25 per week. This "cut-rate" diet, apart from its dollars and cents insufficiency, is of highly questionable nutritional value. Can *you* imagine feeding a family of four on three dollars and fifty-seven cents a day?

mum livable income in certain urban areas, one that the Department admits is somewhat less than the "American standard of living."

The arbitrariness in determining the poverty index and the extremely low dollar figure of presently established poverty-level income suggest, therefore, that the incidence of real poverty is *far greater* than official estimates. It seems entirely probable that *more than 70 million Americans*—over 35 percent of our population—could be classified as poor or "near poor," if the Federal Government were to apply more realistic criteria. It is indeed an understatement to say that the problem has reached a *crisis proportion.*

In retrospect, as a nation, we have scarcely begun to assimilate the lessons of the sixties, especially those involving domestic policies. (It might appear that we should have finally learned something from the great tragedy of our foreign policy in Vietnam—though that is in doubt.) We certainly have yet to turn inward and accept the human wreckage at home. Within the memory of most concerned people are the reports of the National Commission on the Causes and Prevention of Violence (Eisenhower), The National Advisory Commission on Civil Disorders (Kerner), The National Advisory Commission on Rural Poverty, and The President's Commission on Campus Unrest (Scranton). One of the most exotic paradoxes of the past decade is that, as the quality of our reports and studies steadily improved, our urban centers decayed further and racial antagonisms grew worse. It was the blue-ribbon advisory board, chaired by Milton Eisenhower, that poignantly warned us that American cities were becoming a mixture of "places of terror" and "fortresses." The Commission stated that the well-to-do of central cities will, in the not too distant future, live in privately guarded compounds and move about in armored vehicles through "Sanitized corridors" connecting safe areas, while the less well-to-do will possess "tremendous armories of weapons which could be brought into play with or without provocation." It might all seem like science fiction, but one need only glance at the pictorial account of urban living in the December 10, 1971, issue of *Life* Magazine to sense the flavor of things to come. And not even the Vice

President would dare to call Mr. Eisenhower a radical alarmist.

For those who are more inclined to the imagery of the tube or the headline events of the daily newspapers, there were the Watts, Newark, and Detroit riots (uprisings). The crises were ours, as the crimes were ours, and today we are the same society, essentially unchanged from those few short years ago when the convulsions broke out into the open. And there is no reason to believe that the near-catastrophic events of the sixties will not be repeated.

With this in mind the necessity for social change through a coherent and viable economic development policy is self-evident. As was stated, minority and low-income groups have become more politically aware of the economic development issue with all its ramifications. For many it represents a *last chance* for "the system." On the other hand, the quality of interest exhibited by politicians, policy-makers, businessmen, and other "leaders" of the majority community, so far, have been limited to rhetoric or trivia. It would be foolish to predict the future of economic development efforts—both those sponsored by the Government and those of the private sector—other than to say that a vigorous economic development strategy on behalf of low-income citizens is crucial to the future of this nation, as we know it. To pretend otherwise is to behave like the proverbial ostrich, for with the technological and communications revolutions that have occurred, too many people, including the *young, women,* and a growing number of blue-collar workers, are beginning to sense and bitterly resent the social damage and false priorities. Particularly, how benefits and windfalls—at taxpayers' expense—are conferred on the privileged few. How long we can tolerate governments of shoddy slogans, cynical propaganda, and manipulated consensus is anybody's guess, but our estimate is that it's going to become increasingly more difficult to contain the ambiguous forces that will be unleashed if the symbolic hope for economic security does not become a reality—soon.

It would seem self-evident that the establishment in the past has been insensitive to the drift of history. But 75 million poor or near-poor Americans represents a time bomb! And this ominous threat is sizzling on fuses that lead straight back to the board rooms of the powerful corporations and banks and the White House.

2 | CAMPAIGN POLITICS AND BLACK CAPITALISM

If there was one single outstanding feature of the 1968 Presidential campaign, it was that Richard Nixon ran a brilliant advertising campaign. Given the narrowness of his final victory, it is unlikely that he would have won without it. And of all the items in his sample case—Welfare Chiselers, Law and Order, a Plan to end the War in Vietnam—none was as efficiently advertised as Black Capitalism.

By early 1968 a handful of prominent individuals and groups —of diverse attitudes—were beginning to embrace terms like "compensatory capitalism," "green power," "minority entrepreneurship," "economic self-help," "ghetto self determinism," and "community economic development." As we shall see, these slogans meant different things to different people, and the disparities are often shadowed by vague generalities.

Slowly a growing number of politicians, government officials, minority leaders, and the media alike were turned on by the potential of this new approach. Individuals who spoke out included: Dr. Martin Luther King, Robert Kennedy, Jacob Javits, Dr. Kenneth Clark, Whitney Young, Roy Innis, Howard Samuels, and Putney Swope. The organizations ranged from the Black Panthers, Muslims, and CORE through more moderate groups such as the Urban League, the Southwest Council of La Raza, the National Business League, the Black Economic Union, the International Council for Business Opportunity, the Urban Coalition, the National Association of Businessmen to the conservative U.S. Chamber of Commerce and the National Association of Manufacturers.

The potential customers were black as well as white. For blacks, the offer of capitalism was designed to conjure up images of business success, affluence, and power. For whites it was designed to make them forget about integration and the costs of social justice. If the position of political leadership was, at best, vague, popular notions were downright confused. By the fall of 1968, however, things had changed. From Watts to Wall Street, from LeRoi Jones to Richard Nixon, economic development became the new prescription for the ghetto. Everyone seemed to be for it (whatever it was) and they were willing to do something about it (whatever it was that needed to be done). A remarkable turnabout—a solution to ghetto problems was thought to be possible. Not long before James Baldwin had gained universal support for his view that "a ghetto can be improved in one way only—out of existence." What is even more remarkable is that the new issue was catapulted to national prominence by Richard Nixon, the old political pro who stole the show with two dramatic nationwide campaign speeches on "Black Capitalism." Nixon had, at the least, diverted public relations attention from Hubert Humphrey's "politics of joy," and the press ran with it.

The 1968 Presidential campaign, to most interested observers, was not exactly the most thrilling or stimulating experience by past electoral standards. The Democratic primaries, the Kennedy assassination, and the Chicago convention provided excitement, tragedy, drama, disgust, and fear; but by the time Labor Day came around the election campaign itself caught neither the imagination nor the emotions of most Americans.

The Nixon campaign in fact was little more than a political "ad campaign," and it was estimated that he spent $13 million for television alone. In particular, what stood out was his staff's superb use of spot television commercials, several of which were produced by one Eugene S. Jones, head of E.S.J. Productions, of New York. Jones, although he had done a good deal of television work before—including a documentary series called "The World of . . ." (famous people) and produced the "Today Show" on NBC for eight years—was new to the world of political commercials.[1] Thanks to the excellent journalistic account of the campaign by Joe McGinniss (*The Selling of the President, 1968*) we also learned that $110,000 convinced Jones to produce sixteen spot commercials for the Nixon team. Two of those spots "Wrong Road" and "Black Capitalism" offer valuable insights into the kind of pitch that the Republican Party was making for minority votes. The tone and style of the commercials are also crucial in that they provide a jumping-off point for one of the critical questions of this book—did Richard Nixon ever believe that "Black Capitalism" would offer a viable solution to the manifold social problems that beset our nation?

The commercials are:

TWO VERSIONS:
:60 seconds
:40 seconds

E.S.J. #6
WRONG ROAD

VIDEO	AUDIO
1. *OPENING NETWORK DISCLAIMER: "A POLITICAL ANNOUNCEMENT."*	
2. *DOLLY DOWN LS EMPTY ROAD ACROSS WESTERN AREA. DISSOLVE TO MATCH MOVEMENT PAN-TILT IN ON DEJECTED MAN ASLEEP ON PARK BENCH. THEN INTO SCENES OF BOTH URBAN AND RURAL DECAY. THEY ARE THE HUNGRY OF APPALACHIA—THE POOR OF AN URBAN GHETTO— THE ILL-HOUSED MEMBERS OF A FAMILY ON AN INDIAN RESERVATION, SLOWLY BUT FIRMLY THE PICTURE LEADS TOWARD*	MUSIC UP AND UNDER. R.N. For the past five years we've been deluged by programs for the unemployed—programs for the cities —programs for the poor. And we have reaped from these programs an ugly harvest of frustrations, violence and failure across the land.

A SCENE OF FRUSTRATED ANGER, WHICH IS EXPRESSED IN THEIR FACES.

SIGN ON STREETS WHICH SAYS, "GOVERNMENT CHECKS CASHED HERE."

R.N.
What we need are not more millions on welfare rolls—but more people on payrolls in the United States.

3. *MOTIVATES INTO SEQUENCE OF FACES OF AMERICA—ALL RACES, ALL BACKGROUNDS. THERE IS A QUALITY OF DETERMINATION TO THEM, BUT THEY APPEAR SORELY TRIED.*

R.N.
Now our opponents will be offering more of the same. But I say we are on the wrong road. It is time to quit pouring billions of dollars into programs that have failed.

4. *SERIES OF QUICK, EFFECTIVE CUTS OF CONSTRUCTIVE WORK SCENES—A SHIP UNLOADING—A TOWER BEING RAISED—A FACTORY LINE— A BUILDING ERECTED.*

I believe we should enlist private enterprise, which will produce, not promises in solving the problems of America.

5. *DISSOLVE TO SHOT OF CHILDREN STANDING IN THE MUD OF APPALACHIA. THEY STARE AT THE CAMERA. TILT DOWN FOR MATCH MOVEMENT DISSOLVE TO SILO OF LITTLE NEGRO BOY (BACK TO CAMERA) AS HE LOOKS OUT WINDOW. HOLD. FADEOUT.*

MUSIC UP AND OUT.

E.S.J. #13
BLACK CAPITALISM

VIDEO
2. *ESTABLISH MEAN-LOOKING GHETTO AREA.*

AUDIO
R.N.
The face of the ghetto is the face of despair.

3. *BRIEF INDIVIDUAL SHOTS OF MEN, WOMEN, AND CHILDREN. THEY HAVE A WEARY LOOK ON THEIR FACES.*

If we hope to light this face, we must rescue the ghetto from its despair.

4. *LONG AND MEDIUM SHOTS OF SMALL CROWDS OF PEOPLE IN FRONT OF CLOSED STORES OR IN SITUATIONS WHERE THE MOOD IS ONE OF WAITING. THEY ARE POORLY DRESSED.*

But not with more promises. Not with the old solution . . . the handout. We must offer a new solution . . . the handup.

5. *ESTABLISHING SHOTS OF STORES OBVIOUSLY OWNED AND/OR RUN BY BLACK AMERICANS. A BUSY BANK— A CO-OP MARKET—A CLOTHING SHOP.*

With your help, I will begin a new program to get private enterprise into the ghetto and the ghetto into private enterprise. I call it "Black Capitalism."

6. *MONTAGE OF ANIMATED FACES OF BUSY MEN AND WOMEN—ENTHUSIASTIC TEENAGERS, ETC. THE MOOD IS OF BUSY ACTIVITY—BUYING, SELLING, WORKING.*

MUSIC UP FULL.

7. *MEDIUM SHOTS OF PEOPLE IN GROUPS WALKING ON STREETS. STORE-FRONTS, LIGHTED, FILLED WITH PRODUCTS CAN BE SEEN. THERE IS A FEELING OF SUCCESS AND PROGRESS IN THE PHOTOS.*

R.N.
More black ownership of business and land and homes can be the multiplier of pride that will end our racial strife.

8. *SEVERAL SHOTS OF BLACK AND WHITE AMERICANS TOGETHER. THEY ARE TALKING, WALKING, WORKING. ON ONE WE DO A LONG PULL-BACK AND FADEOUT.*

The black man's pride is the white man's hope.

A footnote to the television/commercial aspect of the campaign was provided toward the end of October. While Gene Jones was chatting with McGinniss one day, he mentioned that he was shutting down his business and studio so that he could move out of the country—to Montserrat—permanently. Jones said, and it seems so ironic, after having made those sixteen highly acclaimed spot commercials: "My one qualm about Nixon is that I'm not sure he's got the sensitivity he should. To Appalachia, to the slums, to the poverty and destitution that reside there . . . The hatred, the violence, the cities gone to hell . . . I really don't see any choice, I mean, I don't want my kids growing up in an atmosphere like this."[3]

"The black man's pride is the white man's hope" was a theme that Nixon was to repeat time and again in the next several months. And in case you did not get the message the video part leaves no doubt in the viewer's mind—Richard Nixon is the "great black hope." It was a tough act to beat and Hubert Humphrey was left to tax the credulity of the American public by trying to sell ill-funded and slapdash programs that, thanks to the Vietnam war, had left only resentment and bitterness. The contrast was too much; Nixon gave the appearance of cutting loose from the welfare state while Humphrey was left rechristening Great Society cliches. Nixon's "Black Capitalism" was a commercial success.

Thus, times and circumstances had certainly changed since the last Presidential election. It was then that the Democratic candidate had promised to heal the nation's wounds, resolve differences between races, rebuild the cities, not to enlarge the war in Southeast Asia. The country responded by giving him a whopping popular mandate. It was a landslide. But the history of the four Johnson years proved to be a disappointment, if not a disaster.

In the 1964 Presidential campaign Lyndon Baines Johnson promised the American people the Great Society, i.e. "butter"; in 1965 it became "butter and bullets," by 1966 it was "bullets and butter," and by 1967 it became "bombs and oleomargarine." In 1968, faced with a policy of "bombs and pure corn oil," many of the voices that were indispensable to a healthy and creative government went into opposition over the conduct of the war. The President, in April, looking over his shoulder at the opposition and the historians (not to mention the pollsters and the primary results), wisely decided to remove himself from the more mundane debate over policies.

During this period many low-income and minority groups—particularly the blacks and chicanos—were growing more restive. Their plight and frustrations were well documented and publicized by the President's Commission on Civil Disorders (the

Kerner Report), which actually took its assignment seriously, much to the chagrin of most politicians. In addition, by 1968 the "War on Poverty" was flat out on a stretcher. Most of the anticipated progress in developing new programs (and meeting raised expectations) in housing, education, hunger, health, manpower, welfare, community action, etc., fell victim to the budgetary necessities of the Vietnam war. For those with short memories it should be recalled that many Congressmen, particularly the Dixie-Republican coalition, were relieved to hold these programs hostage.

"Law and order," the clinical definition for keeping minorities in their place in a democracy, became the white preoccupation. And the preoccupation found its standard-bearer in Richard M. Nixon. Hubert Humphrey—who had taken the baton from Johnson, with some vague notions about a "domestic Marshall Plan" and an unspecified commitment to wind down the war—ultimately proved to be no match for Nixon, who had both a secret plan to end the war and a new weapon to solve the problems of minorities in the ghettoes, "Black Capitalism."

Although passing reference was made in the course of a speech in Milwaukee on March 28, the main salvo for Nixon's new domestic thrust came in a two-part nationwide address delivered over NBC radio entitled "Bridges to Human Dignity," on April 25 and May 2, 1968. The April 25 speech was made in Salem, Oregon (during the Oregon primary), and the May 2 speech was made during the Indiana primary. It was then that Presidential-candidate Nixon proposed his bold new approach to the solution of minority problems—black ownership. The principles Nixon espoused in these addresses were immediately picked up by the media, and within days newspaper stories all over the country carried captions saying, "Nixon Endorses Black Capitalism." Nixon defined these principles as follows:

> "To have human rights, people need property rights—and never has this been more true than in the case of the Negro today. (He must have) the economic power that comes from ownership, and the security and independence that come from economic power . . . We need more black employers, more black businesses . . . We have to get private enterprise into the ghetto. But at the same time, we have to get the people of the ghetto into private enterprise—as workers, as managers, as owners."

Another major point which Nixon made was that these changes had to be accomplished with the participation of private industry:

> "Private enterprise, far more effectively than the government, can provide the jobs, train the unemployed, build the homes, offer the new opportunities which will produce progress—not promises—in solving the problems of America."
>
> ". . . we can get a bigger social return on a given level of investment and get some of the jobs done through the market system."

To encourage American industry to participate in these solutions, Nixon proposed tax credits and other incentives:

> "I do not believe that we can expect large private corporate businesses to commit their resources to the problems of the cities without proper incentives. That is why I have recommended a variety of tax credits and other incentives to act as an inducement for business to divert its efforts toward the solution of these problems—many of which industry is demonstrably better-equipped than government to solve."

Finally, Nixon stated that his new approach to minority problems was in line with some black activists' assessments of the situation:

> "Much of the black militant talk these days is actually in terms far closer to the doctrines of free enterprise than to those of the welfarist '30s—terms such as 'self-determination,' 'ownership,' and 'self-help.' What most of the militants are asking is to be included as owners, as entrepreneurs, to have a share of the wealth and a piece of the action. And this is precisely what the central target of the new approach ought to be. It ought to be oriented toward more black ownership, for from this can flow the rest—black pride, black jobs, black opportunity and, yes, black power, in the best, the constructive sense of that often misapplied term."

Nixon's "Bridges to Human Dignity" address left many questions in its wake, however, which were not answered by Nixon's future statements. Vague and sweeping pronouncements without precise solutions seemed to become an occupational hazard of the President-elect. Was Nixon proposing consumer ownership, as in cooperative community ventures? Was he suggesting black ownership of large, profit-making industries in the ghetto? Was he proposing joint ventures between establishment white corporations and newly created black ones? Or was his an offer to increase the number of "mom and pop" storeowners in the ghetto? What was also confusing is that Nixon gave no indication of how organizations already working to increase black entrepreneurship—such as the Interracial Council for Business Opportunity, CORE, the Black Economic Union, the Urban League, and the Federal Government's Small Business Administration's Project OWN—would fit into his plans.

Nixon's computer-happy researchers must not have spent many sleepless nights studying the impact that his Black Capitalism speech would have on the average American voter. One does not doubt for a moment that having researched attitudes toward capitalism they and he knew only too well what the public reaction would be to this "all-American" tack. For every research study has indicated that there is a deep-seated acceptance of capitalism—white or black—in the minds of over 90 percent of our citizenry. As Andrew Shonfield remarked in his book *Modern Capitalism:*

> The United States is indeed one of the few places left in the world where "capitalism" is generally thought to be an OK word . . . Among the Americans there is a general commitment to the view, shared by both political parties, of the natural predominance of private enterprise in the economic sphere and of the subordinate role of public initiative in any situation other than a manifest national emergency.[4]

It must be remembered that in this country, "private enterprise" is dominated by large business corporations. A study published in 1951 by the Institute for Social Research of the University of Michigan suggested a basic public satisfaction with large corporations in this country. The authors report that 76 percent of the 1227 persons polled were of the opinion that the good things about big business outweighed the bad things, while only 10 percent viewed the negative features as prevailing.[5]

These findings were confirmed by a more recent study conducted by pollster Louis Harris for *Newsweek* and the National Industrial Conference Board in 1966. The study indicated that 96 percent of the two thousand individuals eighteen years or over who were polled held the opinion that "free enterprise has made this country great," while 91 percent were of the view that "business in America has changed for the better since the depression days," and 76 percent believed that "most businessmen are genuinely interested in [the] well-being of the country."

The reaction to Nixon's Black Capitalism campaign was immediate and generally favorable, particularly in the white establishment press. For example, *Time* magazine devoted nearly a full page to a verbatim reproduction of the speech. *The Wall Street Journal, The Christian Science Monitor,* and the New York *Times* applauded the principles, editorially. The President was praised highly by conservative dailies and weeklies across the country; and the Dallas *Morning News* roundly applauded his remarks. Tom Wicker, the liberal, associate editor of the New York *Times*—the most powerful "liberal" newspaper in the country—wrote: "Richard Nixon's radio speech on the need for the development of Black Capitalism and ownership in the ghetto could prove to be more constructive than anything yet said by other Presidential candidates on the crisis of the cities." The black press responded more cautiously and with mixed enthusiasm. For example, the influential Chicago *Daily Defender* expressed suspicion of the candidates' motives, although it endorsed the idea of Black Capitalism. The paper asserted that, "Without this base, black power takes on the insignificant aspect of a paper tiger." It fully approved of the "need to build economic independence."

In responding to the Nixon proposals, different people drew different inferences from his speech, and reacted accordingly. Among blacks the response was mixed. Roy Innis and Floyd McKissick, the leaders of the civil rights organization, the Congress of Racial Equality (CORE), were the first to react to Nixon's speech. Innis observed that Nixon made more sense on racial matters than any other aspirant to the Presidency, including Robert Kennedy. Within a month after the "Bridges" speech was made, Innis and McKissick personally met with candidate Nixon for several hours in his Fifth Avenue apartment to discuss his proposals and to relate CORE's programs which were consistent with the theme of "Bridges."

Berkeley G. Burrell, President of the National Business League, an association of black businesses, suggested that by means of major corporations going into the ghetto, "a system of plantationships that is hated will be destroyed." He further stated:

> "What is needed is partnership. We seek (and demand) an equal or better sharing of ownership and operation of the business and commerce of the ghetto. A majority of the business community, as a matter of re-enlightened self-interest, must provide the equity, capital resources, technical capability, guidance, and support that are essential to the growth and development of interracial business within the central city."

Other respected black leaders responded with less favor to the proposal that Black Capitalism might solve minority problems, charging that it implied separatism and the development of segregated economies. Whitney Young, of the National Urban League, said that the "concept of encouraging black entrepreneurship is sound," but he found Black Capitalism to be no more than an empty slogan. Sociologist Dr. Kenneth Clark said that Black Capitalism would lead to a "gilded ghetto" and to a separate, isolated black society, which he strongly opposes.

Robert L. Allen, author of *Black Awakening in Capitalist America*, took Innis and McKissick to task for falling prey to bourgeois nationalism. He said:

> "In summary, CORE and the cultural nationalists draped themselves in the mantle of nationalism, but upon examination it is seen that their programs, far from aiding in the achievement of black liberation and freedom from exploitation, would instead weld the black communities more firmly into the structure of American corporate capitalism. This reformist or bourgeois nationalism—through its chosen vehicle of black capitalism—may line the pockets and boost the social status of the black middle class and black intelligentsia, but it will not ease the oppression of the ordinary ghetto dweller. What CORE and the cultural nationalists seek is not an end to oppression, but the transfer of the oppressive apparatus into their own hands. They call themselves nationalists and exploit the legitimate nationalist feelings of black people in order to advance their own interests as a class. And chief among those interests is their desire to become brokers between the white rulers and the black ruled."

Perhaps the harshest denunciation came in the form of an open letter from Eldridge Cleaver, the exiled Minister of Information of the Black Panther Party to Stokely Carmichael, the former head of SNCC and recently resigned Prime Minister of the Black Panther Party. Cleaver said:

> "As a matter of fact, it has been precisely your nebulous enunciation of Black Power that has provided the power structure with its new weapon against our people. The Black Panther Party tried to give you a chance to rescue Black Power from the pigs who have seized upon it and turned it into the rationale for Black Capitalism. With James Farmer in the Nixon Administration to preside over the implementation of Black Capitalism under the slogan of Black Power, what value does that slogan now have to our people's struggle for liberation? Is denouncing the Black Panther Party the best you can do to combat this evil? I would think that your responsibility goes a little further than that. Even though you were right when you said that LBJ would never stand up and call for Black Power, Nixon has done so and he's bankrolling it with millions of dollars. So now your old buddies are cashing in on your slogan. In effect, your cry for Black Power has become the grease to ease the black bourgeoisie into the power structure."

White observers also drew differing inferences from Nixon's proposals. A Senior Vice President of the National Association of Manufacturers, A. Wright Elliott, defined it as black acquisition of a stake in our society:

> "We must go beyond simplistic slogans and admit that what we are really talking about is *ways that blacks can legitimately acquire a larger stake in our society.*
> "In the economic sense, this means that they must legitimately acquire and control more resources. The concept of private property, which is a major foundation of capitalism, offers no support for color prejudice or special advantage." (ital. in original)

Senator Jacob Javits found the need for ghetto economic development to be analogous with problems of international economics:

> "The crux of this new trend of thought is that the remaking of the ghetto requires a total economic upgrading of the community itself, and that this, in turn, requires the ownership and control of new capital and business opportunities by people within the community. In this view, it is not enough that established businesses come into the ghetto to provide jobs and housing; rather, in an analogy to international economics, the goal is to redress the balance of payments between the ghetto and the surrounding community and to keep capital and profits within the area and under local control."

The AFL-CIO played a cagey waiting game for several months, but it finally issued a bitter denunciation of the Black Capitalism concept.

If Nixon lost a potentially powerful ally in the form of organized labor, he gained some favorable backing with strong editorial support from conservative William F. Buckley, Jr. There are those who would think that it was hardly a fair trade, although others might say that in terms of self-esteem and self-righteousness, Mr. Buckley and the Executive Council of the labor federation are equal. Nonetheless, America's best known conservative columnist and editor issued an immediate rejoinder that took the labor movement to task.

He said of the labor leaders:

> "Now the inflamed gentlemen of the council are clearly thinking as loosely as they write. What makes apartheid objectionable is not that it is anti-democratic, but that it is compulsory. Apartheid means separate development . . .
>
> "The call for special efforts to help the black people especially develop may be anti-democratic in the sense that it imposes special burdens on the white community, but it is surely democratic in the conventional context in that it helps those who need help the most . . .
>
> "Black Capitalism, conceived primarily as government-underwritten credit-easy loans from the Small Business Administration, that kind of thing—hardly needs for its justification participation by the entire Negro community. But scattered successes can give universal hope. Among the objectives should be black-dominated labor unions, which would crack the white hegemonies that deny to Negroes the opportunity to advance in skilled trades."

Buckley concludes by asking, "Why not an SBA loan to blacks who desire to organize a pressure group for right-to-work laws?" It's one of the vagaries of American politics that finds labor opposing what appears to be a black self-help program and William Buckley offering incantations about "universal hope." It just might seem to blacks that they are once again being booby-trapped by both sides, each one with its own special axes to grind. There *are* times when you just can't tell your friends from your enemies.

As the campaign wore on some skeptics labeled Nixon's Black Capitalism speeches as a crass attempt to win over the black vote. Did he have other social programs? Were there any blacks on his staff? Careful research would bear out the view that Nixon's bid for black votes was limited; so much so that it escaped the comment of the national press. Information regarding black participation in the campaign was scant and what there was resembled feeble tokenism. Apparently the only two individuals on Nixon's staff who sought to have contact with the minority community were John McLaughry—a white speech writer who was prominent in drafting the Community Self Determination Act and Leonard Garment, a former law partner and Nixon's "civil rights man." Toward the end of September it was announced that a Minorities Division of the campaign staff was being established under the leadership of Lee Townes, Jr., one of the owners of Virginia Mutual Benefit Life Insurance Company. This tardy effort to enlist black support seemed to have low priority, came conspicuously late in the campaign and even then appeared to be a half-hearted attempt which was ill-financed and hurriedly planned. The strategy called for a series of VIP receptions for Negro leaders, which, incidentally, Nixon himself never attended.

There were very few blacks—certainly none with any political punch—who were associated with this effort. It was not until October 7 that it was announced that a nine-man committee had been formed to advise Nixon on black problems. The members of the committee included: Earl Kennedy (a Detroit businessman and Chairman of the Michigan State Committee); Wilt Chamberlain (the famous basketball star); Jim Alexander (an investment banker from Atlanta); Robert Keyes (an administrative assistant to Governor Ronald Reagan); Samuel Pierce (a former New York State Supreme Court Justice); Samuel Jackson (a Washington lawyer); Hazel Harding of Toledo, Ohio; and Ike Williams of St. Petersburg, Florida. From all appearances the formation of this committee seemed to be an afterthought for show, rather than a serious attempt to appeal to black voters. The only other black of national prominence with whom Nixon publicly conferred was the Reverend Leon Sullivan, and this was a short discussion held at the Progress Plaza shopping center in Philadelphia. Whatever political significance there was to this session was diluted by the fact that Sullivan had also had a similar meeting with Hubert Humphrey the week before. It had been rumored in Washington the Nixon people had asked Reverend Sullivan for an endorsement, offering him in exchange several high government posts—one Republican pol indicated an ambassadorship at a minimum and possibly a cabinet post.

Another and less publicized effort to win black support was to utilize the services of Jan Rus, who became head of the "Athletes for Nixon Committee." Rus (who is white), a former member of the National AAU and Track and Field Committee, turned up in Denver just as the U.S. Olympic team was being outfitted before leaving for Mexico City. In his capacity as head of the Athletes Committee, Rus occupied a suite near the equipment room, where he generously dispensed an ample supply of T-shirts emblazoned with the slogan "Athletes for Nixon." Rus made the shirts available to the athletes, some of whom picked them up after receiving their uniform, thinking they were part of the regular issue.

It was just about this time that the careers and agendas of Rus and Robert "Pappy" Gault began to intersect, and their relationship offers a singular example of the attitude of the Nixon people toward blacks as well as some insights into the personality of blacks who worked for Nixon and who later tried to peddle his Black Capitalism program. Pappy Gault, a former career Marine and Air Force Sergeant was head coach of the U.S. boxing team at the Mexico City Olympics—in fact the first black man ever to become head coach of an American Olympic team. Gault, who became a very strong Nixon supporter after the Olympics, also became a Black Capitalism booster, in a rather odd manner.

In an article entitled "After the Olympics: Buying Off Protest,"[6] Jack Scott and Harry Edwards (one of the founders of the Olympic Project for Human Rights) sought to explain how Black Capitalism worked on a more "practical" level as a *political* effort to buy the endorsements of name athletes for Nixon during the campaign. Scott and Edwards were active leaders in the effort to organize blacks in the field of sports—an arena, for all its superficial brotherhood, known for blatant racism. The year 1968 was important for blacks in their effort to expose the system of "athletic slavery" and the Olympics were a natural target.

The symbolic culmination of these efforts was the raised gloved fists of Tommie Smith and John Carlos while "The Star-

Spangled Banner" was being played and the whole world was watching. Gault, for those who may not remember the rapid events at the Olympics, helped stage a sort of counterdemonstration to the Smith/Carlos gesture. When George Foreman, the heavyweight boxer, was named champion and started to do his traditional victory dance around the ring, Gault stuck an American flag in his hand and pointed him toward the television cameras. Gault was adamant in his efforts to defuse the issues raised by the Human Rights Project and Edwards.

Harry Edwards, who later became a professor at the University of California, described some of the difficulties he encountered during the Human Rights campaign:

> These accomplishments, small as they were in comparison to the problems they sought to correct, were made under the most trying of circumstances. Death threats to myself and my staff [the Olympic Project for Human Rights] were an almost daily occurrence . . . At various times during the boycott movement, I was offered sums amounting to over $125,000 to call the whole thing off—the assumption being that I was one of those rare niggers with brains and that without me the whole protest would vanish. The pressure was always on, and it continued right into Mexico City. Mel Pender, a Captain in the army and a black sprinter on the American team, was threatened with a possible court-martial if he got involved in any protests. Other blacks were constantly harassed and coerced . . .
>
> By the time the Olympic Games were over, we had ample evidence that the American sports establishment was going to fight our protest against racism in athletics with every weapon available to it. It would not even stop short of using black people themselves, as has become clear in the activities of Pappy Gault . . .

According to Scott and Edwards, Gault—as a result of his activities at the Olympics—was flown to Chicago immediately after the Games to address a meeting of the Athletes for Nixon organization at the invitation of Jan Rus. Gault and Rus subsequently scrambled to line up more blacks for Nixon during the campaign.

Edwards accused Gault (who by this time was equally comfortable with either the carrot or the stick) of moving around the track meet "circuit" after the election with the specific intent of buying off black athletes who were militant and outspoken. One example occurred during the Martin Luther King Memorial Games when Gault approached Lee Evans and Tommie Smith with a proposition, that he [Gault] would make sure that they would receive $2,000 over a three-month period, if they would allow him to be their p.r. representative. Gault, it should be noted, denied this charge in an interview with Robert Lipsyte, a New York *Times* sports columnist: "I'd never go for anybody . . . They'd have to come to me. The only time I had anything to do with either of them, I was introduced by an Amateur Athletic union official, and I gave each of them a bottle of whiskey." Edwards also recounted that after Lee told him about the Gault offer he also found out that Sheila Young, a *Newsweek* reporter who had interviewed Gault, said that Gault told her that she'd "wind up in the Hudson River" if *Newsweek* printed a story that would cast his activities in a bad light. In reflecting upon his feelings toward Gault and Black Capitalism, Edwards said:

> In a sense, one could have predicted Pappy Gault—or at least someone like him. For what he is doing is simply a part of the strategy of black capitalism now favored by the establishment: buying off the most vocal elements of black militancy, but doing nothing about the causes of the discontent.

After the election Rus was rewarded by being hired as a special consultant to HEW. His task was to do a study of the President's Council on Physical Fitness. John Wilbern, the chief administrator for the Council, said of Rus's activities, "He has been doing this study for several months now . . . I don't know what he's really doing, but I can tell you this; if you have to spend as much time as he has doing a management-systems study of an eleven-man organization like this one, then someone ought to fire you."

The activities of Rus and Gault on behalf of the Nixon candidates and black capitalism could probably best be summed up in a statement by Rus as he hit the campaign trail. He said, "I want to accentuate the positive in America." Right on!

In their undue haste to clamber aboard the new gravy train, though, Gault and Rus seemed to have fallen headlong into the black capitalism bag, one that ensnared many others, some willing and some not so willing.

But soft sell or hard sell, the blacks were not buying. Richard Nixon received less than 10 percent of the black vote in November 1968.

It is said that the President was disappointed with his showing. Had he spent less time in the television studios he might not have been so surprised. And had he spent any time trying to make a commercial for Black Capitalism himself he certainly would not have been surprised. As McGinniss tells it:

> A couple of weeks later, when Treleaven [Creative Director for Nixon's advertising campaign] told Gene Jones to shoot a commercial called "Black Capitalism," he was surprised to hear that Negroes in Harlem were reluctant to pose for the pictures.
>
> Jones had not been able to find any pictures that showed Negroes gainfully employed, so he decided to take his own. He hired his own photographer, a white man, and sent him to Harlem with instructions to take pictures of good Negroes, Negroes who worked and smiled and acted the way white folks thought they ought to. And to take these pictures in front of Negro-owned stores and factories to make the point that this is what honest labor can do for a race.
>
> An hour after he started work, the photographer called Gene Jones and said when he had started lining Negroes up on the street to pose he had been asked by a few young men what he was doing. When he told them he was taking pictures for a Richard Nixon commercial, it was suggested to him that he remove himself and his camera from the vicinity. Fast. Gene Jones explained to Harry Treleaven.
>
> "Gee, isn't that strange," Treleaven said, "I can't understand an attitude like that."[7]

In spite of his poor showing the President-elect met with six black leaders, just prior to inauguration, to discuss civil rights and other racial problems.* Nixon was quoted by those present as having pledged "to do more for the underprivileged and more for the Negro than any other President had done."

* Those in attendance were: John Johnson, publisher of *Ebony* and *Jet* magazines; Rev. Ralph Abernathy; Hobson Reynolds, Grand Exalted Ruler of the Improved and Benevolent Order of Elks; John Murphy, President of National Newspaper Publishers' Association; Sandy Ray, First Vice President of the National Baptist Convention; and Dr. Nathan Wright, Chairman of the Black Power Conference.

3 | THE POVERTY MARKETPLACE

Had Harry Treleaven taken time out from his career on Madison Avenue to know what was going on uptown, he would not have been so taken aback by the fact that black men in Harlem did not want to pose for his cameras. It was certainly no surprise that black people were hostile to Richard Nixon's candidacy. What was more of a surprise was that many blacks looked upon Hubert Humphrey as simply the lesser of two evils.

In the summer of 1968 one of the authors was in Hough, an all-black ghetto of Cleveland, watching a Hubert Humphrey television team trying to get footage for one of their commercials. The scene was the inside of a store-front neighborhood center whose operations were financed with Federal antipoverty funds. Cleveland was not only a city under Democratic control, but the Mayor, Carl Stokes, was black and a stanch ally of Humphrey. If there was genuine support for Humphrey in any city, Cleveland should have been the one. And yet the director of the camera crew spent more than an hour trying to get a dozen blacks to voice sixty seconds' worth of spontaneous praise for the then Vice President. What about Humphrey's civil rights record, he asked them. What about the poverty program? What about the appointment of Thurgood Marshall to the Supreme Court?

"Oh we'll probably vote for him," said one woman finally, "but we been through enough of these politician promises to know that electing Hubert Humphrey isn't going to make this a better place to live." Several members of the group even argued that the election of George Wallace might not be such a bad thing. At least they knew where he stood. Finally the crew director left muttering that none of the film was usable. Like Treleaven, he could not understand why the blacks were acting like that. After all that the Democratic Party had done for them.

But much of what the Democratic Party had started to do for its black allies in America had been quickly undone by policies of supporting what it thought were its allies in Southeast Asia.

By 1968 Lyndon Johnson's dream of being the President who gave the promise of America to the poor and the racial minorities was in shambles. The war in Vietnam chewed up the money and the energy that otherwise would have been available for domestic programs, and the riots in major cities had turned the country against him.

Moreover, it was apparent that the programs themselves were feeble and impotent against the deep and difficult problems of poverty and racism. In 1964 the Job Corps, the Neighborhood Youth Corps, Headstart, seemed like progressive, sensible solutions to the unemployment of youth and the inadequacies of grade school education. By 1968 it was apparent they were naïve and token responses.

A majority of the poor were white. But many of these were aged or those living in rural areas and not likely to cause much of a fuss. So "The Problem" was 22 million blacks, 16 million of whom were living in the cities; restless, alienated, and getting "pushier" everyday. And what could the financing of a training camp or a pre-kindergarten really do for poor blacks in a society that the President's own Kerner Commission had to label "racist"?

At best, the answer was "very little." The answer was confirmed with the release of the report on the Headstart program by Dr. James Coleman which concluded that children who went through the program lost much of what they had gained in a year because of the inadequate conditions of the public school systems and the intellectually debilitating home life to which most of the children were exposed.

Lyndon Johnson's War on Poverty was essentially a charity program. It was based on the premise that poor people needed welfare services and skill training to equip them with the skills and attitudes—particularly the latter—necessary to enter the Great Society. While whites were certainly guilty of racial discrimination, appeals to the better nature of labor unions, businesses, and local governments could overcome that problem. As is traditionally the case with charity programs raising the spirit was an important part of the strategy. From T-groups to sit-ins in city hall, the War on Poverty offered the black and the poor self-awareness and social action the likes of which middle-class America had never seen. But there were few jobs, and little political or economic power.

There was to be some element of political sharing in the Great Society. But the goodies were to be rationed out by the Democratic Party in return for good behavior and loyalty. Mike Royko tells the story of how young Reverend Jesse Jackson, a protégé of Martin Luther King, came to Chicago with a letter of introduction to the Mayor from the Governor of North Carolina. According to Royko: "Daley told him to see his Ward committeeman, and if he did some precinct work, rang some doorbells, hustled up some votes, there might be a job for him. Maybe something like taking coins in a tollway booth."[1]

After four years of the War on Poverty, the enemy looked as tough as ever. People were still starving in rural Mississippi and Appalachia, the ghettos of Bedford Stuyvesant, Hough, Watts, and East Harlem were still teeming with an army of desperate people. One statistic, that 36 percent of the population between ages twenty and twenty-four in the model cities area of Washington, D.C., was addicted to heroin, sums up the magnitude and horror of urban poverty as well as any.

To be sure, there had been some reduction in the number of poor as defined by government statisticians. But even if one accepted the official definition of poverty, which for an urban family of four is about *one half* of what the U.S. Bureau of Labor Statistics has defined as the cost of a decent standard of living, it was clear that the reductions were due for the most part to the war-inflated economy.

The War on Poverty had added only $2 billion per year to the economy. The War in Vietnam added more than $30 billion, creating jobs and income which eventually trickled down to some of the poor. And when spending on Vietnam was reduced in 1970, sure enough, one million people fell back into the poverty category. Making war is neither a moral nor an efficient way to reduce poverty, but in the America of the 1960s that's the way it worked out.

But even if the money spent on war were suddenly to be made available to fight poverty, there was little consensus as to how it should be spent.

Among the bureaucrats and academics who swarm around Washington, there were two general models of what was wrong and how to right it. Both of them were positions put forth for the most part by white people—since it is they who run and advise the Government—although both propositions had black spokesmen and black supporters.

The first model, the one that the War on Poverty started with, was based upon the fact that the black poor were a minority in this country. Therefore, they would have to work their way out of their second-class citizenship through the system as it existed. This meant that integration—political, social, and economic —had to be the primary goal of any antipoverty effort. Any program that furthered this goal, job training for employment in white-owned businesses, housing to open up in the suburbs, was to be emphasized. Any effort that might tend to "perpetuate" segregation of the races and classes, such as slum housing rehabilitation and development of the inner cities, was to be discouraged.

The emphasis was on dispersing the blacks from the cities into the suburban areas where it was presumed that unskilled jobs were increasing. It was also important to get the black poor out of the ghettos so that what was seen as the "culture of poverty," which engendered negative attitudes toward work and society, could be destroyed.

This was the dominant liberal view of economists and urbanologists in the Johnson Administration. And afterwards it was embraced by officials of the Nixon Administration as well. It was held by W. Willard Wirtz and Wilbur Cohen, by Daniel P. Moynihan and by George Romney.

This dispersal model also held that a major objective of public policy was to convince the outside society to *accept* the integration of blacks and the poor. Since by definition, the latter were in the minority, they could only achieve integration if the larger society agreed to it. For the most part the convincing was to be done on a rational basis. Those with responsibility for making the decisions (Congressmen, businessmen, mayors) would have to be persuaded by appeals to conscience and clear logic that the welfare of all Americans was dependent on the resolution of the racial/poverty crisis.

The job of the poor in this model was twofold. They had to be willing (motivated) to take the opportunities that were given to them, and they had to avoid the kind of behavior that would upset the larger, white society. According to one set of liberal critics the poor had failed, "lost," the War on Poverty, on both counts, *especially the latter*.

"The left has much to answer for in American life," wrote Daniel Moynihan in his book on the Community Action Program, *Maximum Feasible Misunderstanding*, "and not the least for having brought about a too ready rejection by men of the center of any assertion of proletarian cohesion and purpose. We have it from Oscar Lewis that Castro's Cuba solved the problem of juvenile delinquency by giving the machine guns to its delinquents. Were the telescopic sights and mimeograph machines of the community action program so very different?" (page 164).

The second model which we can call the *development* model was in many ways a reaction to the first. Most proponents would have agreed that integration was the desired goal. But they would not have agreed that the only way to achieve this goal was through helping individuals integrate directly into the white man's society.

The basic assumption of antipoverty strategy has been that poor people could be assimilated into the larger economy and society by treating their individual deficiencies, such as lack of education, training, good health, etc., and by moving them to where opportunities were greater. Like the conservatives, the liberal policy makers seemed to feel that the answer to poverty was a sufficiently motivated individual.

The conservatives said the poor were lazy and didn't want to work. The liberals said that they were untrained and had negative attitudes toward society. Liberals might agree that the basic cause was in the environment, *but the solution had to rest with individual blacks.*

As the decade drew to a close, an increasing number of people began to question the assumptions of the "dispersal" position. These assumptions were:

1. Inner city residents would be better off in the suburbs where jobs are growing at a faster rate.
2. Ghettos have no economic potential.
3. Emphasis on developing the inner city would encourage segregation.

Much of the dispersal argument is based on the point that the rate of job growth is higher in suburbs than in the inner city. And so it is. But the issue is not growth rates, but how *many* jobs are open and who gets them.

Charlotte Fremon of the Urban Institute in Washington studied the growth of unskilled and semiskilled jobs in six cities between 1965 and 1967. (These were the only cities and time periods for which the data was available.) She found that in five of the six cities the growth of unskilled and semiskilled employment in the inner city was enough to wipe out total central city unemployment in those cities. The people living in the inner cities did not get those jobs. They were taken by those who live in the suburbs and who commute to town. Now if the poor couldn't get unskilled and semiskilled jobs when they open up in the inner city—where discrimination was least prevalent—how were they going to get them in suburbia?

The assumption that the poor and minority people fared better in the suburbs than they did in the inner city was questioned by another study. Professor Bennett Harrison of the University of Maryland looked at the different effects of education on income in eighteen cities. He found that the value of a high school education meant $25 per week to a white worker and $9 per week to a nonwhite worker. A tragic but not surprising conclusion. But the amazing thing was that when Harrison studied the suburban ring around these cities, the ratios were the same. Nonwhites who managed to break into the suburbs were not able to increase their relative positions at all!

The claim that ghettos have no economic potential rests on the assumption that there must always be a sound economic reason for businessmen to invest or not to invest. Therefore, since businessmen do not invest in the ghetto it is because it is not economically feasible. This leaves economists generally in despair of reversing trends of any sort.

Typical of such comments is that of Robert Levine, former antipoverty official now with the Rand Corporation, who writes: "What it comes down to is the fact that industry plant location is determined by powerful economic factors" and that therefore the Federal Government can only begin economic development at "fantastic cost."

Another analyst of Federal programs, economist Sar Levitan, states that "the problems of the central city are to a large degree intractable."

What these writers generally forget is that the decline of the central city has been caused in no small part by the tremendous subsidy the Federal Government has provided for suburban development. Since the end of World War II billions of dollars have been poured into Federal highway and housing programs which have lured people, white people, out of the central city and into the suburbs. Thus the "powerful economic factors" that determine growth in the suburbs consist to a large extent of conscious and arbitrary decisions by the Federal Government to subsidize growth there. Decisions to subsidize the inner city growth would also be a powerful economic force.

Moreover, if one takes a look at the ghetto, it is not clear at all that businessmen's decisions are themselves all that economic in nature. Two economists made a study of Harlem in 1967–68 and concluded:

> Harlem is well located for the provision of services to a number of other areas in the city. And services are the fastest growing activity in central city areas. It may be asked why, despite its locational advantages, Harlem failed to develop more vigorously. The failure is caused in no small part by the racial situation itself. Many whites have experienced either fear or distaste at the idea of operating businesses in Harlem. The white businesses located there have, for the most part, existed a long

time, and most of them live exclusively off the local market. A more footloose business than, say, a local drugstore is likely to seek a non-Harlem location even at the cost of somewhat more difficult access.[2]

The final argument against development and for dispersal of the black inner city is that, if successful, the former will lead to further segregation. Development, it is held, will draw blacks into the inner city, while whites continue to flee into the suburbs. The result will be a polarized society. Although the concern expressed by many of those who make the argument is valid enough, the argument itself is weak on a number of grounds.

First, if the spread of the racial crisis from the South to the North in the latter part of the 1960s has demonstrated anything it is that resistance to integration is not primarily a matter of race, per se. It is not so much that whites dislike black-skinned people, they dislike poor black-skinned people. To working-class whites, poor blacks represent a threat to their marginal economic status. To middle-class whites, poor blacks represent a threat to their middle-class value system. The hysterical protests of mothers in Jackson, Michigan, of Chinese in San Francisco, and of otherwise liberal Jewish housewives in the Forest Hills section of Queens in New York City in 1971 were not aimed at middle-class black people, but at the fear that welfare families with large numbers of tough children with lower-class values would destroy the schools and overrun the neighborhood with crime. And as long as no one can guarantee that they are wrong, they will continue to oppose, successfully, any large-scale dispersal of poor blacks.

It follows that the path to integration may not be through the immediate dispersal of welfare families into middle-class suburbs but through the same process of integration and assimilation that previous immigrant groups went through. That is the process by which people develop middle-class skills, values, and confidence in a protected ghetto from where they then move off to integrate with the rest of the middle-class society. At that point not only is the surrounding society more ready to accept them, they themselves are tougher and more capable of surviving the race and ethnic pressures that still exist.

The Irish, the Italians, the Poles, the Jews, the Chinese, and so forth all went through that same process. For some the process took years, for others generations, and for some the journey out of the ghetto is not over. It is a process of "up and out"; rise up in the ghetto and move out into society. The dispersal theory attempts to stand the integration process on its head with an "out and up" strategy.

The fear that economic development would lead to a segregation of the races also underestimates the pull of the economy at large. As fast as ghetto enterprises can take the unskilled, uneducated black men and provide them with the training and experience they need, the same men will be lured off by the better opportunities in the larger economy. It is precisely the process of developing salable skills that will integrate the black man. Integration requires that black families move into the white middle class as *equals,* not as isolated charity cases.

There were of course major differences between the ghetto of the late 1960s and that of fifty years before. For one thing, the blacks were visibly different. For another, much of the family and social cohesion of the black man had been destroyed by the centuries of slavery. Finally, the ghetto itself did not offer the economic opportunities that it had in the past. The years of high demand for unskilled labor to man the industrial boom were past and the ghetto no longer served as a great labor market. Moreover, the concentration of economic power in the hands of food, drug, and department store chains made it almost impossible for ghetto businesses to survive the competition from these giants, who, while usually not physically located in the ghetto, were close enough to draw the patronage of its residents.

History could be expected simply to repeat itself. In order for individual blacks to follow the "up and out" path massive Government aid would be necessary to lift the inner city ghetto out of the economic depression into which it had sunk *as a result of past Federal programs.*

The final question between the proponents of the dispersal and development strategies was cost, always the final question when white America considers its racial problems. Proponents of dispersal claimed that development would be a tremendous cost. Proponents of development claimed that moving millions of people into the suburbs when the country was already undergoing a severe housing shortage was impossible. When dispersal people claimed that these millions could be transported to work sites in the suburbs and then back home at night, development people said the cost would be prohibitive even if it were a reasonable idea—which it wasn't. Given the complexities of both positions, neither side could come up with any meaningful cost estimates.

This then was the debate among scholars and government officials as to the future of the black ghetto. In theory, the dispersalists predominated. Everyone was philosophically in favor of opening up the suburbs. But no one was willing to open up *their* suburbs. While Cabinet officers proclaimed bold plans to force housing integration, the plans were quietly and sometimes not so quietly eviscerated in the HUD regional office when protests from suburbanites began to appear. As Secretary Romney soon found out, he was almost ridden out of one suburban community (in his home state of Michigan) on a rail. He beat a hasty retreat and amended his "dispersal" policy directive. The result was that nothing happened. Political reality prevented the dispersal while the lack of money prevented the development of the inner city.

A few efforts were made in the direction of development programs by the Johnson Administration between 1966 and 1968. In 1967, for example, Hubert Humphrey received the President's blessing to persuade defense contractors to establish facilities in the inner city. Part of the rationale was that defense contractors should have been willing to spread the benefits they were receiving from the war to the ghettos which, in terms of restricted domestic budgets, were paying for it. Companies like Aerojet-General, General Dynamics, Lockheed, Thiokol, AVCO, North American Rockwell, and Fairchild-Hiller—all major defense/space contractors—set up subcontracting facilities in black ghettos and Mexican-American barrios to please their number one customer.

Their heart was not in it, however. A few unskilled jobs were created by the Federal contracts but with one or two exceptions little in the way of a permanent employment emerged. When the defense companies complained to the incoming Nixon Administration that it was too much trouble for them to work on Government contracts in the ghetto, the program was quickly shelved.

In 1968 the Labor Department decided to lure firms into the inner city to employ the hard-core unemployed by giving grants to these firms. In Brooklyn three firms received over $3.5 million to hire and train twelve hundred people for at least six months. At the end of two years all three firms had closed down the ghetto sites and between them had managed to employ only three hundred people for more than six months. In Los Angeles the Labor Department gave approximately $1 million to each of five firms for locating in the Mexican-American barrio of East Los Angeles and hiring 1,580 local residents. As a result, one of the firms moved closer to the barrio, three moved and ended up the same distance away, and one took the Federal money and moved farther out.

Then there was the Model Cities program, the Great Society's major effort to pour resources into poor inner city areas. Between 1967 and 1970 one billion dollars had been appropriated to Model Cities, but by June 1970 only 10 percent of the money had been spent. Incessant conflicts between city halls which had the power over the program and the neighborhood groups that had been organized under the antipoverty program had brought the effort to a standstill. Originally, directives were issued which called for local "citizen participation," but they were soon reversed.

All of these programs for inner city development had one common characteristic. *They were controlled and operated by outsiders.* Like the Urban Renewal program before them, money was being given to white outsiders to do something for the ghetto dwellers. Many blacks and chicanos saw in these programs the same kind of process by which underdeveloped countries were being exploited everywhere—colonialism. In the words of black sociologist Kenneth Clark, black ghettos were "social and political—and above all economic—colonies."

The colonial parallel runs through the writings and speeches of black and other minority leaders, and with the disappointments of the War on Poverty, it became more credible.

As a psychological concept the parallel is compelling; race prejudice and exploitation are clearly the cause of much suffering and deprivation among individual blacks. And the assertion of a black pride and self-respect—a psychological nationalism—is essential for blacks to free themselves from the crippling effects of racism. But as an operating political and economic principle it is less clear. Does it mean the establishment of a separate state? Or a separate economy? If so, how can such a separation be managed?

Robert S. Browne, a black economist and director of the Black Economic Research Center, opened a National Black Economic Development Conference in Detroit in 1969 with a discussion of the colonial analogy. After describing the economic development planning in the Soviet Union and in India, he asked: "Does such an economic plan have meaning for black people in America?"

His own answer was yes and no. "The answer is no because this type of plan assumes the existence of a nation which has title to a cluster of contiguous resources and which exercises sovereignty over both itself as a community and over its members . . .

"Black America clearly fails all of these tests . . . We are not yet a consciously cohesive community; we do not have sovereignty over ourselves as individuals; we do not have sovereignty over ourselves as a community."

And his answer was yes because only by planning and operating as a unit, politically as well as economically, could black people hope to achieve a measure of economic self-reliance. Browne went on to say that ". . . the first step in black economic development is not economic at all, but political. There is no question of 'pulling ourselves up by the bootstraps.' We have no bootstraps. We are starting with so few economic resources of our own that our tactic must be to utilize cleverly what strength we do have, namely, the political force of 25 million potentially united black minds."

Browne's view, which reflected those of many of the younger black leaders, suggested that society is a collection of group powers. Although individuals have their own characteristics, the ability to integrate into society depends for the most part on one's ability to become part of a group with power, such as a corporation, a professional class, a labor union, etc. The problem for the blacks was that they had no group power and therefore were always at the mercy of what Lester Thurow of the Brookings Institution called the "monopoly power of whites."[3]

For many black leaders, given the nature of society, blacks *as individuals* could not hope to integrate in any large numbers. The lesson of the 1960s was that equality and justice could only come when blacks obtained independent power. Stokely Carmichael called it "Black Power," Roy Innis called it "Self-Determination."

One way to power was through votes. And in Northern cities, blacks began to organize themselves in the traditional style. Cleveland, Gary, and, later, Newark elected black Democratic mayors. In the South the Voting Rights Act gradually began to have its effect, and counties with black majorities like Hancock County, Georgia, and Greene County, Alabama, and cities like Fayette, Mississippi, began to elect black leadership.

But there are limits to the search for power through the electoral process when your constituency numbers only 15 percent of the population. Furthermore, political power is not necessarily a function of voting strength. In cities like Chicago there were plenty of black votes, and Mayor Richard J. Daley's indifference to the interests of black people was well known. And yet in election after election the black wards poured huge majorities for the Daley Machine. The saying on the South Side of Chicago was that Congressman Bill Dawson, the Democratic machine leader in the black wards, paid a chicken for every vote.

If black men were ever going to stand up tall on the streets of Chicago, they were going to have to outbid those chickens of Daley's. Thus, the final, and perhaps in the end the most important, reason for black economic development programs was that they provided support for the drive of black people to political power.

And so black ghetto leaders all over the country were turning to an economic development strategy to gain both jobs and income for their people—and to lay a foundation for political power. In Chicago, Jesse Jackson, who had been offered a job at a toll booth if he behaved himself, started Operation Breadbasket to feed the poor and to create black business.* In Roches-

* By 1971 Jackson had created an "economic development" organization with enough political importance to bring Mayor Daley to a Breadbasket conference where he enthusiastically embraced the erstwhile ghetto militant.

ter a militant black organization called FIGHT had established an electronics plant, in Philadelphia the Reverend Leon Sullivan had moved from street demonstrations and boycotts into development of a black-owned shopping center, in Los Angeles a group of unemployed blacks were running a toy factory making black dolls, in Chicago black youth gangs had formed a development corporation whose first venture was a wastepaper reprocessing plant.

And for the first time the white business establishment seemed to be taking seriously the efforts of blacks to develop their economic power. The Xerox Corporation was helping the FIGHT organization, General Electric had assisted Leon Sullivan's group, and the Mattel Toy Company had invested $250,000 in the toy factory which was to be wholly owned by a black community organization.

And reluctantly the Johnson Administration was being pulled into making some response. Howard Samuels, a wealthy businessman/politician was named head of the Small Business Administration in early 1968 and proceeded to begin a drive to enlarge the number of loans and assistance given to black businesses. He made a tour of banks and businessmen in cities all over the country to persuade them to enlarge their portfolio of black loans.

And in Bedford-Stuyvesant perhaps the most interesting experiment of the Johnson Administration was taking place not under the sponsorship of the President, but of the late Senator Robert F. Kennedy.

In 1966 Senator Kennedy made a tour of the Bedford-Stuyvesant section of Brooklyn where he was confronted by a bitter and hostile group of local black residents. Stunned by the reaction and determined to find a way to bring some hope to a hopeless population, Kennedy sent his aide Adam Walinsky to create a program for the neighborhood for which Kennedy in turn would get public and private support.

The program was based on the conclusions of Kennedy and Walinsky that the poverty program had been insufficiently concerned with generating employment and income where the poor lived, that it was foundering on city politics, and that the approach to the poverty program was piecemeal. What was required was a comprehensive strategy ("we must grab the web whole," Kennedy said in a 1966 speech on poverty), and a major role in solving poverty problems for the business community.

The last notion came from several sources. First, Kennedy saw, as Lyndon Johnson was to see shortly afterwards, that the Vietnam war was going to drain away the funds that had been promised for major domestic purposes and he thought that the private sector might be persuaded to pick up the slack. Secondly, championing the role of business in the poverty program was seen as helping to moderate the hostility toward Kennedy among businessmen. Finally, the presence of influential businessmen in a ghetto development program would free the program from dependence for political protection on local politicians. Thus the program embodied an alliance of businessmen and ghetto residents and specifically minimized the influence of the city and the anti-poverty bureaucracies.

This alliance was reflected in the structure of the project that emerged from the interplay between Kennedy's staff and the residents of the neighborhood. Two corporations were set up to run the program: the Restoration Corporation, composed of twenty-six leaders from the Bedford-Stuyvesant community, and the Development and Services Corporation, composed of twelve white establishment figures. In addition to Kennedy himself and his fellow Senator, Jacob Javits, the D&S board included Thomas Watson of IBM, Douglas Dillon, William S. Paley of CBS, George Moore of the First National City Bank, and Benno Schmidt of J. H. Whitney & Company.

To finance the program, Kennedy and Jacob Javits introduced and succeeded in passing Title I-D to the Economic Opportunity Act which established a Special Impact Program.† In the first year the program provided the Bedford-Stuyvesant program with almost $7 million.

The Johnson Administration was cool to Kennedy's idea. The President had no enthusiasm for a program with Kennedy's name on it, the politicians wanted to keep control of anti-poverty programs at city hall, and the Federal bureaucrats had a distaste for self-help.

† See Chapter 9.

Kennedy persisted. He was convinced of both the political and program logic of ghetto development. In the California television debate with Eugene McCarthy in June 1968 he took the development view while McCarthy maintained the "liberal" dispersal position. And much of his campaigning in California among the blacks and chicanos drove home messages of people having more control over their economic destinies. But the assassin's bullet ended it. And after June the chance for what might have been a national debate on the future of the cities and the black poor was gone.

Thus, as the election year of 1968 rolled in, there was discernible discontent with the Great Society among a number of blacks. And there was developing a body of ideas and experience that would have had an answer for that discontent. And among some, there was the hope, or fear, that Richard Nixon, the renowned political opportunist, would capture that discontent for his own use, to build a black base for himself and the Republican Party.

4 | THE RISE AND FALL
OF THE COMMUNITY
SELF-DETERMINATION ACT

"The Community Self-Determination plan jointly evolved by CORE and Republican legislative technicians and just introduced under Republican sponsorship in the House of Representatives is an imaginative proposal aimed at the same objectives outlined in my radio address 'Bridges to Human Dignity'. . .

"The program is one for economic development, within the ghetto, for building pride and independence, for enlisting the energies of private enterprise and creating new institutions by which private capital can be made available for ghetto investment. I am glad to see it under Republican sponsorship, and I hope it receives full and careful consideration by the appropriate committees of Congress."

RICHARD NIXON, June 12, 1968

One morning in December 1968, a month after the election of Richard Nixon and a month before his inauguration, several hundred people gathered in a ballroom of the Washington Hilton at the request of four United States Senators. White capitalists and black capitalists, labor leaders and Mexican-American organizers, outgoing Democrats and incoming Republicans, they met to discuss a proposed piece of legislation Richard Nixon had endorsed during the campaign. It was, so they thought, the President-elect's program for the blacks.

The bill that brought them all together was the Community

Self-Determination Act. It had been introduced in July 1968 with support from a bipartisan coalition of thirty-three Senators (nineteen Democrats, fourteen Republicans) and thirty-six members of the House (all Republicans). The coalition ranged in the Senate from Gaylord Nelson—a liberal Democrat who had been one of only three Senators to oppose the Vietnam appropriation bill in 1965—to John Tower, conservative Republican from Texas. The Senators who had convened the Washington meeting besides Nelson were Fred Harris, a Democrat from Oklahoma, and Jacob Javits of New York and Charles Percy of Illinois, both Republicans.

The Community Self-Determination Act was a product of a number of minds, conservative as well as liberal. The major ideas came from Roy Innis, black Chairman of the Congress of Racial Equality who had met with Nixon in May. Much of the work was done by John McClaughry, a Republican, and Gar Alperovitz, a Democrat, both formerly staff aides to several Congressmen and Senators. In addition, a host of community organizers, lawyers, and tax specialists worked on the 180-page bill for several months.[1]

The bill they came up with was an attempt to combine the growing demand of poor and black people for control over the stores, businesses, and houses in their neighborhoods with conservative traditions of local autonomy and self-reliance. These notions were combined in the community development corporation (CDC), the key institution set up by the Act. The CDC was to be a private profit-making corporation operating in a poor urban or rural area. Any resident of the area sixteen or over could buy a share in the corporation at par value of five dollars. But no matter how many shares a person had, he was only entitled to one vote in corporation elections. The shares did not pay any dividends.

In McClaughry's words: "The corporation would own a family of businesses which might range from a shoeshine stand to a major factory. With the profits from these enterprises, the community corporation would finance community service projects of the people's own choice, such as day care centers, basic education, legal aid, nonprofit housing, health care, and the like."

A companion local institution, the community development

bank, was to be wholly owned by the CDC. This bank would finance CDC businesses. The bill also created a United States Community Development Bank, as a secondary financing institution serving the local banks.

In addition to the community development bank, the other major financing for the program would come in the form of tax benefits. The major beneficiaries would be established business corporations, primarily through turn-key programs.

A turn-key program, based on some experiences of American firms in underdeveloped countries, is one in which an existing business corporation would establish a business facility and train local people to manage it. After a specified period of time the outside firm would sell the business to the local community development bank. The bill provided a series of tax benefits to encourage private corporations to enter into agreements with the CDC.

The principal authors of the Community Self-Determination Act represented three different political forces concerned with domestic policies in 1968. And each brought to the bill their own ideological motives.

For Roy Innis, Floyd McKissick, and other members of CORE, the bill represented their views on what American blacks needed most—economic power. From being a leading integrationist organization in the early 1960s, the Congress of Racial Equality had turned away from concern with civil rights to an all-absorbing interest in how blacks might obtain the economic base that alone would give them equality.

Innis calls this, "Separatist Economics." He maintains: "We live in a setting where one group—not our own—controls the institutions, and the flow of goods and services. We can change our condition by liberating ourselves and placing these vital instruments of social and economic destiny in our own hands. This is what we mean by separation—quite a different matter from segregation."[2]

Innis thinks that black ghettos such as Harlem were in many ways similar to underdeveloped countries. But since the ghettos lack the political boundaries that would permit them to protect their own industries they needed to create special protections to assure the loyalty of black consumers and to assure that the profits will be used for the best interests of the black community rather than the enrichment of a few individuals. The Federal Government should therefore forego conventional welfare programs in favor of assisting blacks to develop power independent of the white establishment. "We are past the stage," he wrote, "where we can talk seriously of whites acting toward blacks out of moral imperatives. That does not work."

Why should the white establishment help the blacks attain independent power? Innis' answers: "Enlightened self-interest on the part of those who hold real power in society. Not the liberal politicians, or the labor bosses who had been the black man's ally up until this point, but the corporate businessmen, who have a greater stake in avoiding racial warfare than anyone else." Innis' position suggested the theme of Robert Kennedy's Bedford-Stuyvesant program, an alliance between ghetto blacks and businessmen.

If Roy Innis represented that part of the black community that was ready to turn its back on traditional liberal social objectives and their traditional liberal allies, John McClaughry represented the kind of enlightened conservative Republican who Innis might have hoped was listening.

McClaughry, now a Republican state legislator in Vermont, had worked several years on Capitol Hill for a variety of Republicans, including Senator Charles Percy. In the spring of 1968, while a Fellow at Harvard's Institute of Politics, he was a major supplier of domestic program ideas for Richard Nixon, later joining the Nixon campaign staff as Special Assistant for Community Affairs. He was a force behind Nixon's "Bridges to Human Dignity" speeches, and was responsible for the May 1968 Nixon-Innis-McKissick meeting.

McClaughry is a conservative who labels himself a "Jeffersonian Republican." He believes in limited government, reliance on "free market" solutions to economic problems, and decentralization of legitimate government functions to the lowest feasible level. For McClaughry, the New England town meeting—small, democratic, relevant—should be the foundation of government. Only in this way, he feels, can the citizenry effectively take care of their own problems without spawning a faceless and expensive bureaucracy.

In addition to this strong reliance on local decision-making as opposed to Governmental action at higher levels, McClaughry also emphasized the vital importance of maintaining a widespread ownership of private property, even through Government aid if necessary. He is fond of quoting Daniel Webster, John Adams, and James Madison to the effect that the concentration of property and economic power into the hands of a few must inescapably lead to despotism, followed by either political or forceful revolution, all anathema to the traditional conservative.

McClaughry also saw that his Republican Party badly needed to acquire a foothold in the minority community. The Republicans were unlikely to outdo the liberal Democrats in civil rights, open housing, racial balance in schools, and the like. As the interests of blacks, Spanish-speaking and other minorities shifted to economic means, however, he saw an opportunity for the Republicans to provide them with a political home by helping them obtain property rights, which would make them more conservative.

Like Innis, McClaughry believed that the Republican officeholders and leaders of the large corporations could be persuaded that helping propertyless minority groups to acquire ownership and control of their economic fortunes was a highly desirable means of advancing conservative goals and strengthening Republican ranks.

Gar Alperovitz, the third co-author of the Community Self-Determination Act, represented the interests of those who wanted to hold the gains the Great Society had made for the poor in the face of a Republican Administration and an increasingly conservative Congress. He reasoned that much of the institutions created by the War on Poverty—the community action agencies and the model cities programs—might be saved if they could be placed under the protective coloration of a business-oriented antipoverty effort larded over with Republican ideology.

Alperovitz also had another, more personal motive. He was interested in the notions of community control of business, not only as a device to help the blacks and other minorities to achieve power, but as a way of restructuring society.

He saw both Republicans and Democrats drawing close together into a corporate socialism controlled by a technocratic elite. A similar fusion of interest was happening in other advanced countries, both communist and capitalist. Only through the development of decentralized local economic power could a technological dictatorship be avoided. For Alperovitz, the Community Self-Determination Act was a step in that decentralized direction.

The fusion of interests around the President-elect's vague references to Black Capitalism was neat. Innis would bring in the blacks, McClaughry the businessmen and the conservative politicians, and Alperovitz the liberals.

Too neat. They had not at all reckoned with the power of the labor liberals, nor with those who had little ideology or political persuasion but who wanted desperately to be capitalists and who just happened to be black.

Organized labor, whose support of social welfare legislation is essential to muster the Democratic votes necessary for passage, was opposed to any programs that took away their power to control the pace and direction of the integration of blacks into the mainstream of the American economy.

The leadership of the AFL-CIO, the United Auto Workers, the Teamsters, and other labor unions see industrial labor as the primary road through which new immigrants to American society must travel. Thus they support Federal investment in programs to give poor black vocational training. Such programs are operated by the U.S. Department of Labor, and by State Labor Departments, where organized labor has its greatest influence. As a result, the billions of dollars that have been poured into manpower training programs are concentrated on training the poor for low-paying marginal menial jobs such as nurse's aides, short-order cooks, etc., and until recently scarcely any funds at all have gone to support the training of the poor for jobs in the better-paying industries, such as construction.

Labor leaders also see the political strength of organized labor as the basic political protection for blacks and other minorities. And in fact it is organized labor which in Washington and in most state governments provides the bulk of votes on issues of critical importance to the black community. In recent years the Carswell and Haynsworth defeats, passage of all major civil rights legislation, and the survival of the poverty program would not have been accomplished but for the lobbying strength of organized labor. In return for this support, the civil rights leadership gave labor a tacit agreement not to interfere with the pace of labor union integration. The classic situation occurred in 1970 when Clarence Mitchell, Legislative Director for the NAACP and the most influential black lobbyist in Washington, refused to join the Nixon Administration's attempt to force labor unions working on Federally financed construction projects to speed up the pace of integration. Mitchell's rationale was that he could not afford to break up the alliance with labor which had served the blacks so well in the past.

The promise of Black Capitalism was to provide blacks with a political base, founded on their own economic power freeing them from dependence on organized labor and other liberal groups. For most of organized labor,* Black Capitalism is bad enough, but the vision of community development corporations which are almost explicitly established to concentrate power in the hands of black institutions was completely unacceptable.

The position of organized labor is reinforced by the views of a class of liberal academicians who form the core of academic advice to the bureaucracy and to liberal Democrats and Republicans. Many of them are economists who are very uncomfortable with questions of power shifts. Economists tend to take questions of power as given and therefore rarely come to conclusions that disturb the status quo. In addition, economists tend to want to quantify problems; they find it very difficult to quantify political power relationships and almost impossible to computerize them. Finally, many of these academicians have come to positions of influence by doing their work in labor-oriented research. Between 1964 and 1970 the U.S. Department of Labor alone spent millions of dollars in grants for research given to colleges and universities. There arose a whole category of manpower economists, whose loyalty to the primacy of manpower training programs in the array of domestic policies is very strong. In a small way it is

---

* Some of the more progressive labor unions, it should be noted, have recognized the need for political organization among poor minority people. The UAW in recent years has devoted time and resources to minority organizing efforts in various parts of the country.

a parallel to the military-industrial complex. The spending of money on research to assist manpower programs has created a constituency for the continued support of such activities.

The second group to oppose the Community Self-Determination Act were those who represented black businessmen's organizations and who were beginning to appear more frequently in Washington now that a Republican Administration was about to come to power.

These were organizations like the National Business League, founded by Booker T. Washington in 1900, and the Interracial Council for Business Opportunity, supported by donations from the Rockefellers. These groups represented the marginal entrepreneurial spirit that managed to survive in the black community despite the many obstacles to a black man getting into business. Their membership tended to be older and more conservative in their outlook than most black civil rights organizations. And they were often estranged from or at least uninvolved in the mainstream of the black movement in the 1960s.

In the literature of black society written by black people themselves two characteristics of black businessmen became clear. First, they have been forced, as a result of being excluded from white markets, into a position of exclusively exploiting their fellow blacks. As Kenneth Clark points out in his book *Dark Ghetto:* "Most Negro wealth comes from businesses that white society did not wish to control or from services particularly personal—newspaper publishing of the segregated press; real estate and insurance, which grew out of Negro burial societies; an undertaking which owes its Negro monopoly in the ghetto to the fact that white undertakers did not wish to handle Negro bodies."[3]

Second, the Negro businessman, like other middle-class Negroes, had a history of estrangement from black society. "The psychology of the Negro of wealth," Clark continues, "like that of the Negro poor, is in its own way a psychology of insecurity. The wealthy Negro is not sure that his wealth will bring power though he sees that money often brings power in white society. He uses most of his psychic energy to protect his wealth; he is conservative and careful of his wealth and does not easily share it with the ghetto community at large."

"The ghetto pathology includes an unwillingness to make any

personal sacrifice beyond those already required by the ghetto itself. The ghetto fails to prepare one for voluntary sacrifices precisely because it demands so many involuntary ones . . . Whatever the source of wealth, those who attain it tend to divorce themselves from the community itself and refuse to assume generally any responsibility to the community."[4]

The picture that Clark draws is one of a small isolated business community, unsure of itself in terms of both the outside white society and of the ghetto population. Traditionally the leadership in the black community has not fallen to the business community, but to the ministers and churchmen who can offer spiritual solace and a social structure to the black masses.

One of the most surprising aspects to these descriptions of black society is the absence of the businessman as a figure of power. In his discussion of the black power structure, Clark talks of ministers, lawyers, teachers, and politicians, but only once mentions a businessman. And even this businessman attained power through a career as a local political leader. It would be unthinkable for someone writing of a white American power structure to leave out the businessman.

In America, business power has long been the foundation of political power and the absence of businessmen from the black elite is an insight into their powerlessness. Clark comments on the failure of a small Harlem middle-class group which tried to form itself into an informal power structure to gain protection and influence for Harlem. "Only two," Clark says, "were totally independent in the sense of freedom from reliance on elective or appointive office. No one in the group had achieved the level of economic independence that would permit him to be publicly identified with the conflict at issue."[5]

Lacking a genuine business class and recognizing their weakness, middle-class blacks developed a myth of business success to give themselves a sense of accomplishment. E. Franklin Frazier, in his brutally honest dissection of the black bourgeoisie, writes:[6]

> In escaping from identification with the masses, the black bourgeoisie has attempted to identify with the white propertied classes. Since this has been impossible, except in their minds, because of the racial barriers, those identified with this class have attempted to act out this role in a world of make-believe. In the world of make-believe they have not

taken over the patterns of behavior of white-collar and professional white workers but the values and as far as possible the patterns of behavior of wealthy whites. With their small earnings, their attempt to maintain the style of living of the white propertied classes has only emphasized the unreality of their way of life. Faith in the myth of Negro business, which symbolizes the power and status of white America, has been the main element in the world of make-believe that the black bourgeoisie has created.

The stirring in the black masses caused by the Civil Rights movement and the Antipoverty programs of the 1960s to some extent broke down the traditional isolation of the black middle class. By the end of the decade of the sixties black lawyers, black architects, and other black professionals were working for and with the black poor and their organizations all over the country. A greater sense of unity and black pride among many segments of black society were among the major achievements of the sixties.

The black businessman was an exception to this. Freedom rides, civil rights marches, demonstrations, political organizing were alien to him, as they are to most small businessmen. Furthermore, since the black businessman is typically an exploiter of a segregated market, integration is an economic threat. The small margin which enables the black-owned barbershop or funeral home to survive would be wiped out in the event of quick integration. Thus many black businessmen felt threatened in that the opening up of black society to whites meant the closing down of their monopolistic, although marginal position.

For the years of the sixties then, the black businessmen and their spokesmen watched as the ministers, the lawyers, and the black politicians grabbed the fancy of white society and the black masses. Frazier had noted that "the Negro leaders who propagate the myth of Negro business are uncompromising enemies of any radical doctrines."[7] The heady demands for change sweeping through the black community were leaving the uncompromising enemies of radicalism behind, with the bitter label of "Uncle Tom."

As befits a group that would seek to emulate the behavior patterns of the white propertied class, many of the black businessmen were Republicans. And thus the election of a Republican Administration dedicated to Black Capitalism meant that it was now "their turn" to become the spokesman for black society. Men who a few years before cringed at the sound of Stokely Carmichael shouting "Black Power" were now prepared to receive the responsibility from the white Republican Administration for transforming that revolutionary slogan into a respectable business-oriented path. Everyone knew, or thought they knew, that the President *had* to have a program for the blacks—that he couldn't rule without reconciling himself to such a large and potentially disruptive group. And Black Capitalism had been the only thing he had offered during his campaign. He would therefore have to turn to those blacks whose instincts were conservative and Republican and who still believed in the capitalist dream of Andrew Carnegie.

The black business community saw the Community Self-Determination Act as an attempt by what they thought were black radicals to muscle in on Black Capitalism. The last thing they wanted was to see that slogan used to further the interests of community organizers and civil rights marchers.

The program of the Washington Conference confirmed the fears of the black bourgeoisie. Featured speakers were people like Roy Innis and Franklin Florence, militant minister from Rochester, New York. Alex Mercure, director of a migrant worker education program in New Mexico, another nonbusinessman, represented the Mexican-Americans.

The purpose of the meeting was to gather up support for the Community Self-Determination Act and to create a committee of businessmen and minority people to lobby for the bill with the new administration. The Senators lent their names to the effort because they had been convinced that there was a groundswell of support for the proposal.

But halfway through the proceedings it was clear that there was anything but unity among both whites and nonwhites. In the audience labor representatives were complaining loudly to all around them that the bill was a Nixon Administration ploy to kill the poverty program. And then halfway through the morning, things began to open up. William Hudgins, President of the black-owned Freedom National Bank in Harlem, said that he would not agree to any community development banking scheme that would undercut the established black banks. Dr. Edward

Irons, head of the National Bankers Association, a trade association of black banks, rose from the audience and also criticized the bill.

Darwin Bolden, the truculent head of the Interracial Council for Business Opportunity, rose to say that the bill would have the effect of destroying the black businesses that were already in the ghetto. Several other blacks joined in the chorus of criticism with the labor union people following each remark with applause.

Then the Reverend Franklin Florence, of the FIGHT Corporation in Rochester, one of the models for the Community Self-Determination Act, surprised everyone by attacking both the bill and Innis. Florence indicated that he personally had not been consulted. He shouted: "If this is to be a community self-determination bill," he said, "then we better start by letting the black community determine what should be in this bill."

The Senators began to look uneasy.

Roy Innis rose. A dramatic orator with a West Indian accent, Innis described his own vision of a separatist economics and then proceeded in a bitter denunciation of his critics in the black community. To get black participation, he said, "I will send my lieutenants into the black community to get their ideas." And as for who was running the show, he reminded them: "This is *my* bill. And if no one likes it, let them get their own bill."

The fate of the Community Self-Determination Act was sealed there. Clarence Mitchell, chief lobbyist for the NAACP walked out of the room. And the Senators, who thought they were sponsoring something that the black community wanted, found themselves in the middle of a bitter dispute between blacks and quickly withdrew. And shortly afterwards labor lobbyists let their liberal Senator friends know that they were not happy with the proposal.

Two months later the Executive Council of the labor federation at its winter meetings at Bal Harbour, Florida, issued a scathing attack on Black Capitalism:

> At its worst, Black Capitalism is a dangerous, divisive delusion authored as a panacea by extremists, both black and white, some businessmen who see a chance for profit, and a few well-intentioned but misguided liberals . . .

The union leaders made no mention of Nixon's sponsorship of the concept but there was nothing ambiguous about their condemnation. They viewed any such effort as "apartheid, antidemocratic nonsense" and "attempts to build separate economic enclaves" which they viewed as being regressive and self-destructive.

Although opposing *large-scale* "separatist" economic ventures, the Council did endorse low-interest loans and technical assistance for *small* businesses. Quite clearly "big labor" was making it known that it was prepared to exercise its political muscle to ensure the defeat of any new legislation consistent with Nixon's Black Capitalism promises.

The businessmen's committee, headed by Joe Wilson, President of Xerox, was nominally formed, to keep up appearances, but slowly dissolved afterwards as it became clear that the political interest had waned. The committee's one accomplishment was to commission a paper by Dr. Sar Levitan, a manpower economist from George Washington University who was mildly critical of the proposed bill. Senator Goodell reintroduced the bill without a great deal of enthusiasm when the Congress came back in January 1969, but hearings were never held. The bill was later extensively rewritten as the Community Corporation Act of 1970 but was not introduced again.

The Community Self-Determination Act died by the hand of an unlikely coalition of labor liberals and black businessmen. But that is not quite the whole story. As the conferees filed out of the meeting room, one labor lobbyist said: "You know, if there had been some evidence that Nixon was really interested in any of this, none of those blacks would have jumped on it like they did. They would have tried to work something out beforehand. I think this is a side show, and everybody senses it."

True or not, the words were an accurate foreshadowing of the future of Black Capitalism.

5 | THE BLACK SHARE
OF THE $ PIE

The History

"We see more and more clearly that economic survival for the Negro in American means . . . that he must employ labor, that he must organize industry, that he must enter American industrial development as a group, capable of offensive and defensive action, and not simply as an individual, liable to be made the victim of the white employer and of such of the white labor unions as dare. . . . We cannot depend on God or his vice-[regent] the White Man."

W. E. B. DuBois

On April 27, 1699, a bill—no doubt written by the ancestral forefathers of the Urban Coalition—was presented to the Colonial Assembly.

A Bill for facilitating the conversion of Indians and Negroes (which the King's instructions require should be endeavored to be passed), would not go down with the Assembly; they [the assembly, consisting of landed gentry, merchants, et al.] had a notion that the Negroes being converted to Christianity [would alter the heathen's status in the eyes of God], would [then] emancipate them from their service, for they have no other servants in this country but Negroes.[1]

Thus on the theory that Christianity was likely to infect the healthy supply of labor for domestic service, the bill was defeated.

For two hundred seventy years, between 1699 and 1969—when President Nixon signed Executive Order 11458*—a business-as-usual policy of economic servitude prevailed with regard to blacks in America. Many volumes of history have been written and many more can be compiled with all the necessary supportive evidence to document this pattern of systematic discrimination. We have attempted, within a limited space, to cull information and facts from relevant materials so as to present current dilemmas within the context of a historical framework.

For the average middle-class white American—schooled in the history of the Negro as a passive figure plodding along in the shadows of American life—contemporary black militancy and strident demands for a "piece of the action" are viewed as a threat to his own political and economic security. Moreover, as a result of miseducation he feels no guilt. Most Americans comprehend neither why blacks aren't satisfied with their lot nor why they haven't used middle-class methods to achieve their newly acquired goals. In retrospect it is difficult for mid-America to comprehend fully the brutality and horror of slavery and the tragedy of black history. So painful and degrading was America's systematic slavery that upon reflection one is amazed that the blacks managed to survive it at all.

In recent years, social scholars have begun to deal with the economic and political realities of black history in America. As black consciousness has risen, economic and political expectations have taken on an entirely new meaning. Blacks have every intention of gaining the dignity and economic security that was denied them by the circumstances of their own history and the willful exploitation by European powers and later by American corporate and political interests. For a better understanding of the brutal and repressive nature of black political/economic history one need only refer to leading scholars such as John Hope Franklin, David B. Davis, Carl N. Degler, Milton Cantor, Staughton Lynd, Stuart W. Bruchey, Douglass C. North, Benjamin Quarles, Kenneth M. Stampp, and C. Vann Woodward.

Almost all black businesses *since our nation gained independ-*

---

* The Executive Order which created the Office of Minority Business Enterprise, the super-agency which was to coordinate all Federal and private-sector programs.

ence have been established to serve the personal needs of the black community; principally because white businessmen have found them *unprofitable* and, therefore, have refused to provide these services for black people. In those fields where white merchants have found it most profitable to serve the black community—such as furniture, appliance, and department stores and food markets—black businessmen have generally found it too difficult to compete. As a result, by 1967 nearly 90 percent of black-owned businesses are beauty shops, barber shops, mortuaries, restaurants, cleaning and pressing stores, repair shops, tailor shops, and the like. (It is of no small coincidence that even in 1856 *Colored Weekly,* a magazine published in New York, reported that the economic opportunities open to blacks were restricted to: barbers, tailors, cooks, stewards, shoemakers, waiters, servants, and laborers.) White merchants, in or outside the ghetto, have offered all other services and most basic goods for sale. With some exceptions, this has been true throughout the history of black people in America.

In a book entitled *The Circle of Discrimination,* Herman Bloch—a black economics professor and former union organizer —identifies, analyzes, and documents the historical patterns of discrimination that led to the black man's economic subordination in the New World. He starts in the Colonial era under Dutch and English rule, when the Afro-American's "outsider" status was institutionalized, and carries his study to the present day. In a devastating critique Bloch places particular emphasis on the role of employment—although he offers valuable insights into ownership also—and gives ample documentation to support his theme of overt discrimination and deliberate suppression.

One is struck by the studied ingenuity of both trade unionists and businessmen as they competed with one another to assure that the black man was systematically kept out of the mainstream of the American economy.

In his classic book, *Folkways,* William Graham Sumner noted that:

> the habits of the individual and customs of the society which arise from efforts to satisfy needs [in the case of the American colonies, the lack of an indigenous population, the territory, plus the white man's need to emulate the estate system prevalent in Europe]. In time [these

individual habits and customs of society, arising from needs, won] authority, [became] regulative for succeeding generations and [took] on the character of a social force.[2]

Although historians and sociologists differ as to which came first, legal slavery or institutionalized discrimination—it depends upon whether you read Mary and Oscar Handlin's *Race and Nationality in American Life* or Carl N. Degler's *Slavery and the Genesis of American Race Prejudice*—life for Afro-Americans under the Dutch rule (1625–64) was bad and under the English (1664–1777) it became worse. The main difference being that the Dutch offered a limited degree of social mobility and the occasional opportunity for land grants while the English did not. As early as 1702 the English passed an act entitled "An Act for Regulating Slaves"; A. J. Northrup in *Slavery in New York* told of how some folks resisted the English "noblesse oblige." The language of the act stated that "Negro Americans have been found oftentimes guilty of confederating together in running away, or other ill practices." (More recently, Rap Brown and others have stood charged with similar "offenses.")

Thus, on the eve of the American Revolution the relative position of the Afro-American relative to the white freeman was described as follows:

> In general, . . . slaves were forbidden to assemble without permission and presence of responsible whites, were not to own, or carry guns of any kind, were not to trade, buy, sell, or engage in any other economic activity without permission of their masters, were not to be off the plantation grounds at any time, or on the streets after 9 or 10 in the evening without written permission, were not to practice, or administer medicine, were not to lift their hands against any white person, were not to be taught to read or write.[3]

The white man's attitude toward the Afro-American was determined by basic economic needs. Colonial America lacked an indigenous labor supply and Afro-Americans were forcibly transplanted to the New World to provide cheap labor. At the same time social and economic needs determined that the slave labor force was to be treated as racially inferior.

The Revolutionary War provided black slaves and freemen some freedom of movement in their efforts to gain access to the trades. Since there was an urgent need for manpower to fight the war, the labor shortage became aggravated. Blacks were therefore allowed to achieve more economic mobility. An additional factor was the effort of the revolutionary leaders to offer freedom to those slaves who joined the Revolutionary army after pro-British, Tory slave owners had offered slaves this freedom if they fought the colonists.

The condition of the black man, however, did not change substantially after the war.

> By the time the colonies had succeeded in overthrowing English control, slavery had become a national institution, fully implanted in all 13 colonies, and the newly formed political confederation did not change the Afro-American's second-class social, economic, and political status.[4]

Remarking on the kinds of institutionalized discrimination that occurred Abigail Adams wrote John Adams (her husband) that:

> I have been much diverted with a little occurrence . . . which serves to show how little founded in nature the so much boasted principle of liberty is. [Specifically, she was referring to the exclusion of Afro-Americans from the skilled trades.][5]

Prior to 1820, those blacks, freed by their owners or having purchased their own freedom, took part in urban businesses, as owners, craftsmen or employees. Their situation deteriorated, however, as blacks in large cities lost out to the influx of foreign immigrants for jobs, housing, mobility and business. Beginning with the Scottish and Irish, who immigrated in the 1820s, blacks were continuously confronted and attacked by successive waves of immigrants until Congress passed the Immigration Exclusion Acts in the early 1920s.

Legally, many of the blacks' rights were lost in the courts, and the combination of economic discrimination and prejudice destroyed the blacks' position in most Northern urban centers. In Philadelphia, for example, an 1836 state court ruling deprived Negroes of the right to vote, ending forty-six years of full citizenship. Legal discrimination also had an economic impact. Black-owned businesses decreased from 344 in 1838, to 111 in 1849, to less than 20 just before the Civil War. Public opinion was so much against the blacks that legislation to limit southern

Negroes' migration into Pennsylvania was introduced in the legislature although it failed to pass.

After the Napoleonic Wars in Europe, a new wave of immigration to America intensified the discrimination against blacks since the immigrants desperately needed jobs, trades, and status in a strange land. Leon F. Litwack[6] traces the exclusion of blacks from trades and professional activity as well as from their unskilled jobs when in competition against whites. Blacks were restricted to the most menial occupations after slavery was abolished in the Northern states.

Litwack summarized the double standard employed by the Abolitionists:

> Of what use was the right to vote, attend school, and to enter the homes of the abolitionists if it was still impossible to gain access to any but the most menial employment. The economic condition of the Negro was at best deplorable, and the new waves of immigrants, competing for many positions which Negroes had long monopolized, only made matters worse. Although some white abolitionists had agitated vigorously in the areas of civil rights and educational opportunities, little had been done in the way of economic assistance, except to call upon Negroes to improve themselves.[7]

Most "history books" pictured the growth of the Abolition Movement as a rather glorious page in the "struggle for equality." J. M. McPherson sheds more realistic light on this period:

> When the militant phase of abolitionism began in 1831, the status of Northern Negroes was deplorable. Shut out from white schools and churches, forced to live in city slums and ghettos [Five Points, formerly common land, is one area referred to], denied equal civil and political rights, . . . confined to menial occupations, almost universally despised as members of an inferior race, the Northern Negroes' lot in 1830 was a harsh one. In some respects their status actually deteriorated [further] in the next thirty years. The huge influx of immigrants in the 1840s and 1850s drove colored people out of many of their former occupations and subjected them to the mob fury of socially and economically insecure immigrants.[8]

By the 1850s the blacks were being squeezed out of manual labor by the German and Irish immigrants. Dr. Charles Wesley, a black historian pointed up the failures of the antislavery movement in bettering the economic lot of blacks.

> The antislavery movement would destroy slavery, but it neglected the more practical task of creating an economic future for the free Negro population in industry. Many Negroes were physically free, and yet, they were enslaved and placed in degraded economic positions by the apathy of their friends and the hostile attitude of their fellow workers. Racial toleration in industrial occupations was rare. In the majority of places where Negroes and whites worked together there was a sullen suspicion which soon gave opportunity to the whites to force the Negroes out of employment, either by means of economic pressure, or by legislation. The conditions of Negro free labor which were brought out by the Civil War did not end economic strife between the races. They served only to increase the struggle between white and black labor in the United States.[9]

According to the eminent historian C. Vann Woodward, Thaddeus Stevens, the foremost champion of freedmen and leader of Radical Reconstruction, was not prepared to enfranchise the Negro freedman in 1866. Stevens was also the leader of the Republican House majority. Stevens, however, did change his mind in 1867, though the reasons are unclear and debatable. Woodward offers his own interpretation of events in *The Political Legacy of Reconstruction*. These views are fascinating, both in their historical context and as they relate to the striking parallel circumstances of the GOP and candidate Nixon's position in 1968.

Woodward wrote that:

> Thaddeus Stevens, foremost champion of the freedmen, master of the Republican House majority, and leader of Radical Reconstruction, was advocating some extremely radical measures.
> In addition to "the party purpose" so frankly avowed by Stevens, there was another purpose which was not frankly declared. It was more often disavowed, concealed, deprecated. This was the purpose of the business community. Although there were significant divisions within the community, a powerful group saw in the return of a disaffected and Democratic South a menace to the economic order that had been established during the absence of the seceding states from the Union. On nearly every delicate and disturbing economic issue of the day—taxation, the National Bank, the national debt, government bonds and their funding, railroads and their financing, regulation of corporations, government grants and subsidies to business, protective tariff legislation—on one and all the business community recognized in the unre-

constructed South an antagonist of long standing. In combination with traditional allies in the West and North, the South could upset the new order. Under these circumstances, the Northern business community, except for the banking and mercantile interests allied with the Democrats, put aside conservative habits and politics and threw its support to Radical Reconstruction.

Neither the party purpose, the business purpose, nor the two combined constituted a reputable justification with which to persuade the public to support a radical and unpopular program. But there was a purpose that was both reputable and persuasive—the philanthropic purpose, the argument that the freedmen needed the ballot to defend and protect their dearly bought freedom, their newly won civil rights, their welfare and livelihood. Of their philanthropic argument the Radicals could make a persuasive and cogent case. And it is undoubtedly true that some of the Radicals were motivated almost entirely by their idealism and their genuine concern for the rights and welfare of the freedmen. What is doubtful is that these were the effective or primary motives, or that they took priority over the pragmatic and materialistic motives of party advantage and sectional economic interests. It is clear at any rate that, until the latter were aroused and marshaled, the former made little progress. On the whole the skepticism of Secretary Gideon Welles would seem to be justified. "It is evident," he wrote in his diary, "that intense partisanship instead of philanthropy is the root of the movement."

This ulterior motivation, then, is the incubus with which the Negro was burdened before he was ever awakened into political life. The operative and effective motives of his political genesis were extraneous to his own interests and calculated to serve other ends. If there ever came a time when those ends—party advantage and sectional business interests—were better served in some other way, even in a way destructive of the basic political rights of the race, then the political prospects of the Negro would darken. Another incubus was the strongly partisan identifications of his political origins. The major national party of opposition took no part in those origins, regarded them as wholly inimical to its interests, and consequently felt no real commitment to the movement nor to the preservation of its fruits. If there came a time when that party was in the ascendancy, even locally, the political future of the Negro again would darken. To these evil portents should be added the strong resistance to Negro suffrage in the Northern states, the obvious reluctance and hesitance of radical leaders to commit the party to that course, and the grudging acquiescence of the North in the coercive use of it in the South.[10]

It is clear from Woodward's interpretation that the political freedom which was granted to Negroes was motivated by political and economic considerations that would give advantages to white business and corporate interests; and that the argument was couched in idealistic and moral tones. One of the remarkable ironies of history is that Nixon's "Bridges of Dignity" speech was made a hundred years later.

Just as the Republican Party promised political freedom to Negroes in 1867 the GOP candidate in 1968 pledged to give economic freedom to blacks. Whether the stated and underlying motivations and concerns are parallel in nature and scope are questions that will be answered as this book progresses.

Until the 1880s it was the Northern European immigrants who inhibited the upward mobility of the blacks. After 1880 the circumstances changed, but not for the blacks. A new wave of immigrants, this time from Eastern and Southern Europe—Greeks, Italians, Slavs, and Jews—reached the American shores. Thus, until World War I the black remained in the same position of competition, displacement, and discrimination; but during this period his "competition" was not the Irish and Scots, but the new immigrants.

Those hit hardest by burgeoning American racism were the blacks who had been in urban centers first. They had worked hard, received a measure of success and accommodation from the white majority, then suddenly saw that advance destroyed by both the influx of European immigrants and the "great migrations" of untrained and uneducated Southern blacks, with whom they had little in common. Rather than setting up new communities, the new black arrivals migrated to established black neighborhoods and turned minorities into majorities, racial enclaves into urban slums.

W. E. B. DuBois, for example, advised that Negro fugitive slaves should not be sent to Pennsylvania, as the effects would be detrimental to the existing colored population. He described the changes taking place as follows:

> . . . A mass of poverty-stricken, ignorant fugitives and ill-trained freedmen . . . rushed to the city, swarmed in the vile slums which the rapidly growing city furnished, and met in social and economic competition equally ignorant but more vigorous foreigners. These foreigners outbid them at work, beat them on the streets, and were enabled to do this by the prejudice which Negro crime and the antislavery sentiment had aroused in the city.

In 1898 DuBois observed the marginal nature of black-owned businesses, saying that the Philadelphia Negroes of that time "(held) no conspicuous place in the business world." In the first national study of black-owned businesses, made in 1898, DuBois showed that the average capital investment for the surveyed businesses was only $4,600 and the majority of these were retail and service establishments. Later studies indicated that the average of the annual sales of over four thousand black businesses in a dozen cities was less than $3,400. Nearly half of these stores were retail outlets, half were service businesses, and the remaining few were scattered small businesses.

In the two decades before and after the turn of the century, Booker T. Washington began to put forward his proposals for the advancement of black people through Black Capitalism. Washington, the most influential black man of his time, was the focus of a national uproar when President Teddy Roosevelt invited him to dinner at the White House. But Washington was no militant integrationist. He felt instead that only through the acquisition of economic power combined with a willingness to accept at least temporarily the then current racial attitudes of whites toward blacks would his people become free. In 1896 he wrote:

> Friction between the races will pass away in proportion as the black man, by reason of his skill, intelligence, and character, can produce something that the white man wants or respects in the commercial world . . . Let us go on for a few more years knitting our business and industrial relations into those of the white man, till a black man get a mortgage on a white man's house that he can foreclose at will. The white man on whose house the mortgage rests will not try to prevent that negro from voting when he goes to the polls. It is through the dairy farm, the truck garden, the trades, the commercial life, largely, that the negro is to find his way to the enjoyment of all his rights. Whether he will or not, a white man respects a negro who owns a two-story house.[11]

As with today's version of Black Capitalism, Washington's vision was a favorite with the large, white capitalists. Andrew Carnegie was a particularly strong admirer: "Booker Washington," he wrote, "is the combined Moses and Jehovah of his people . . . He contends that good moral character and industrial efficiency, resulting in owner-ship of property, are the pressing needs and the sure and speedy path to recognition and enfranchisement. A few able negroes are disposed to press for the free and unrestricted vote immediately. We cannot but hope that wiser policy will prevail."[12]

The black scholar, W. E. B. DuBois, rejected Washington's views as condoning the loss of the black man's political and social rights. DuBois claimed that Washington's doctrine "tended to make the Whites, North and South, shift the burden of the Negro problem to the Negro's shoulders and stand aside as critical and rather pessimistic spectators; when in fact the burden belongs to the nation . . . So far as Mr. Washington preaches Thrift, Patience, and Industrial Training for the masses, we must hold up his hands and strive with him . . . But so far as Mr. Washington apologizes for injustice, North or South, does not rightly value the privilege of duty of voting, belittles the emasculating effects of caste distinctions, and opposes the higher training and ambition of our brighter minds—so far as he, North or South does this—we must unceasingly and firmly oppose them."[13]

Another criticism of Washington's Black Capitalism came from a source at the other side of the political and racial spectrum from DuBois. Thomas Dixon, Jr., Baptist minister and author of the racist novel *The Clansman*, thought that Washington's Black Capitalism was the most effective path blacks could take toward integration—and thus it was a menace. In 1905 Dixon wrote in the *Saturday Evening Post*:

> Mr. Washington is not training Negroes to take their place in any industrial system of the South in which the white man can direct or control him. He is not training his students to be servants and come at the beck and call of any man. He is training them all to be masters of men, to be independent, to own and operate their own industries, plant their own fields, buy and sell their own goods, and in every shape and form destroy the last vestige of independence of the white man for anything . . .
>
> The Negro remains on this continent for one reason only. The Southern white man has needed his labor, and therefore has fought every suggestion of his removal. But when he refuses any longer to work for the white man, then what? . . . What's to be the end of it if the two races are to live side by side in the South?

Whether Washington's proposals were plans for integration or perpetual bondage we shall never know. He founded the National Business League in 1900 to further his dreams of creating a black business class and built a university at Tuskegee. But Black Capitalism did not flower.

Conforming to what was becoming a fixed historical pattern, black businesses (as well as employment) grew during the prosperity generated by the First World War. Estimates of black businesses rose from 15,000 in 1910 to 24,000 in 1920, but then dropped back in the twenties. During the period blacks almost exclusively served a segregated market. But even there they could not compete. Black businesses are estimated to have accounted for less than 10 percent of the black market during the decade of prosperity.

The Depression caused the collapse of large black businesses and greatly reduced the overall dollar value of black enterprises. Chicago had supported some three thousand black businesses prior to the Depression, including two banks and four insurance companies. By 1933 most of the larger businesses were wiped out, both banks were gone, and only three of the insurance companies were still operating. By 1938 the number of black businesses was down to twenty-five hundred.

The black population in the urban centers continued to go out of business as the white-owned businesses, though hurting and losing outlets, picked up a greater share of the black consumer market. By 1938 Chicago's remaining black enterprises were receiving less than 10 percent of the money spent by blacks. In Harlem, the largest urban concentration of blacks at that time, the situation was much the same. More than 80 percent of some ten thousand Harlem businesses were owned by whites; and the black-owned businesses were, for the most part, personal service and restaurant establishments.

The permanent black ghettos began to take shape during the 1940s, and by the end of World War II segregated housing patterns had left most large cities with sections that were virtually all black or all white. World War II brought another temporary surge of prosperity to black people, many of them moving North to fill job shortages. It also brought one of the first demonstrations of black political power in the threat by A. Philip Randolph to march on Washington in 1941 with a hundred thousand blacks if they were not provided a semblance of equal opportunity in defense work. In face of such a threat, Franklin Roosevelt signed Executive Order 8802 setting out Federal policy against discrimination in employment.

After the war, however, it was business-as-usual. Although the depression that many had been predicting did not occur, the extreme job shortages of the war were relieved and many blacks were bumped back out of the job market. Black-owned businesses, being concentrated in the retail trades, mirrored the fortunes of the black work force. And like black residents of the inner cities, black businesses were among the prime victims of Federally sponsored urban renewal programs referred to as "urban black removal." Of all businesses which were "urban removed" out of their present locations, over 30 percent do not open up again, and of those that do, half fail within the first five years. Black businesses were also the victims of the growing power of large retail chains which during the 1950s and '60s drove hundreds of thousands of small enterprises, black and white, out of business. As a result of all of this, the number of black businesses in the United States actually declined by 20 percent between 1950 and 1960.

In 1964 a Drexel Institute study of small businesses in Philadelphia found that in seventy years the situation of black businesses had not changed significantly. Approximately half of all Philadelphia black businesses were hairdressing, barber and luncheonette shops, with median annual sales of $2,500, $4,400, and $6,800, respectively. There were only thirteen small manufacturing firms among the city's 4,242 minority group businesses. Although ten of these thirteen were profitable, most minority-owned businesses were marginal in profit-making, stability, and physical condition. Almost all of the black-owned businesses were in predominantly black areas, but even in those areas, more than 60 percent of all businesses were white-owned.

In the past several years numerous cultural interpretations have been presented to explain why blacks have not been more successful as entrepreneurs. Some sociologists and anthropologists have maintained that the lack of a history of business, a tradition of enterprise, is the principal factor contributing to the historical absence of black entrepreneurs. To support their arguments they cite how Chinese have become businessmen here and in other countries; Armenians have been involved in the business of importing and retailing rugs; and Jews in America have been closely associated with the clothing industry and retailing. They make the point that these non-English-speaking immigrants faced discrimination, even if discrimination against them was not as intense as that against the blacks. They also had to surmount a language barrier.

But the success of the immigrant businesses may well have been an important reason for the failure of black business. In the nineteenth century, blacks were overwhelmed by the European immigrants—often two or three times the black populations in each urban center. The community cohesion of blacks—weak because of the years of slavery—died quickly under the mass of immigrants who outnumbered them, outbid them at jobs, beat them in the streets, and took great advantage of the prevailing attitudes of racism. By limiting the economic and employment opportunities of the black, the white majority assured the black's social subordination. This social subordination tended to create in turn a crippling psychological bind. Sense of inferiority and failure—imposed by the dominant culture—became internalized and self-perpetuating, at least, until the sixties.

In addition, most of the immigrants possessed centuries-old traditions in trade and business among their own people and with outside majorities. The blacks were workers, slaves, and products of a dependency culture which did not breed aggressive, money-oriented, competitive attitudes.

As Nathan Glazer explained:

> As slaves, Negroes were stripped of all opportunity for independence, as well as after slavery, when efforts at independence were regularly punished. They include the related experience of the Negro family . . . also marked by slavery and post-slavery traumas . . . which presumably provided little support for nascent business enterprise, in contrast to other families from entrepreneurial cultures.

The black American, newly freed from a slave culture and a life of dependency, was not as well prepared to compete in

American business as the newly arrived immigrant. The poorest European peasant or the persecuted Jew from the "old world" ghetto had been allowed to trade with his own people, and often with the established classes in Europe; he came to this country knowing how to market his products and how to manage his small resources. Moreover, because slaves are not paid any wages, the freed blacks came to the cities completely without financial resources or experience in dealing in a money economy. This complicated their struggle to get capital, stock, or space to rent.

Culturally, black Americans were Americans, not possessors of a distinct foreign culture which might provide a market for special food, wines, clothing, and the like. The Italians needed pasta, so Italian manufacturers made pasta in all shapes and sizes—and created a market worth over $300 million in 1967, spread over 250 companies in America. The Jewish people needed their special kosher foods, so the Goodmans, Meyers, and Manischewitzes made the foods, and had built by 1967 a market of over $60 million. As of this writing, there is still not a meaningful market for "soul" foods, and when there is, it is likely that the manufacturers involved in marketing them will be white, not black businessmen. The Chinese have provided an additional example of economic mobility by building an economic base in laundries and restaurants, sufficiently strong to develop economic security. It is estimated that the income of Chinese merchants from Chinese-owned businesses is, in relation to their numbers, forty-five times greater than the income of blacks from black-owned businesses.

Finally, of course, there is racism. Whites allowed white immigrants, but not the black migrants, to trade with them. When the immigrants were not allowed to trade with established Americans, by sheer weight of numbers and through their political and social structures, the immigrants forced permission. The blacks, lacking these numbers, lost the right to trade, even among their own. Racism also boxed the black businessmen into ghettos where they could not take advantage of the rising American prosperity, even if they had the financing and technical knowhow. As a result, black business was, in 1967, about where it was in 1890. The general effect has been to make the blacks a consuming but not a producing market. Just as the blacks could not develop a comprehensive economic structure, so they were not able to establish political or social organizations with significant economic power.

Traditionally, the white community has thought of the black community as a monolith, with one leader or a group of leaders echoing the sentiments of all the black people. Although this is not true, and probably has never been true—just as no white individual can speak for the white community at large—the myth of black leadership has persisted.

Certainly there is today no single leader who can speak for all blacks concerning ghetto economic development, black entrepreneurship, Black Capitalism, or any other program. Even those historically important national black groups, which have at times represented the interests of the black community, have little relevance to the strategies of black economic development—although some more recently have made this effort a higher priority.

For more than fifty years the National Association for the Advancement of Colored People (NAACP) has conducted a vigorous and successful campaign against the legal restrictions imposed by the white society on black Americans. The National Urban League has focused its efforts on developing jobs for black Americans at all levels of American industry as well as concentrated on expanding educational opportunities and, in this sense, has helped to increase the number of black professionals. More recently the League has initiated a program "New Thrust" in the area of ghetto economic development, which is supported from a grant from the Ford Foundation.

CORE, which was the initiator of the desegregation sit-ins, emphasized direct confrontation tactics as a means to dramatize a variety of different civil rights problems in local communities. One of CORE's most important accomplishments was the desegregation of interstate terminals after sponsoring "freedom rides" across the South in 1961. CORE has, since 1967, placed a high priority on minority economic development.

The Southern Christian Leadership Conference (SCLC) was the first civil rights organization to concentrate on the South. It began in 1957, primarily to implement, through nonviolent means, the Supreme Court decisions against school and bus segregation in the South. SCLC and Dr. Martin Luther King, its Executive Director, had become synonymous. Since Dr. King's assassination in Memphis in April 1968, SCLC has been seeking to redefine its priorities. The Poor People's Campaign was one such effort. Most observers would agree that although the Reverend Ralph Abernathy has been a competent leader, he simply does not have the stature and charisma of Dr. King. In recent years SCLC has also had financial problems.

Prior to Dr. King's death, SCLC made a major policy decision to concentrate activities in an effort to broaden their base in northern urban centers. As a result of this effort economic development did become a high priority. Consistent with this strategy the Reverend Jesse Jackson set up "Operation Breadbasket" in Chicago which called for economic integration and, where necessary, direct boycotts.† In addition, Hosea Williams began supermarket development work in Memphis and nearby cities.

The Student Non-Violent Coordinating Committee (SNCC) was started by college students at Shaw University in North Carolina in 1960. The organization was successful, specifically, in setting up voter registration drives and, generally, in shaking up the southern white establishment. Today SNCC seems to be dormant and its former leaders have struck out in new directions. John Lewis, Julian Bond, James Foreman, Stokely Carmichael, and H. Rap Brown were all former "SNICK" leaders.

The Black Panthers gained national prominence in 1968 by organizing for direct political action—self-defense, they called it —in northern ghettos. Their efforts in the field of economic development, however, were very limited; although in their "manifesto," allusions were made toward people's control of the economic system.

More recently Panther organizations in various cities have been deterred from their "grass roots" self-help projects for they

† In early 1972 Reverend Jackson split from *Breadbasket* to organize *Operation PUSH*—People United to Save Humanity. At that time Jackson emphasized that "economics must be the No. 1 item on the agenda for black people in 1972 and beyond."

have had to defend both their local neighborhoods and their lives from what appeared to be a systematic effort on the part of national law-enforcement authorities and local police to repress them.

From 1965 through 1969 the American public was barraged by what can best be described as a tumult of "frantic tokenism." The flowery rhetoric flowing from public figures on how much was being done to help the nation's minorities literally swamped all the media, including billboards and buttons adorned with such slogans as "Give a Damn." To say the least the "urban crisis" was overkilled on the conference circuit. Government officials at all levels announced new crash programs. Corporation presidents proclaimed their organizations' resolve to leap immediately into the thick of things, using private-sector know-how to "clean up the mess" and get things moving.

In addition, at well-contrived press conferences, public affairs officers of corporations, government agencies and nonprofit organizations piously intoned the success of their efforts. And they displayed reams of statistics and graphs to prove it. There was almost no effort to verify these claims. Two nonprofit organizations‡ which specialized in urban economic development finally decided, in late 1969, to make a systematic analysis of these claims as they applied to minority-owned businesses. They conducted, in New York City, what they termed "a reality study of minority economic development." The project was *business-oriented*. Every effort was made to avoid the jargon of social scientists who interpret history, economics, sociology, etc., from an academic viewpoint. It was the first one of its kind, and the case studies shed light on both.*

As George Bernard Shaw said in *Man and Superman:*

> We laugh at the haughty American nation, because it makes the Negro clean its boots, and then proves the moral and physical inferiority of the Negro by the fact that he is a shoeblack.

‡ The groups are: Capital Formation, Inc., a nonprofit organization set up to aid minority businesses, and JPM Associates, Inc., a private firm specializing in urban economic development. Both of these organizations are involved daily in finding practical solutions to immediate urban problems.

* See Appendix, p. 275.

THE NUMBERS

Americans as a breed seem to be obsessed with figures, statistics, and percentages. A foreigner visiting our country for the first time might well think of us as a people whose mentality resembles that of a neighborhood butcher (always weighing on the scales), with the soul of a statistician and the political imagination of a pollster. Figures, statistics, and polls seem to be such an important part of our political reportage and literature. The behavioral studies of our social scientists, the style of our major weekly news magazines such as *Time, Newsweek,* and *Business News* as well as our influential dailies such as the New York *Times* and the *Wall Street Journal,* and America's increased reliance on marketing are all factors which heavily contribute to this obsession.

As black people in America have begun to demand a larger share of America's great wealth there have been various plans and formulas put forth as to what constitutes a fair "piece of the action" and how to reach that goal.

Too often in the past the hard-nosed businessman has avoided abstract and theoretical arguments relating to social problems. Taking him at his word, then, we have gone to the bottom line to gather "the figures." We trust that corporate leadership will read them with care for they add up to a damning indictment of the private sector.

It has been argued by some that black people should own businesses in America in the same proportion as they are represented in the population. Quite apart from the theoretical basis for such an argument there exists a huge gap between population and ownership.

Estimates of black population in the United States have ranged from 11 percent to more than 15 percent.† Using, for our purposes, the lower count, it might be argued that blacks should

† It has been claimed that census takers often do not go into black communities for their counts, and that census figures grossly underestimate the black populations in America, for that reason.

own around 11 percent of the five million businesses in the United States, or 550,000 businesses.

Employment figures for minority-owned business provide no source of encouragement either. In 1969 the civilian labor force reached eighty million. Since most minority-owned businesses are small the employment generated by minority-owned businesses is less than 1 percent of the civilian labor force.

An obvious inequity exists, but the fact is that there is no rational basis for the assertion that 11 percent of the population should own 11 percent of the business. Studies of other minority groups would probably not show a direct correlation between the group's proportion of the population and its share in business. The significance of the blacks' low proportional representation in the business world is that the gap itself is so enormous, and has been so throughout recent history. A recent Federal study reported that blacks in America own about $382 per family in all financial and capital assets as against $5,924 for the average white family.

These figures take on added significance because blacks traditionally have not had other sources of income, such as land ownership or large-scale agricultural production, nor have they had the kind of full-scale employment that produces a minimum of savings.

Thus, the discrepancies above are reflected in the generally low family incomes among blacks. Although blacks represent 11 percent or more of the population, they have less than 6 percent of the aggregate income.

The late Whitney Young, Jr., who was Executive Director of the National Urban League, has cited figures to show that this gap in income is getting worse, not better:

> The income gap that separates white and black Americans is, despite all the efforts of recent years, *growing*. (In 1968) for example, amid much fanfare, the Government announced that Negro family income, as a proportion of white income, rose sharply. Negro family income was now 59 percent of that of white family income, said a Federal press release—a 4 percent jump in only two years. But in 1952, Negro family income was 57 percent of that for white families—so the proportionate gain was a mere two percentage points in a decade and a half.

And the dollar gap between the two groups actually grew. In 1950, median white family income was $3,445; median black family income $1,169—a dollar gap of $1,576. By 1967, after widely heralded social reforms, white income had soared to $8,318. Negro income was $4,939 —and the dollar gap was now $3,379.

Moreover, there are discrepancies in the nature of black business that are every bit as disturbing as the discrepancies in black income. SBA estimates of industrial distribution illustrate that minorities are concentrated in low income-yielding, marginal types of enterprises. The great majority of minority-owned businesses are small retail and service businesses, employing an average of three to four people with gross sales of less than $100,000. Obviously, none are among Fortune's top five hundred businesses.

For example, according to the SBA, more than 42 percent of minority-owned businesses are in services, as compared with 27.6 percent of white-owned businesses. Nearly 30 percent of black-owned businesses are involved in personal services alone, compared with only 7.3 percent of white businesses. The small size of these businesses is indicated by the fact that only 19 percent of the black businesses have annual gross receipts of more than $100,000 a year.

If an analysis is made entirely within black communities, representation of blacks by industry is even worse. This is most easily seen in the analysis of ghetto business in Washington, D.C., where "services" represent 60.7 percent of all black businesses.

As Howard Samuels observed:

> Of 28,000 businesses in Washington, only 2,000 are owned by blacks, and half of these are beauty parlors and barber shops. In a city nearly two-thirds black, there simply isn't a black business community worth talking about.

In Harlem and in San Francisco ghetto areas, service and eating places represent, respectively, 59.9 percent and 48.6 percent of businesses owned by blacks. In 1968 a survey of businesses in Harlem revealed that, of all businesses in Harlem employing ten or more persons, fewer than fifteen were owned by blacks. Comparative figures from the same survey indicated a decline in minority ownership during the preceding ten years. In all of

New York City, the most commercially active metropolis in the country, with a large black population, only one out of a thousand blacks can be classified as an independent entrepreneur. Among whites the percentage of entrepreneurs is forty times greater.

Another interesting fact about black business is its geographical location. Almost 60 percent of black-owned businesses are located in the South, with less than 15 percent in the populous, industrial Northeast. Nearly 30 percent of all black businesses are owned and operated by women, with 32 percent of all southern black proprietors being women.

In 1969 the U.S. Bureau of the Census reported that there were 322,000 minority-owned firms in the United States. Of these 163,-000 were owned by black people and 100,000 by Spanish-speaking minorities—Mexican-American (who accounted for 70,000), Puerto Rican, Cuban, and Latin American. The total number of minority-owned firms represented slightly over 4 percent of all firms in the United States.‡ Their receipts came to less than 1 percent of the receipts of all American businesses. Table 1 in the Appendix compares the number and receipts of minority-owned firms to the totals for all businesses in the major industrial categories. (Note that the industries do not include farming, medical or legal services.)

Average receipts per firm are $200,022 for all U.S. businesses compared with $33,040 for minority firms. As Table 2 illustrates, most minority firms, both black and Spanish-speaking, are "mom and pop" stores without any paid employees. The average annual receipts of such enterprises is $7,000. The Census counted one hundred minority-owned firms with more than a hundred employees. Of these, forty-one were black and twenty-three were owned by the Spanish-speaking minorities. Table 3 shows the cities in which firms owned by black and Spanish-speaking people are most numerous. Table 4 shows the ten most important industry groups of minority-owned firms. Major differences between the industrial pattern of businesses owned by blacks and the Spanish-speaking are that the blacks are more heavily concentrated in personal services and in the category of "special trade

‡ The data for all U.S. businesses is as of 1967 but there is no reason to expect that there was any change in two years.

contractors" (plumbers, plasterers, etc.). Black-owned firms obtained 58 percent of their receipts from retail and service trades, while the Spanish-speaking received 65 percent of their receipts from these businesses. It is worth noting that financial institutions critical to the economic development of a community, with the exception of black insurance companies, are not represented among the leading minority businesses.

Those institutions generally regarded as "successful" by blacks and whites alike are the black banks, savings and loan associations, insurance companies, and newspapers. They are "successful," however, only when these organizations are compared with other black businesses. Using any other benchmark, such as white banks or insurance companies or newspapers, the success of the black operations is rather difficult to prove.

Consider the black savings banks as one example. Although six black-owned commercial banks were founded before the Depression, most of them were begun after World War II. According to a U.S. Department of Commerce report, there were fourteen black-owned banks in 1951, with total assets of $32 million; eleven of these banks were located in the South. By 1958 this number had decreased to ten banks, but assets had increased— slightly—to $38 million. At the end of 1967, there were seventeen black-owned commercial banks, eleven of these in the North, with assets of just over $162 million. White-owned banks finished 1967 with assets of almost $370 billion; this is more than two thousand times the assets of the black institutions. By 1968 the National Association for Black Bankers, for example, has a membership of twenty-one banks, with assets of $207 million. The assets of white-owned banks in 1968 exceeded $400 billion, which is two thousand times the assets of the black-owned banks.

In 1968 there were forty-five black-owned insurance companies, with assets of $400 million. White-owned insurance companies' assets are 3,300 times that figure, or $1,320,000,000,000. In 1968 there were thirty-six black-owned savings and loan associations; there are 6,100 white-owned savings and loan associations, with assets of $150 billion.

Ownership of black-oriented newspapers provides a similar example. In 1948 black ownership of black-oriented newspapers was estimated at 169, one half of which were published in the

South. Circulation was approximately 2,000,000 weekly, and total valuation of these publications was estimated at about $10 million. By 1967 there were only eighty-five newspapers oriented to the black community of which blacks owned 85 percent. Total circulation was down to 1,177,000 weekly, with less than 27 percent in the North, 42 percent in the South, and 31 percent in the West. Total estimated value of these newspapers is *$30 million.* By comparison, the total white daily newspaper circulation of 2,300 papers is more than fifty million, and their share of advertising revenues is more than $1.5 billion annually, as opposed to an estimated $15 million annual revenues for black-owned papers.

The most successful black-oriented publication is *Ebony* magazine, published by John H. Johnson. Black owned, operated, and staffed, the magazine currently has a national circulation of more than 1 million, and is growing. The Johnson corporation also publishes *Jet,* a pocket-size news weekly with national news of pertinence to the black community, and *Tan,* a "true confession and homemaking" magazine, appealing to housewives. Their combined circulation is 451,000 blacks nationally. A fourth black-owned national magazine for blacks is *Sepia,* a *Life*-format monthly, with a small circulation of 58,000. *Tuesday,* a two-year-old publication, is put out and sold by white businessmen for black readers of general-readership Sunday newspapers. Best classified as a Sunday supplement, like *Parade* and *This Week, Tuesday* has a national circulation of 1,540,000 and is growing, with approximately 80 percent of its readership in black homes. There are several other small black magazines, with limited circulations and moderate assets.

For comparison, 1967 advertising revenues for the general-audience magazine and newspaper supplements owned by white corporations were over $2.5 billion, and they reached 95 percent of all U.S. homes. Total revenues for black magazines and newspaper supplements combined were considerably less than 1 percent of all sales.

A staggering example of the meager role of blacks in business is provided by the situation of black-oriented radio stations. Since World War II, radio stations programming rhythm and blues, gospel and folk, as well as special news to the black community, have burgeoned. As of 1968, more than 105 "soul" stations in 61 cities, with a potential coverage of 93 percent of black consumers, were programming "black sounds" full time. Additionally, there were more than 150 stations programming part-time to this market, anywhere from two hours per day to two hundred hours per week, in some 61 cities and 40 other areas.

Until recently, not one of these "soul" stations was owned by blacks. Even as late as 1967, there were only five of these 105 full-time stations which were owned and operated by blacks. Further, these stations represent only a small fraction of total radio programming for the more than five thousand stations in the United States. Thus, of the $900 million spent on radio advertising in 1967, none of the money effectively went to black owners or managers.

Relatively few (14 percent) of all "soul" stations are located in northern urban areas; 58 percent are in the South, and the remaining 28 percent are in the West.

Few black Americans own manufacturing, distribution, or industrial facilities; the capital required has generally not been available to black businessmen. The largest black owned and operated manufacturing and distribution business is Motown Records Corporation, a $30 million Detroit record company, built on the national popularity of two black vocal groups, the Supremes and the Temptations. The largest food manufacturing concern owned by blacks is H. G. Parks, a Baltimore-based sausage and meat processing company, grossing over $6 million in 1969. Other manufacturing companies, mostly cosmetics firms catering to black customers, produce gross sales of less than $3 million each annually, and average fewer than twenty-five employees.

Although many blacks have made a great deal of money in the sports and entertainment fields, few have begun business ventures not dependent upon their star status. Exceptions are James Brown Enterprises, Inc., owned by soul-singer James Brown and Tetragrammaton, owned by comedian Bill Cosby. Brown Enterprises, earning $1.5 to $2 million annually, is concentrating on the communications industry, and currently owns "soul" stations WJBE in Knoxville, and WRDW in Augusta,

with plans for further investments in this area. Tetragrammaton's main claim to fame, thus far, is the distribution of John
Lennon's naked album cover "Two Virgins"—with generally
clandestine sales. Other performers and athletes, such as Ray
Charles, Sammy Davis, Jr., Bill Russell, Wilt Chamberlain, and
Jimmy Brown, have made business investments, but relatively
few have been geared to black businesses as such.

Black ownership of other capital-intensive businesses, such
as automobile dealerships, shopping centers, supermarkets, and
the like, is almost nonexistent. Out of some thirty thousand auto
dealerships in the country, only one was black owned and operated in 1965; by 1968 there were seven. Black ownership of
shopping centers is limited to three, each of which was started
within the last few years in ghetto areas. Even with foundation
and public-supported groups working to increase black ownership of large-volume supermarkets, only three black-owned
supermarkets in the country were doing a weekly gross of more
than $25,000. In general, more than 90 percent of every black
food dollar is spent in white-owned supermarkets and grocery
stores.

A more recent study entitled "Black Capitalism and the Ownership of Property in Harlem"[14] determined that outsiders, non-
residents of Harlem, own more than 85 percent of the total
assessed valuation of the properties there. The report, prepared
last year by Dr. Michael Zweig of the State University of New
York, was a working paper for the Economic Research Bureau.
The report based its findings on a random survey of ownership
of 25 percent of all the blocks in Central Harlem—an area
bounded by 110th Street, Third Avenue, the Harlem River, and
a string of parks along Morningside Heights.

The study found that of all residential buildings examined,
the assessments of those owned by Harlem residents totaled
$17.4 million, compared to $115.8 million owned externally.
The value of assessed store buildings was $5.35 million for out-
side ownership compared to $1 million for Harlem residents.
In addition residents pay about $13 million in taxes annually
on their local property incomes, presuming an average rate of
30 percent for individual and corporate incomes together, and
that they retain about $29 million annually. According to the

study, then, "This is roughly $115 a person for each of the quarter of a million people who live in Harlem."

Zweig, on the basis of his findings, went on to attack the Black Capitalism programs of the Nixon Administration and warned that this policy was a diversionary tactic designed to channel black leadership into entrepreneurship programs rather than have them put their efforts into establishing cooperative institutions which would legitimately serve the needs of the community.

One of the most significant groups of entrepreneurs in many black communities is the Black Muslims. Complete economic independence from the white community is the final goal of the Muslims. As interim steps, they have established black businesses and industries to minimize black-white contacts, to provide jobs and capital, and to offer the sense of group security necessary for an independent people. Today in Chicago, Muslims own department stores, restaurants, several apartment buildings, and other service businesses; in Michigan, Iowa, and Georgia they own large farms; and in every city where there is a temple, they own restaurants, beauty or barber shops, clothing stores, and other businesses. All of the Muslim ventures are well run and efficiently managed. A conservative estimate of the economic earning power of the Black Muslim membership would be around $600 million. Total financial holdings of the Nation of Muslim are estimated to be between $75 and $100 million.

No analysis of black business, no matter how brief, would be complete without reference to illegal activities. Organized crime is big business. Although there are few reliable estimates, it is clearly in the order of billions of dollars. In 1967 a Presidential Commission on Law Enforcement and Administration of Justice reported that from gambling alone, "Estimates of the annual intake have varied from $7 to $50 billion. Legal betting at racetracks reaches a gross annual figure of almost $5 billion, and most enforcement officials believe that illegal wagering on horse races, lotteries, and sporting events totals at least $20 billion each year. Analysis of organized criminal betting operations indicated that the profit is as high as one third of gross revenue—$6 or $7 billion each year."[15]

The impact of organized crime on the ghetto is staggering. The chairman of the joint legislative committee on crime of the New York State Legislature estimated that the gross income of the "syndicate" from New York City poverty areas is "equivalent to more than 80 percent of the welfare funds poured in by Federal, state, and city agencies."[16]

Although these rackets are still controlled for the most part by the Mafia-linked organizations, blacks have in the past decade taken over responsibility for much of the action in ghetto areas. While again, figures are hard to come by, black numbers and policy operations probably are the largest employers of black people in many areas. They are also a source of capital for the more legitimate businesses. Since black businesses have difficulty getting financing from white-controlled banks and other financial institutions, they often turn to the rackets for venture capital, which of course does not come for free. It is estimated that over 25 percent of black businesses are financed in this way. One of the most successful is the black sausage manufacturing firm of H. G. Parks. According to Milton Moskowitz, the financial columnist, "The only reason the company got started in the first place was that it got financing not from a bank but from 'Little Willie Adams,' king of the numbers racket in Baltimore."

The black crime entrepreneur is more often found around the margins of his industry. He is the hustler. Black Congressman William Clay describes the economic life of the hustler:[17]

> He may be a pimp or a numbers writer, a purveyor of hot goods, or a numbers banker, a procurer of women or a narcotics pusher. He may even be a "con expert," "flim-flammer," "three card monte expert" or just a plain hustler off government programs . . .
>
> This doesn't mean that the hustler is lazy. He can't be if he is going to make it. It's just that the system is not "economically feasible." It's possible for a ghetto black with $100 initial capital to live on his stake for months just by the fast turnover in so-called "hot stuff." That is the trade name for stolen merchandise but in many cases it isn't really hot at all. It sells better and faster under the label—"hot" . . .
>
> Blacks have developed a network of crime completely acceptable to the white majority. That system of survival is clearly outside the law, clearly in violation of the law, but certainly with the tacit ap-

proval of the decision makers. This sub-economy (an economy within an economy) accounts for approximately 15 percent of black income in some urban areas.

The acid test was whether or not corporate America was willing to lend its enormous economic and political powers to rearrange the deck, one which it had stacked, systematically and self-servingly. If it was found unwilling, the cheated minorities would surely look for a new dealer.

Is corporate America willing to shift its emphasis, to provide the massive assistance necessary to rectify the economics of misery, the legacy of generations of corporate poaching? It was noted several years ago, with regard to the economic and political power of American corporations, that:

> There is an elusiveness about power that endows it with an almost ghostly quality. It seems to be all around us, yet this is "sensed" with some sixth means of reception rather than with the five ordinary senses. We "know" what it is, yet we encounter endless difficulties in trying to define it. We can "tell" whether one person or group is more powerful than another, yet we cannot measure power. It is as abstract as time yet as real as a firing squad.[18]

How long must the "other America" stand blindfolded before the firing squad?

6 | BIG WHITE BROTHERS

The Private Sector

"Now all you Gentlemen who wish to lead us
And teach us to desist from mortal sin
Your prior obligation is to feed us;
When we've had our lunch, your preaching can begin."
BERTOLT BRECHT

The summers of 1966 and 1967 were "pretty hot." The impact of the riots which erupted in Watts, Detroit, Newark, and scores of other American cities brought home to most Americans what the nonviolence of all the boycotts, marches, and pleadings of many, many long cold winters had failed to accomplish. The "other America" exploded and with it all the myths, symptoms, and stereotypes that "white America" had, for so long, taken for granted. The sickness of institutional racism had finally broken out into the open and with it all the realities of the existence of two very different cultures, one white and one black.

Americans were reminded daily, without letup by the blare of commercial television, radio, the newspapers, and billboards of what American was supposed to mean—it meant having just about

what you wanted, when you wanted it, even if it *was on credit.**
On the other hand, the black (and brown) culture was pretty
much stuck with failure, disease, miseducation, dilapidated housing, violence, and death. Many whites passed alongside the ghettos to and from work—on the freeways or in commuter trains—but
the psychological distance of uncounted miles was further than
most whites had been willing to travel.

The rumblings of the discontent of earlier summers had
brought social workers, academic researchers, VISTA volunteers,
data collectors, and other assorted social science types by the
droves into the nation's ghettos. Though well-intentioned, these
sociological commuters could not control the seething anger
that had swept through the ghettos and barrios of our country.

The hopes and promises of the "War on Poverty" programs
were becoming unhinged. And when fall of 1967 finally came,
the major domestic policy question was: what could be done to
prevent a repeat performance of last summer's tragedy? The
drafters of social programs in Washington got back to their drawing boards while the grafters of local programs, the mayors and
city councils, began to increase their police and "social control"
budgets. Instead of creative social programs, most local officials
started talking about riot control techniques—dogs, barbed wire,
new kinds of gases, dumdum bullets, helicopters, and even tanks.
By early 1968 the mood was divisive. It was cool, but tension and
fear were in the atmosphere.

The medicine that might have begun a cure for the economic
and social sickness of the ghetto was expensive. The Johnson
Administration and its allies on the Republican right (including
Richard Nixon) were spending money on other things in Southeast Asia. And so the bureaucrats and the mayors were told
that new ideas were welcome—as long as they did not cost anything.

As a result the President, Government officials, and the media
began to turn toward a new doctor (or fireman as the case may
be)—the private sector—one that previously had exhibited little
interest in dealing with social problems. And business leaders

---

* Most estimates indicate that the average middle-class white family is
two and a half years in debt, but they still consume all the junk that the
mass media peddle them.

themselves were beginning to make some noises about the need to accept more social responsibility. Out of the ashes of the slum neighborhoods that were gutted during that summer of '67 sprang the Urban Coalition. It was organized by an emergency convocation of two thousand national leaders. Although there was a generous sprinkling of labor, religious, and minority group leadership, it was clearly dominated, and financially supported, by the business community. Members of the convocation were asked to return to their communities and to organize local chapters. Within months chapters were formed in forty-two cities across the country. A new "awareness" had begun to take hold.

Unlike earlier Government programs, the new ones *had* the blessings of the private sector. This newly accepted responsibility by the business community was summed up in an article by Max Ways in a special issue of *Fortune* Magazine—the bible of corporate America—devoted to "Business and the Urban Crises" (January 1968). Ways discussed business' new-found interest in the racial crisis. First noting the "sluggishness and ineptitude" with which the Government and most social institutions had responded to the crisis, Ways went on to write:

> . . . Since midyear of 1967, and largely as a response to the race crisis, [the] business attitude toward the problems of the city is shifting. The ardent efforts of the nation's business institutions will be especially needed, because they have qualities demanded by the double crisis of the Negro and the city. Modern corporations are flexible and innovative. They are accustomed to sensing and meeting and evoking the changing desires of the public. Above all, they practice the difficult art of mobilizing specialised knowledge for action—i.e. the art of managing change.

Moreover, Ways wrote, business could succeed where the Government had failed because "business is the one important segment of society Negroes today do not regard with bitter suspicion." A bit presumptuous, but relatively true.

In the past, corporate community interest had, for the most part, taken the form of giving the "united way" through Community Chest. There were corporate deviants, however, who donated funds to the Boy Scouts and the Little League, or those who gave to the alma maters (prep school, university, or graduate school) of their board chairmen or even their favorite opera, theater, art group, or hospital of the wife of the chairman of the board. Through gift-giving, major companies, particularly in corporation towns, could manage also to influence social policy. The success or failure of private programs or community groups were more often than not dependent on the good graces of those who gave the donations. And you can bet your bottom dollar that prior to 1967 there was not a farthing given to groups that were considered gadflies in their community—that is unless it involved a quid pro quo, a payoff for good behavior. They were not exactly bribes, but they certainly greased the right wheels. At any rate, blacks and other poor folk were not at the top of the list and what they did receive was on the order of turkeys for Thanksgiving or some buckets of coal for the winter.† One community organizer who had gone the corporate donation route in New York City remarked in late 1967 that "the annals of corporate sponsorship of minority programs is about as thick as the 'Blue Book of Puerto Rican Millionaires.'" It is interesting to note that with the exception of Congressman Wright Patman —the maverick populist from Texas—critics of the big corporations, including Ralph Nader, have not yet turned their attention to corporate donation policies.‡ Nor did Congressional investigations of the large foundations seriously focus on corporate philanthropy until 1969. Jules Cohn has suggested that a study of the techniques, management, and decision-making processes of big business donors would provide revealing and useful information for students of corporate urban affairs efforts, as well as for the donors themselves.[2]

† The topic reference "Poverty" in the 1960 Public Affairs Information Service Index (the index of periodical literature for public affairs) says, "See also—Beggars and Begging," and has only two listings.

‡ Congressman Patman charged that most of the large, private, and family-controlled foundations "appear to be afflicted with charitable myopia, if not outright blindness." He further stated that "while Puerto Rican children in Harlem fell behind in their studies because of language problems, the Lilly Endowment, Inc., of Indianapolis, sent $15,000 [to a university in] Mexico City . . . and a Rockefeller-controlled foundation . . . sent $311,280 to [an English-language program in] Tokyo." Similarly, "while our central cities fell into decay and Negro youths rioted in our streets, the Bollingen Foundation (a Mellon family foundation in New York City) sent thousands of dollars abroad to uncover the dust of centuries and study 'Roman and Etruscan town plans.'"[1]

It would be misleading to ignore the fact that although the record of corporate responsibility was bleak before 1967, there were at least some notable rhetorical exceptions. As early as 1961, George S. Moore, then President of First National Bank, declared:

> Today's institutions—banking or business, public or private—cannot exist in modern society without reacting constructively to (1) the goals of society, and (2) the economic, technological, social, and political forces that mold that society . . . social responsibility . . . is an indispensable act of profitable growth from which the American public has benefited incomparably. It consists of enriching society today so that interacting interests of both business and society will endure tomorrow.[3]

In 1965 the Chairman of the Board and President of International Telephone and Telegraph Corporation, Harold S. Geneen, bullishly intoned:

> Now some of you wonder why a major, profit-making corporation like IT&T wants to join the war on poverty. The answer is threefold:
>
> 1. We in industry owe it to our society to use our resources to cure social ill that has been with us too long.
> 2. We in industry must maintain for ourselves and the nation a trained labor force.
> 3. We in industry have the capital, the manpower, the skills, the technology, and the desire to get the job done.[4]

And on that stirring note, "to get the job done," Mr. Geneen led IT&T into the "War on Poverty," along with many other corporations—as contractors to run Job Corps Centers.

Some cynical observers of the education/manpower scene in Washington at the time offered other explanations as to why certain corporations were so hot on getting Government contracts. Critics pointed out that one rationale was a less than humane desire for companies to enrich themselves with Government Research and Demonstration (R&D) dollars; for "Education and Learning" was becoming a big business and what better way was there to experiment on developing new educational materials and techniques than with Federal funds using hardcore poor youngsters as guinea pigs. The defense "hardware syndrome" had its newer counterpart in the "software" people industry. And, as one corporate executive said, "There's only one thing worse than having a government contract; that's not having it."

There is a bitter irony in relating the aforementioned statements of Geneen to a story concerning Richard Nixon, who, by 1966, had acquired an obsessive faith in the private sector and who was also—as never before in his career—enjoying the rewards of the free enterprise system as a Wall Street lawyer.

Three years after the Geneen statement, candidate Nixon, in laying the political groundwork for what was considered to be a future effort to dismantle the Office of Economic Opportunity, used a classic stand-up comics' routine. It was employed several times during the campaign and was designed to titillate what some reporters called his kind of "Hertz rent-a-crowd." The favorite line was to ask himself, and the audience, "Do you know how much it costs to keep a Corpsman in a Center each year?" Silence . . . pause . . . "Well, I'll tell you, $12,000 annually." Gasp, longer pause, then, "And it only costs $2,600 to send a youngster to Harvard!" Pause, laughter from the audience . . . a smile on the candidate's face . . . serious again, "And I promise you that if I am elected President, I will eliminate this kind of program that is a drain on the American taxpayer." Large applause . . . Cheering! A genuine crowd-pleaser.

It was either out of ignorance or sheer cynicism that Nixon, the free enterprise candidate, singled out the Job Corps for his attack. And it is hard to believe that the candidate was so ill informed; so one can only assume that he was cynical enough to believe that his audiences were ignorant. (Nixon had, very early in his career, elevated the half-truth to an art form.) For, ironically enough, ITT *was* one of the contractors which ran a Job Corps Center as were AVCO, Westinghouse, Litton Industries, IBM, and Xerox. It just so happened that the Job Corps was the only one of the poverty programs that was run by the very industries which had "the capital, the manpower, the skills, the technology," and the desire to "get the job done." In spite of the fact that they were operating on a cost plus overhead basis, they failed—miserably. In particular, one of the leaders of a teachers' strike at the Camp Kilmer Center managed *by ITT* remarked that "the business/management types who run the operation know absolutely nothing about education . . . and couldn't be less interested in the problems of the kids. If they had their way totally, this place would become a cross between a concentration camp and a prep school."

And who ultimately paid the price of suffering because of private-sector ineptitude? The ghetto kids, of course; for one of Nixon's first acts as President was to fulfill his campaign pledge by ordering the closing of more than thirty Centers which, in effect, dumped twenty thousand youngsters back into the searing slums and ghettos for the Fourth of July weekend (1969). How's that for planning? Just in time to celebrate Independence Day . . . and the beginning of another long hot summer which saw unemployment of black teenagers rise to 28 percent in most large cities. An interesting Alphonse and Gaston act between the GOP candidate and a highly "enlightened" private-sector leader; perhaps when President Nixon and Mr. Geneen met, they considered the possibility of exchanging speech writers.

The digression is particularly illuminating in that at no time during the campaign—when Nixon was exploiting the full potential of the issue—nor, for that matter, during the period prior to the closing of the Job Corps Centers, did the press pick up on the issue or the irony of the connection between campaign and corporate rhetoric. Somewhere between the fashion pages and the racing results one could locate a short filler item recording the outraged protests of Congressman Carl Perkins of Kentucky after Moynihan told him about the "shifts of administration priorities," for management reasons, which finally resulted in the closing of the Centers.

With the exception of the Job Corps and programs for "research and demonstration" in developing educational material, job recruiting and training, and building and managing public housing development projects, there had been little corporate participation in "social" programs during the early years of the Johnson Administration.

Furthermore, most of the companies which were enlisted to participate did so as a result of pressure by the Johnson Administration, with promises of more goodies to come in the future. Others became involved for the profit motive. For example, certain corporations—which required labor-intensive markets, with too-few job applicants—found that recruitment programs aimed at unemployed minority persons gave them a new and useful resource for potential workers at Government expense. Other companies perceived an expanding market, both in the ghettos and in the Government, for products or services related to social objectives. For, if there ever was to be a "peace dividend" after the Vietnam war, products helpful to slum renewal, job training, housing, medicare, and programmed education would have an important, big, Government-financed market. Finally, the threat loomed large that the Government might exclusively take over the area of public problems, thus eliminating businesses' political influence in local communities. Hence, some companies recognized the opportunity to improve their public images while, at the same time, maintaining or improving their political leverage.

It should be stressed that, prior to 1967, corporations rarely established projects themselves in the area of economic development. Rarely, therefore, did they allow for minority community ownership.

Job Opportunities in Business Sector (JOBS) was the *first* major private-sector program to aid the ghetto economy. It was announced by Johnson in his last "State of the Union Message" in 1968. Johnson described the program as "a new partnership between government and private industry to train and hire the hard-core unemployed." Under the partnership, the Government—through its Concentrated Employment Program (CEP) —would identify and recruit the unemployed, and the companies through the coordination of the National Alliance of Businessmen (NAB) would train them and offer them jobs. Each company was to bear the "normal" costs of hiring, but the Government was to pay the employers for "extra costs," such as transportation services, courses in reading and writing, correction of health problems, and counseling. The goal was to place at least a hundred thousand men and women in jobs by June 1969.

How many "hard-core" were really placed in jobs by this program is anyone's guess. Estimates vary widely, depending upon the sources. The National Alliance of Businessmen reported at least 84,000 placements as of September 30, 1968, and 125,000 by the end of 1968. By December 2, 1969, one NAB executive* was claiming that nearly 300,000 hard-core had been trained and placed by the program. As the figures mounted, however, so did the complaints. Directors of CEPs, community action agencies, and even participating companies had begun to accuse the NAB of padding, counting double, and generally playing a phony numbers game. In Pittsburgh, for example, NAB reported that 1,800 were hired through the program. The figure given by the Pennsylvania Employment Service was 884, while the director of the CEP program for the city, Dave Epperson, said that his agency could verify a figure of only 135.

An extensive study by one of the country's major research organizations reported in 1969 that "the pressure to report numbers of recruits was resulting not only in companies reporting as hard-core personnel those whom they would have hired anyway, but also in rewarding companies with higher turnover, by enabling them to report more recruits."

One director of a CEP program in a large midwestern city said, "Those figures given out by NAB are about as reliable as Westmoreland's body counts."

Joseph Loftus of the New York *Times* took several weeks to prepare a careful survey of the performance of NAB in 1968. He reported that:

> Staff people at the Alliance know, or at least have an impression of how most of the cities are performing and where the significant exaggerations about placements are . . .
> Los Angeles, for example, had been claiming placements in the colossal tradition of a Hollywood press agent. The latest word from Los Angeles was that it was starting afresh and had no placement figures to announce at all . . .
> Memphis has made a reputation here for exaggerated figures, too. Honolulu's campaign, not claiming much, has been called a "disaster." El Paso is not much better. New Orleans and Philadelphia are among those that have fallen short of their marks. New York's results are termed unsatisfactory.[5]

Another detailed field analysis by a "blue-chip" management/consulting firm disclosed that the majority of those counted by

---

* Leo Beebe, a former official of the Ford Motor Company.

one manufacturer—who was the single largest "hard-core" employer with almost 20 percent of the NAB total—has been processed through regular personnel, and had not received any special training. The report indicated that some companies simply changed their regular discriminatory hiring policies, hired qualified blacks, and reported them as hard-core unemployed. In other words, they hired qualified people whom they should have been employing all along; and got the extra bonus of publicity and subsidies.

A General Accounting Office report on the program in 1970 showed that more than two thirds of the JOBS enrollees dropped out. Of those that remained more than half were earning salaries of less than $3,000 per year. The GAO report also identified instances of firms pocketing the money earmarked for training employees and putting it into such items as rugs and air conditioners for their offices.

Unfortunately, the hard-core jobless who were hired in Detroit were subjected to yet another setback, as layoffs in the auto industry which represented 25 percent of the total national quota. In an effort to offset the "last to be hired, first to be fired" syndrome, the United Auto Workers union proposed a reverse seniority program to the Ford Motor Company. In announcing Ford's rejection of the plan, Vice President for Labor Relations Malcolm Denise said that Ford's "commitment to the hard-core remains as broad and resolute as ever." Henry Ford II was head of the NAB!

The paradoxical antics of the auto-manufacturer and the head of the NAB—coincidentally having the same name—are reminiscent of Andrew Hacker's whimsical and apocryphal tale of the corporation without shareholders and employees whose ten directors (the only humans involved with the organization) freely acknowledged that "at least eight of the ten of us, as private citizens that is, did not favor the legislation we were supporting . . . in the company's interest."[6]

It requires little imagination to come up with similar instances of conflict between a corporate executive's personal interest and the policy of his company. How often have you heard a corporate officer say, with earnest conviction: "You know I'm opposed to the war, but that's our Government's foreign policy and *we* can't help it if we're prime contractors. Somebody has to do it," or "I'm sure dead-against air and water pollution but we'd go out of business if the Government didn't provide the subsidies to *allow us* to change equipment," or "There's nothing I'd rather do than give a loan to the first Negro that walks into our bank, but the Government has all that red tape and forms; *they* strangle you"?

Such are the platitudes of the corporate elite; just plain old spokes in the wheel who have figured out how to get to the top of the executive heap but don't know how to fight their way out of the plastic bag of rhetorical paradoxes. What is far more insidious is that these are the "new breed" of corporate executives whose faces appear on the covers of *Time, Newsweek, Fortune,* and *Business Week.* They are the men whom Kenneth Galbraith trusts so explicitly in *The New Industrial State,* whom Charles Reich would lead us to believe, by virtue of "Consciousness III," are going to head a new revolution that will ultimately benefit us all (replete with bell-bottoms, peace symbols, and copies of the last Nader Report in their hip pockets), and whom Richard Nixon surrounds himself with (all the p.r. and advertising guys like Haldeman, Ehrlichman, Zeigler, and whatever their names are).† *Who is conning whom?*

In another sense one almost longs for the good old days when —at the very least—you knew where people stood. Where have all those tough-nosed "Public Be Damned" corporate managers gone—men like Charles E. Wilson ("Engine Charley"), the former G.M. executive and later Secretary of Defense under Eisenhower, who said quite forthrightly, "I always thought that what's good for General Motors is good for the country"?

The ascendancy of slick public relations or urban affairs officer (the "image makers" and "front men") at most corporations must really rankle the tough-minded marketing and sales people. For example, as recently as 1963, Dr. Theodore Levit, marketing adviser to Standard Oil, in an address at the Harvard Business School, stated:

† *Newsweek,* with dazzling imagery, quoted a White House insider who had devised what he called the In-Box Gauge of Personal Clout in High Places in order to identify "movers" and "shakers."

"The point is this: the businessman exists for only one purpose, to create and deliver value satisfactions at a profit to himself. He isn't and shouldn't be a theologian, a philosopher, an Emily Post of commerce. His job is ridiculously simple. The test of whether the things he offers do indeed contain value satisfactions is provided by the completely neutral mechanism of the open market. If what is offered can be sold at a profit (not even necessarily a long-run profit), then it's legitimate . . . The cultural, spiritual, social, moral consequences are none of his [the businessman's] personal concern.[7]

Corporate America is in a double bind, one that involves the distance between word and deed and they know! How they get themselves out of it (or even if they care to) is another story, one which only obliquely affects the theme of this book. It is difficult to resist the temptation to continue exploring this issue, but at this point it is more valuable to return to the central concern of this chapter, that of examining corporate activities.

LIFE INSURANCE COMPANIES

The life insurance industry by the end of 1967 had investments of more than $37 billion in various income-producing projects throughout the country. In September 1967 the industry committed—by way of an announcement from the White House—$1 billion to rehabilitate blighted urban areas. In the language of the declaration it was "to improve housing conditions and to finance job-creating enterprises and needed services for those in city-core areas." Investments under this $1 billion program—the most dramatic commitment by private enterprise—were to be those which, because of type, location, or risk would not ordinarily be financed by life insurance companies. These investments would, except under extraordinary circumstances, carry *Government guarantees* or insurance for members. These investment loans are generally offered at interest rates no higher than the regular market rates.

As of December 31, 1968, the life insurance industry had committed $943 million‡ to this program. Eighty percent of this money was to be invested in job-creating and service facilities. More

‡ Within a short period of time, therefore, the figure went well over a billion.

than one half of the total was supplied by the industry's big five: Prudential, Metropolitan, Equitable, New York Life, and John Hancock.

Although this program was not directly aimed at the minority entrepreneur, he would benefit to some degree. If $1 billion is not a large sum of money, relative to the life insurance industry's total investments, it is certainly the largest amount of private-sector money that has ever been directed toward disadvantaged citizens' business efforts.

The most long-term significance of this program is that the insurance industry finally awoke to the fact that there might be an important investment market in the inner-city areas. Since an overwhelming percentage of its funds will be in housing and other Federally guaranteed areas, the risk for the insurance companies seemed to be small; the rewards, both financial and social, are equal or are better than other investment opportunities.

By early 1968 there appeared to be some dissension in the ranks over the interest-rate ceilings of FHA mortgages, which was not the kind of profit ratio that insurance companies had become accustomed to; and there were indications that the initial enthusiasm had begun to wane. Some companies were even talking about dropping out; but at least, for the time being, one industry had put its best foot forward.[8]

One expert on urban real estate pointed out that "All that glitters is not gold. Although this step apparently represents a big commitment on the part of the industry, don't lose sight of the fact that the policy decision is consistent with the long-range interests of those companies involved. They *must* protect the market value of downtown real estate in urban centers . . . and besides these new investments are all subsidized."

Performance of $1 Billion
Urban Investment Program
December 31, 1968

HOUSING	$715,620
JOB-CREATING/SERVICE FACILITIES	228,036
TOTAL	$943,656
Housing Units	59,300
Jobs Created/Retained	26,566

BANKING

For the overwhelming number of commercial banks across the country the problems of minority group entrepreneurship might just as well not have existed. To begin with, small loans to ghetto businesses were not exactly the traditional banker's cup of tea and substantial loans to minority individuals were unheard of. Historically, commercial banks have operated successfully by providing low-risk money at low-interest terms to qualified borrowers. A loan to a minority entrepreneur—particularly a ghetto businessman in an urban center—was inconsistent with low-risk banking policy; it represented a high risk at the same low rate of return. The banker not only shared other corporate institutions' prejudices against minority investments; he also had a well-bred sense of what is called a profit maximization.

Since the typical loan officer is trained to make sound loans he is not inclined to concern himself with the minority entrepreneur. In business-as-usual terms a larger commercial loan to a reliable white manufacturer means less homework and paper-shuffling. The loan officer knows only too well that his own success and promotions depend on good business judgment; i.e., keeping his desk neat and keeping his default rate as low as possible.

More often than not when a black businessman walks through the door of the bank the loan officer *assumes* that the loan is going to be more trouble than it's worth. He prefers instead to see a "familiar" face, for that kind of recognition reinforces the assumption that loans to "traditional customers" are well backed by credit ratings, plant facilities, and personal knowledge of the individual and his business needs. Some would say that these are just good business practices; others would maintain that they are highly discriminatory (or racist). Both are right.

While bank presidents and board chairmen such as David Rockefeller* and George Moore were making commendable speeches and wearing "Give a Damn" buttons these sentiments are hardly ever translated into workable strategies and meaningful programs for local branch offices or divisions. Local branch

* Rockefeller even suggested that the private sector could get the job done without the help of Government.

managers have been unwilling to take their bosses at their word and make loans that would raise their branch's default rate and efficiency quotient. Very few branch managers could be described as anything but hard-nosed. That's why they've got their jobs.

So, a paradox exists. Top brass was publicly committed to freeing money and middle management hasn't been told how to get out of its prescribed role.

There are more than fourteen thousand commercial banks throughout the United States and a *conservative* estimate of their total investment in minority business enterprise over a twelve-month period (January 1, 1967–December 31, 1967) is less than $8,000 per bank. As one black businessman in San Francisco said, "I can get $6,700 for a new Cadillac but they wouldn't give me the same amount to start a new business." The percentage of the total bank assets devoted to minority loans is $1/20$ of 1 percent—the figure is appalling. There are exceptions to this pattern but they are rare. Those banks which have made a special effort to develop new management techniques and deal with the discriminatory factors can be counted on the fingers of one hand. The pace-setters are: the First Pennsylvania Banking and Trust Co. of Philadelphia; the Citizen's and Southern National Bank of Georgia; and the Hyde Park of Chicago. Six New York banks with combined assets of $69 billion refused to put aside a joint fund of $15 million for minority loans in early 1968. They were publicly committed to civic betterment but not $2\frac{1}{4}$ to $4\frac{1}{4}$ percent worth.[9]

CORPORATE SPIN-OFFS

There was much talk and publicity in 1967 and 1968 about the success of "corporate spin-offs." This involves a technique whereby a new corporation, with community or minority group ownership and management, combines with an establishment company's financial resources, technical and management expertise, or with a captive contract. Eventually, the newly formed corporation is "spun-off." This occurs when the participating minority entrepreneur or community group acquires control of the stock from the parent corporation through a prearranged turnkey agreement. All of the projects—there were about twenty in the country—were still in their infant or adolescent stages, so it was premature to make judgments as to their chances for long-range success.

Some of the corporations involved were: Warner and Swazey in Cleveland, Crown Zellerbach in San Francisco, E.G.&G. in Roxbury, Massachusetts, Avco in Dorchester, Mattel Toys in Watts, Eastern Gas and Fuel in Boston, Harris Intertype in Cleveland, Commonwealth United in Venice, California, Aerojet-General in Watts, Martin Marietta in Washington, Western Electric in Chicago, and Xerox in Rochester. In many ways these experiments are useful. However, it should also be pointed out that most are artificial and poorly planned. It is almost as if the sponsors had said, "Okay, here's the check, use our name and get out of our hair." Maybe this is overstated, but the fact is that most of the companies appear to be no more than holding actions, with the exception of Xerox, Mattel, Harris Intertype and perhaps two or three others. The reason for the initial success of the exceptions is that there was a true partnership—from the outset—between the corporation and the community group in all phases of planning and execution. Those that failed took the paternalistic, begging-for-the-bone approach. What has been learned from these experiments is that private industry must develop new and creative techniques of investment and organization to allow for the special problems that can be expected to emerge from operating a minority- or community-controlled company. Investment must be managed in such a way that control of the company is primarily in the hands of minority people, yet the equity interest of the private investors must be sufficiently large to induce them to actively assist in the running of the business.

Probably the best incentive to persuade corporations to undertake spin-offs or to locate in poverty areas is to offer some form of Government subsidy. Several bills have been authored in the Senate toward that end; none has been passed.† Most of the corporations mentioned above have received some Federal funds, usually in the form of job-training subsidies. Those firms that did

† Senator Robert Kennedy introduced the "Urban Employment Opportunities Development Act of 1967," which is probably the one that is best known.

undertake some form of spin-off were large, well-established companies that could afford to risk losses.

In summary, the participation of various corporations in "community-minded" programs varied industry by industry. An extensive research study‡ documented that those industries which had most to gain by keeping on good relations with the government and those which were involved in labor-intensive markets were most enthusiastic. The highest percentage of participation was achieved by aerospace corporations, financial institutions (including banks, savings and loan companies, and insurance companies), and companies manufacturing electronic and computer equipment. Those corporations which either stated that they weren't interested in participating or whose efforts were so meager that they couldn't even be called tokenism were predominantly in merchandising, metal manufacturing, petroleum, farm and industrial machinery.

The factors which motivated corporate involvement are many and varied. Though not necessarily in order of importance they are:

(1) Compliance with Federal or local regulations;

(2) Fear of future riots that could either jeopardize existing investments or be disruptive to normal business, particularly when a plant is located in a ghetto (like Warner & Swazey in Hough);

(3) A desire for favorable publicity;

(4) An effort to create a long-run market or to increase profits for their particular product (U.S. Gypsum's and Alcoa's interests seem to be of this nature);

(5) A sincere belief in corporate social responsibility, that private-sector objectives and public interests are convergent. If the corporate executive is genuinely committed to the well-being of the community, it then seems logical that enlightened corporate interests would be consistent with the best interests of society; and

(6) The desire to preserve for corporations the greatest latitude of autonomy in relation to other competing social interests. Corporate America wants to retain the concentration of political, economic, and social power that it has acquired. This interest coincides with point three—favorable publicity—since it is consistent with the interests of the private sector to maintain a positive image in the eyes of the American public. For many years corporate interests have taken great pains

‡ For complete details on the authoritative study see: Jules Cohn, *The Conscience of Corporations.*

to emphasize that the identity of corporate and local social interests are one and the same; just as it has made every attempt to assure the citizenry at large of the commonality of corporate and national interests.[10]

The explanations offered by executives of corporations which did not participate were varied and candid. The President of a new conglomerate, after admitting that his company wasn't interested in getting involved in social problems, stated: "Don't compare us with aerospace or insurance. The insurance companies have more cash than we do, and those in aerospace had to go out of their way to be good citizens simply to keep the Government money flowing." His point is well taken as several studies of defense industries have demonstrated how most aerospace corporations are totally dependent upon the Government for their existence. Another executive, the President of a large retail chain wryly remarked that "it wasn't until after the Detroit riots that the automobile makers got busy. If their factories were in East Cupcake, they wouldn't be so energetic."

FEDERAL AGENCIES
AND THE BUREAUCRACY

Ballad of a Receding Goal

Lyndon Johnson took an axe,
  To make inflation bygone,
He gave the budget forty whacks
  and sent the chips to Saigon.
While war and space go on apace,
  Each funded in entirety
Matters of poverty and race
  are of the chopped variety.
For each man kills the things he loves.
  Farewell oh Great Society.

—An unidentified black teenager in the Job Corps.

In order to comprehend the full dimension of the problems facing low-income and minority groups it is essential to gain some insights into the bureaucratic programs that have been established to "help them." Some time ago a highly respected magazine, *The Washington Monthly*—which views its own role as that of "journalistic ombudsman" covering for the Federal Government the Office of the President, the Senate and House, Federal executive agencies, and regulatory agencies—began to publish a "Memo of the Month." The publication of these memos provides in an instant more graphic insights into the "ways" of the Federal bureaucracy than volumes of scholarly research documents.

The one presented opposite is not atypical.

Such are the "working conditions" within the Federal bureaucracy. More often than not there is usually an inverse proportion between the productivity and the "chickenshit"—such as depicted in the "Memos." Federal career civil servants *are not,* as Ronald Reagan would have us believe, "the invisible army on the Potomac that is determined to socialize the country." But, by and large, at the middle-management level, they are a far sturdier breed than state, county, or municipal bureaucrats. Local governments, and their bureaucracies, as Joseph Lyford observed in *The Airtight Cage,* are far more inefficient and unresponsive than Federal agencies. He wrote:

New York City government is like the Empire State Building without elevators. Somewhere up on top is the administrative apparatus, the public is in the basement, and in between is a vast air space occupied by the civil service. The consequence of this three-tiered arrangement is that the unaffiliated citizen lives in nearly total bewilderment about his government and, on their side, the administrative officials work in general ignorance of what their own bureaucracies are doing to the citizen. A different style of frustration lies in wait for the citizen who thinks he can accomplish something by interrogating public officials at public meetings. An individual who tangles with the head of a bureaucracy will find himself fighting out of his class; any commissioner will tell the citizen that the citizen is "not in possession of all the facts." The common thread that stitches all the official responses together is their irrelevance to the questions. Such confrontations give the bystander the feeling of traveling through one of those amusement-park concessions where iron bars turn out to be rubber and where mirrors make a man seem seven feet tall or seven inches short. The citizen might try to barge into the bureaucratic establishment and demand an audience, but that is tantamount to wandering through a pitch-black cave, full of hollow voices telling the citizen he has the wrong department.[11]

dpo PERSONNEL MANAGEMENT LETTER

OFFICE OF THE SECRETARY

U.S. DEPARTMENT OF HEALTH, EDUCATION, AND WELFARE

OCT 14 1970

DPO PERSONNEL MANAGEMENT LETTER NO. 70-3

SUBJECT: Proper Office Attire

TO : All Employees, Office of the Secretary

We are frequently asked what the Office of the Secretary policy is with regard to proper dress. Because styles and attitudes about clothing have been changing so rapidly in the past several years, there is often doubt as to what is proper and acceptable dress for the office. We believe that some not-too-rigid guide-lines in this area would be helpful to all employees.

It would be impractical to attempt to establish a definitive list of all acceptable and unacceptable items of clothing for office wear. Certain items would clearly fall within one group or the other, but there are many which are not so easily categorized. Often, the nature of the work being performed, where it is being performed, and the season of the year will greatly influence dress.

As a general policy, employees should exercise good judgement and good taste in their dress. They should be groomed in a manner fitting to the surroundings into which their assignments take them. In any event, it is prudent to avoid extremes in both fashion and style.

When questions arise, it is the responsibility of each Division head to give guidance to his employees on matters of appropriate dress.

E. Hicks, Jr.
Director, Division of Personnel
Operations
Executive Office

INQUIRIES: Employee Relations Branch, Room 4338 North, Extension 34925

DISTRIBUTION: All Employees, OS

In any analysis or presentation of the role of Governmental agencies—be they Federal, state, county, or municipal—it should be stated quite forthrightly that no agency or department, national or local gave a hoot for low-income or minority groups until the Economic Opportunity Act (EOA) of 1964 created the Office of Economic Opportunity. The highest order of endeavor on the local level was the proclaiming of "Brotherhood Week" or the establishment of Human Rights Commissions which neither had subpoena or enforcement powers—they were, in fact, provisional exercises in group therapy somehow designed to provide outlets for vocalizing local tensions. The main thrust of what was then referred to as "social services" was carried out by local welfare agencies who viewed their clients as charitable wards and treated them accordingly.

With the creation of OEO as an advocate agency for the poor over a thousand Community Action Agencies (CAAs) were established throughout the country. Local governments were bypassed as "grant in aid" funds were given directly to the CAAs. In this manner local agencies and departments were for the first time forced to deal with low-income community groups as an institutional force in their communities. In most cases, efforts were made by local public officials to either gain control through local co-option or by collective efforts (by mayors and governors) to pressure the Administration and Congress to change the legislative intent of the Economic Opportunity Act. These pressures were realized in late 1967 when a crippling amendment to the enabling EOA legislation, the Green Amendment (sponsored by Congresswoman Edith Green of Oregon) was adopted by Congress. The sense of the Amendment was to give local officials the option to take over control of local CAAs.

If local officials were outrightly hostile to the plight of poor people, the attitude of most Federal agencies was that of studied indifference. HEW, the Department of Labor, the Department of Agriculture, and the Department of Commerce among others each had their own constituencies and they did not perceive low-income groups as an appropriate clientele. As late as the spring of 1967 these other agencies still refused to integrate their efforts with those of OEO, the one agency which had a legislative mandate to coordinate programs that affected the lives of low-income people. One of the mechanisms that was employed by the Administration to facilitate the interfacing of programs and the linkage of efforts was the creation of Federal Executive Boards (FEBs). These Boards were composed of the directors of all Federal agencies (including district military commands) or their representatives in the nine major cities in the United States—where Federal agencies maintained their regional offices. At the direction of the President, monthly FEB meetings were initiated with a high priority assigned to the problems of minority and poor people. One high official of OEO reported that most of the time spent at FEB meetings centered on discussions which ranged from the excessive utilization of paper clips to that of riot control and that the directors of other Federal agencies were most inclined toward protecting their own turf. They simply were not concerned with efforts to coordinate programs with OEO and become more sensitive to its problems and responsibilities. (Rather than deal with immediate and pressing problems, they devoted several of those meetings to informal "talks" by guest speakers from the State Department informing the officials of domestic agencies how they could galvanize support for the President's Vietnam effort.)

In most local communities the limits on policy decisions and political options are set by a small and informal coalition of business, real estate, and trade union leaders as well as a limited segment of the formal political leadership. This group usually exercises a considerable amount of control over the mass media. The power is very subtle but effective. It is almost exclusively used to protect the vested interests of the privileged. The power brokers simply do not like anything that threatens the existing, institutional arrangements.

The poor and the blacks have systematically been excluded from institutional decision-making. They are rarely represented on public bodies: school boards, welfare departments, urban planning committees, utility-regulatory commissions, or even anti-poverty boards. And where they are represented it usually is because the project involved is worth peanuts.

With this view of civil servants and bureaucracies (Federal and local) in mind, we can now proceed to analyze the policies and efforts (administrative and bureaucratic) of those Federal agencies which are responsible for providing grants and guidelines, programs and priorities for low-income and minority groups, especially in the areas of economic and business development.

Economic Development Administration

The Economic Development Administration (EDA) is an agency of the U.S. Department of Commerce, established in 1965 to encourage economic development in certain "lagging communities" throughout the country. In order to convince private industry to locate in these communities, EDA has various programs designed to "sweeten the pot" for private investment.

In its effort to stimulate industrial growth in areas with high unemployment or low family incomes EDA can offer public works grants and loans, direct business loans, and technical assistance grants. They have tended to concentrate in small towns and rural areas as well as making substantial business loans. The fiscal average loan in fiscal 1969 was $1,004,000. Usually, they refer smaller borrowers to the SBA and private sources. EDA has also given support to other Government agencies and has generally participated in projects when supplementary funding is available from other Federal agencies.

Although EDA has concentrated its $250 to $300 million dollars per year on lily-white programs it has recently been involved in establishing several major urban projects, including those in Los Angeles (Watts) and Oakland, California, in the "stockyards" of Chicago, and in Brooklyn, New York, at the old Navy Yard.

After the Watts riots in 1966, industry was reluctant to move into the area. EDA underwrote a technical assistance study to determine the economic feasibility of development, and concluded that the area could, under normal circumstances, be a natural center for industrial development. Watts was well served by utilities and transportation, and had a large supply of under-utilized industrial and commercial land. Watts also had a strong industrial market, and God knows a large labor pool available for diverse industrial jobs.

EDA proposed that a Local Development Corporation (LDC) be created with establishment business and financial leaders from the Los Angeles area, both black and white, to administer the development. EDA stipulated that the LDC be independent of any local community groups, and that community participation be kept to a minimum. The agency rationalization was that business acumen was more important to community development that was "relating to the community." Various community groups felt otherwise and suggested that the whole project was another shuck to help major corporations and improve the status of a handful of Negroes who "were on the make." From its inception most community groups felt left out in the cold.

Thus, Watts Economic Resources Corporation (ERC) was formed in June 1968, with nine LA trustees, and was empowered to buy and sell land, machinery, buildings, and equipment, to borrow money, and to guarantee third-party loans. EDA arranged for an OEO grant of $3.8 million to the project, which EDA matched, for programs subject to EDA approval.

Watts's ERC has since created a 45-acre Watts Industrial Park, with EDA approval. Lockheed Aircraft agreed to be the first major tenant, and promised to provide jobs and training for the unemployed. It is generally agreed that the project is not a success. Lockheed seems to have a poor track record for delivering on promises.

The City of Oakland was designated as an EDA target area in 1965 because of persistent unemployment. EDA sponsored an interagency "task force" in Oakland—with the participation of Small Business Administration, Departments of Housing and Urban Development, Health and Labor, and the OEO—charged with developing a coordinated Federal and local strategy to help poor people. Since Oakland's problems were critical, EDA established a program to reverse the unemployment trend in four areas within the city before the "task force" had completed its strategy. In addition, EDA committed funds for public works loans and grants, business loans and technical assistance; including a ten-million-dollar grant to World Airways, which promised to train minority individuals.

The Oakland project can best be summed up in the words of

journalist Murray Kempton in an article, "Land of Dreams—Oakland, California":

> The salvation of Oakland, like so many great undertakings in America, is rather going to be done.
>
> Its disaster is the one common to cities: In the last ten years its overall population has declined 5 percent, and its Negro population has increased 73 percent. It is a city of considerable amenity. Only 15 percent of its housing units are substandard.
>
> Oakland is also a tight union town, and the Labor Department estimates that one third of its labor force is unable to earn a decent living.
>
> It is ridiculous to quarrel over whose fault this is, although the city and the special Federal team which has been sent in to repair the damage seem to have spent a good deal of time quarreling about almost nothing else . . .
>
> Oakland strives for its reclamation pretty much as Americans . . . always do—by building edifices for the wonderment of nonresidents. Its port commission has a higher budget than the entire city government. The 30 percent of the white population which has moved out in the last ten years kept its construction union cards in Oakland, of course; the Federal Government has a rule of thumb that 58 percent of the wages paid on its Oakland construction projects go to people who live outside of Oakland.
>
> The city is, of course, concerned about its poor and not just because nowadays it isn't easy to get Federal money without attaching a rider certifying that somewhere in the plans there's a little grease for the hard core. The Government will shortly grant $10,000,000 to World Airways to expand the local airport. The president of World Airways was listed recently as in the $100,000,000 class, which would suggest that he might be able to find $13,000,000 around the money market somewhere; but the Government came rushing to his relief because he promised that his new facility would train and hire Oakland Negroes.[12]

Eugene Foley, then Director of EDA, seemingly satisfied with the agency's effort said, after the commitments in Oakland:

> We need bold and imaginative action in each ghetto and we offer inducements to obtain it. If we can devise schemes for a legitimate profit to be made in the ghetto then we will see the vast economic and talent resources of American business begin to apply themselves to the solution of urban problems.[13]

One source in Oakland, a leader of a community group, indicated that at last count fourteen individuals—hard-core blacks—

had been trained by World Airways. The inducements that Foley felt were so conducive to "bold and imaginative action" were, to say the least, generous. Port Authority officials point out that some day in the future there will be more jobs. EDA officials maintain that they are sure that the Port Authority and World Airways will work out reasonable agreement concerning training and employment. One executive at World Airways stated that to the best of his knowledge not one black had been hired by his company as a result of the project but that by September of 1972 a program would be initiated.

Another EDA project was its funding of Walt Disney's Mineral King project. Another "hard-core" company, Disney's assets were listed as $267.6 million as of October 1970.[14] This project—a ski resort—was billed as a means to help the rural poor of California by stimulating economic activity and jobs.

The Mineral King project is not only a typical example of EDA's coziness in subsidizing big business or political friends of the Administration. It is, too, a symbol of the Federal bureaucracy's indifference to America's environment and ecology. Walt Disney Productions had been granted permission from the U.S. Forest Service to despoil an untouched part of the Sierra Valley, surrounded on three sides by the Sequoia National Park. The distinct financial advantage was that the resort's location was approximately halfway between Los Angeles and San Francisco.

At the center of the ensuing controversy over Disney Productions' attempt to rape the Mineral King area, one of the most beautiful in the West, were the right of the Forest Service to license those kinds of projects without holding public hearings; the propriety of the Government's leasing large tracts of national forest land to private, profit-making resort speculators; and the decision to put a highway across a national park to give subsidized access to a corporate speculator. The Sierra Club has challenged the Mineral King plan, and it is expected that the final decision will be made by the Supreme Court in early 1972. The groundwork for Federal participation through EDA was laid back in 1966 and 1967.

Originally, Interior Secretary Stewart L. Udall was opposed to the plan, which would run the road across Sequoia National Park. One article cited the fact that:

California's highway engineer J. C. Womack said the Mineral King road could be built only "at the expense of other critical (road-building) projects." He added that the use of funds set aside for other road-building projects would be ". . . very disruptive to previously approved planning and scheduling of projects in the Southern Counties" of California.[15]

The deal that was finally arranged between Governor Ronald Reagan (it was reputed that Disney had contributed heavily to his '66 gubernatorial campaign) and the Feds was that the Democratic Administration issue a permit *and funds* to allow for construction of the road while Reagan would assure that the Feds would receive the necessary acreage to establish the Redwood National Park.[16] The permit was finally issued in 1967, and EDA came across with three million bucks for the California Highway Commission on the grounds that the Mineral King "winter wonderland" resort was essential to the state's economy—and would ultimately help poor folk. From ski slope to trickle-down, the poor and unemployed of California were snowed-under once again.

OFFICE OF ECONOMIC OPPORTUNITY

The War on Poverty was officially launched with the creation of the Office of Economic Opportunity (OEO), which was the major handiwork of the 1964 Economic Opportunity Act.

In its effort to alleviate the poverty of millions of Americans—urban and rural, black, white, Mexican-American, Puerto Rican and Indian—OEO was given program responsibility in wide variety of areas, including manpower, housing, health, legal aid, education, etc.

> . . . which provided services, assistance and other activities . . . to give promise of progress toward elimination of poverty or a cause or causes of poverty through developing employment opportunities, improving human performance, motivation, and productivity, or bettering the conditions under which people live, learn, and work; . . .[17]

Some of its better-known programs were VISTA, Headstart, Legal Services, Upward Bound, the Job Corps, the Neighborhood

Youth Corps, and Foster Grandparents. But at the gut of the entire antipoverty effort was the Community Action Program, which was designed to give low-income Americans an opportunity to identify, design, plan, and initiate their own priorities and emphases in more than a thousand communities across the nation.

> . . . which developed, continued, and administered with the maximum feasible participation of residents of the areas and members of the groups served; . . .[18]

Toward this end, OEO-funded Community Action Agencies (CAAs) were designated as local-initiative programs. They were given demonstration grants and "required" to maintain a measure of community control in their planning.

> . . . which is conducted, administered, or coordinated by a public or private nonprofit agency . . .[19]

In succeeding amendments to the Act, Congress cut the heart out of community action and all but eliminated local initiative. In addition, by acts of Congress and decisions of the White House, some of OEO's most effective programs were "spun-off," or transferred administratively, to old-line agencies, where it was *assured* that their effectiveness would be severely diminished. The *central purpose* for creating OEO was that the other Federal and state agencies had failed in their efforts to deliver services to low-income and minority groups. Such was the fate of Headstart, Neighborhood Youth Corps, and the Job Corps, among others. While the political base and programmatic effectiveness of OEO was being reduced, however, the 1966 and 1967 amendments to the Economic Opportunity Act upgraded OEO's role in the area of economic development. It gave the agency authority to establish "Special Impact" programs in selected low-income communities.

The Title I-D amendment to the Economic Opportunity Act (co-sponsored by the late Robert F. Kennedy and Jacob K. Javits) of 1967 stated forthrightly that communities have the right to control and to direct the improvement of a whole variety of business and social opportunities. The community-owned corporation was the key to the whole concept. As Robert Kennedy said in December 1966:

> The measure of the success of this or any program will be the extent to which it helps the ghetto to become a community—a functioning unit, its people acting together on matters of mutual concern, with the power and the resources to affect the conditions of their own lives. Therefore, the heart of the program, I believe, should be the creation of community development corporations [CDCs] which would carry out the work of construction, the hiring and training of workers, the provision of service, the encouragement of associated enterprises—The community development corporations . . . would find a fruitful partnership with American industry . . . A . . . critical element in the structure, financial and otherwise, of these corporations should be the full and dominant participation by the residents of the community concerned . . . Through CDCs, residents of the ghettos could at once contribute to the betterment of their immediate conditions, and build a base for full participation in the economy—in the ownership and the savings and the self-sufficiency which the more fortunate in our Nation already take for granted.

Some CDCs have set up factories or shopping centers. Others run maintenance services, cattle feeder lots, fish co-ops, catfish farms, woodwork and toy co-ops, strawberry producer co-ops or stores. Other community development corporations operate local services, as well as perform municipal services under contract from local government. The community development corporation can be set up by civic groups and churches, by a Model Cities Board or poverty program Community Action Agency, or by any group of individual residents of that community. It really merits the title of community development corporation, however, if any community member may join.

In principle, this inclusiveness distinguishes the community development corporation from ordinary private businesses, such as those mentioned in programs for minority business enterprise, as well as from branches of large corporations in poor neighborhoods. In these ordinary private businesses, a limited group of individual owners or partners or shareholders run the corporation, and receive the profits for their own private use. In a community development corporation, the profits accrue to the community, and the community decides what to do with them.

Community development corporations, thus, are a possible form of organization for a community that has economic, social, or political needs, and is interested in working out new ways for its members to cooperate with each other in meeting them.

Initially, most of the CDCs were in economically depressed black and chicano urban neighborhoods, but more recently CDCs have been established in rural Indian, chicano, and white communities as well as urban low-income white neighborhoods.

SMALL BUSINESS ADMINISTRATION

In late 1963 a review of loans made by the Small Business Administration showed that in the ten-and-a-half-year period from 1953 to 1963, only seven loans had been made to Negro businessmen, as against 425 loans to white businessmen. Moreover, the SBA was, at the time, the only Government agency to which minority businessmen could turn, if they could not get financing from regular commercial sources. Between 1963 and 1968 SBA made limited efforts to expand their outreach to minority entrepreneurs, in both the number of agencies offering assistance and the amount of funds granted. However, these programs have failed to produce substantial headway in the minorities' fight for parity in business ownership and in employment.

The Small Business Administration is a permanent, autonomous agency of the Federal Government. It was established under the Eisenhower administration in 1953, by the Small Business Act. The agency was authorized to provide financial and advisory aid to small businessmen who could not get reasonable financing elsewhere, and a $275 million revolving fund was provided for loans. By 1967 the fund had been increased to more than $400 million.

Although SBA efforts are linked to the Departments of Commerce, Labor, Housing and Urban Development (HUD), the Department of Defense (DOD), and the Office of Economic Opportunity, it is independent of all of these organizations, and has its own Presidentially appointed chief administrator and staff. By 1968 there were over seventy-five SBA field offices, operating in every state, with the assignment of providing financial and management assistance to small businesses. With the exception of investment, speculative firms, and communications media, any small business would be eligible for SBA assistance so long as it did not exceed certain statutory limitations on income ceilings and the number of employees.*

The SBA was the first Governmental agency to attempt to promote minority economic development. In 1964 the SBA launched in Philadelphia a special program to offer loans to small businessmen, and especially to Negro businessmen, on more liberal terms than usual. It was called the "6 × 6" *Pilot Loan and Management Program* and it offered loans of up to $6,000 for up to six years. Additional SBA programs oriented to minority businessmen included the *Equal Opportunities Loans Program* authorized by the 1964 Economic Opportunity Act. The Act (which was the OEO, antipoverty legislation) authorized the funds for loans but delegated the authority for administering the program to SBA. It is generally agreed that the program was a bureaucratic mess and the result was, of course, minimal help to the minority community.

This pilot program was deemed so successful that it was expanded by Congress in the Economic Opportunity Act of 1964, and the SBA was permitted to make loans of up to $25,000 for fifteen years, with low interest rates (4¾ to 5½ percent). These Equal Opportunity Loans were made available to low-income or minority borrowers and, as with the "6 × 6" loans, financing was made on the basis of character and potential, rather than collateral. It was obvious that the loans were, once again, too small to help any but those "mom-and-pop" businesses, and the volume of the loans remained relatively small.

When "Black Capitalism" became a topic of political conversation in late 1967 and early 1968, President Johnson encouraged SBA Administrator Howard Samuels to expand the use of SBA programs. Samuels developed and initiated a crash program which he inaugurated in August 1968. It was designed to activate the agency bureaucrats and to make SBA loans—particularly Equal Opportunity Loans—more accessible to black capitalists. It was called Project OWN. Although other existing loan programs had been opened up and new ones initiated for minority business-

* (1) Wholesale firms had to have annual incomes under $5 million; (2) retail firms had to have annual incomes under $1 million; (3) manufacturing firms had to employ fewer than 250 persons.

men, they were limited in scope and design. By past SBA standards, Project OWN was the "great leap forward." From its
inception, the SBA had a reputation for being a bureaucracy that
was generally unresponsive, if not specifically hostile, to the needs
of minority individuals and groups. SBA officials by and large had
a smalltown white merchants' viewpoint which definitely did not
include providing any kind of a competitive advantage to blacks
and Mexican-Americans.

The first goal of Project OWN was to increase the number of
loans to minority businessmen from 1,700 in fiscal 1968 to 10,000
in fiscal 1969, and 20,000 by June 1970. To facilitate this increase,
Samuels demanded that paperwork for loans be simplified and
that the time necessary to obtain loans be reduced. In a further
effort to expedite the total process, involvement with local minority organizations was to be established to help identify new
entrepreneurs. Consistent with this effort, Samuels laid the
groundwork for developing future SBA programs which would
make the bureaucrats more responsive and sensitive to the needs
of the minority community as well as increasing the capacity
of the agency to mount and coordinate management and technical assistance by volunteers or retired businessmen.

Project OWN did make significant progress toward achieving
its goals in fiscal 1969; loans to minority businessmen were increased to 4,120 in this period. The paperwork for loans and loan
guarantees was reduced, but the forms were still lengthy and
complicated, and the *minimum* application-to-decision time was
six weeks (some took eight months to a year).

In addition there were several other SBA programs which,
though potentially useful, were almost exclusively directed toward assisting white businessmen. For example, the SBA was
authorized to lend up to $350,000 for up to fifteen years at 5⅝
percent maximum interest, for construction, expansion, or modi-
fication of small business facilities. SBA also can offer participation to minority business ventures by guaranteeing bank loans
for applicants who could not meet commercial collateral requirements. The SBA had the power to guarantee up to $350,000 or
90 percent of a commercial loan, whichever is less, and can also
directly lend up to $150,000. Generally, applicants would go

directly to the SBA, which then would pass the information on to a commercial bank for approval and lend at a locally allowable interest rate.†

OTHER FEDERAL PROGRAMS

Model Cities has been another potential source of funds for economic development programs. According to a number of responsible officials, though, they were not encouraged, administratively, to initiate new projects. Although its supervisory agency, the Department of Housing and Urban Development, finally issued guidelines in late 1970, limiting community representation, there were already growing numbers of local, individual Model Cities agencies that initiated economic development programs. By 1970, however, local community leaders were so bogged down in their efforts to merely interpret HUD guidelines and regulations that it seemed too difficult to mount any serious programmatic efforts.

The efforts of the Bureau of Indian Affairs (BIA) have been consistently atrocious since its inception in 1824. The mentality of the agency's bureaucrats generally has been that of protecting the stockade, rather than of acting as advocates on behalf of the Indian tribes they are paid to serve. Specifically, the practice of licensing white "trading posts" on the reservation has been commonplace. The traders, for the most part, are allowed to mark up their goods at considerable profit. In addition, on certain reservations the white traders not only own the only gas station and have the only telephone, but in certain instances they run the local post office. In disputes over monies owed to the store, some white traders have been known to open envelopes containing Federal checks to individual Indians.

† The exact relationship between the banks and the SBA is often unclear. One example of the kinds of bureaucratic game-playing that occurred involved a minority contractor, an SBA regional office, and one of the country's largest banks. The processing of a black contractor's application was held up for six weeks while the SBA office and the bank's loan department exchanged five letters in a jurisdictional dispute as to *who* should type the form.

One example of BIA failure relates to their policies regarding the Navajo Reservation, the nation's largest reservation encompassing the northern third of the state of Arizona, parts of New Mexico and Utah. Ever since the U.S. Government assumed its trusteeship of the Navajo people it has endeavored to make them economically self-sustaining, with very little success.

Those policies began as early as the Treaty of 1868, by which the Navajos were freed from captivity at Fort Sumner and returned to their former homelands. In that treaty it was recited that each Navajo was entitled to receive "seeds and agricultural implements" to cultivate the soil. However, given that the Navajo lands are in high desert without irrigation, the promise was rather meaningless and, needless to say, the Navajos never developed an agricultural economy. As a response to the earlier failure the BIA then devised an "Employment Assistance" program, which turned out to be a euphemism for relocating the Indians into the ghettos of American urban centers where they were to be trained for jobs which rarely existed in those cities. As a result most of the Indians returned to their homelands—trained as plumbers and steam fitters—to herd sheep and live in poverty.

Furthermore, the BIA has systematically discouraged and prevented Indian groups from establishing their own co-ops, on the reservation, to compete with the white trader. The conditions on the reservations are tantamount to human bondage.

With regard to rural economic development programs sponsored by the Federal Government, low-income and minority groups have fared far worse than their urban brethren. Most Federal efforts are clearly stacked in favor of the wealthy farmer or the corporate "agri-business." The concentration of wealth in the hands of a small number of rich farmers and corporations, as well as vertical conglomerates, is accepted as Department of Agriculture "official policy." This, of course, is done at the expense of the poor and minority individual farmer as well as those seeking to establish low-income cooperatives.

In testimony before the Senate Sub-Committee on Employment, Manpower and Poverty in August 1968, an article which appeared in *Fortune* Magazine by Roger Beardwood was read into The Congressional Record.[20] It offers some excellent insights into the plight of the rural poor and the institutional power—political, economic, and bureaucratic—that perpetuates these tragic conditions. Beardwood wrote that:

> Big farmers in the South not only make decisions that leave hired hands and sharecroppers jobless, homeless, and penniless. They also have a powerful voice in the formulation and execution of farm policies and programs that vitally affect the survival of independent Negro small farmers. In 1950 some 492,000 Negroes in the South were classified as farm proprietors and managers; by 1960 only 167,000 remained in that category. There are fewer now, and if the trend continues unabated, almost none will be left by 1975. Many of these small farmers and their families could be helped to stay on the land for at least another generation. But three things are against them: their farms are very small, they lack the money to mechanize, and they do not have a Washington lobby.
>
> The big farmers' control over small farmers' destinies rests on two facts of political life. First, the key agricultural committees in Congress are largely controlled by the Southerners; some of them, like Senator James Eastland of Mississippi, are farmers themselves. Second, the most important Agriculture Department programs are administered by state and county groups that are dominated by whites. The black farmer is helped where the administration is fair and unprejudiced, and hindered where it is not.
>
> The Negro farmer's troubles frequently start with the Agricultural Stabilization and Conservation Service. The A.S.C.S. is at the very heart of the farm program, that complicated structure which supports prices, sets production and marketing quotas, conserves land by taking it out of intensive cultivation, and allots the number of acres on which farmers may grow crops such as cotton, tobacco, and corn.
>
> By its very nature, the A.S.C.S. system works best for large farmers. For the land on which they do not grow crops, farmers are compensated according to their past production; large farmers have usually had a higher crop yield per acre than small farmers. Moreover, large farmers can take out of production their least fertile land; small farmers do not have that margin. And on the land they do continue to cultivate, large farmers can continue to increase income by using modern technology. Small farmers, in contrast, lack the capital and knowledge to mechanize, irrigate, or use the latest pesticides.
>
> Theoretically, the A.S.C.S. is highly democratic, operating through a pyramid of state and local groups. At the top is the state committee, appointed by the Secretary of Agriculture after consultation with farm organizations, state directors of agriculture, deans of agricultural colleges, and political leaders. Under the state committees are three-man county committees that are elected by community committees chosen by farmers themselves.

But Negroes sit on only five southern A.S.C.S. state committees. And there are only 454 Negroes among the 37,000 community-committee members. Most important, no Negro sits on any county committee (four have been elected as alternate members). And it is these all-white county groups that hire the A.S.C.S. staff that administers the Federal program. This year only 310 Negroes had permanent full-time jobs in 2,892 county offices in the entire nation, and no office had a Negro manager.

In the last several years there has been a slow, minimal improvement in the administration of Agriculture Department programs, brought about by pressure from the civil-rights groups, a firmer Federal policy, and by Negro farmers themselves. Burke County, Georgia, is one of many places where the pressures are rising. The A.S.C.S. office is a small, red-brick building in the county seat of Waynesboro. Recently, while three Negro farmers waited to talk about crop allotments, the acting manager, Frank S. Cates, described things as he saw them. "I'll admit the small farmer is more vulnerable than the big one," he said, "but these minority people who live in these shacks don't want to work. They'd rather go off somewhere and get on relief. You know this white-black thing. We never had any problem until these outside agitators came in. I don't know what the younger generation will come to, but the older people get along just fine. There's nothing an ordinary man can do about the situation. J. Edgar Hoover knows it's the Communists."[21]

If the American corporate community—by the end of 1968—had done nothing, then bureaucratic officialdom in Washington had accomplished next to nothing. In point of fact the call for retreat in the War on Poverty was loud and clear. With few exceptions most Federal agencies were involved in holding operations, with each bureaucracy jealously guarding its own turf waiting for the new administration to take office. The "enclave theory" was a bust in Vietnam, but it was a resounding, if unintended, success in dealing with America's poor and minority groups. They were being isolated (literally) and strangled (figuratively).

Under Samuels' administration, SBA had established a Black Advisory Council which was supposed to maintain communications between the agency and the black community. Whether the Nixon Administration would capitalize on this new-found credibility was in question. As one EDA official candidly remarked, "Our programs were never meant to directly help poor or minority individuals or groups. If the 'trickle-down' theory works, okay; if not, that's the way it is."

OEO was continuously running out of money or having programs taken from them. By and large, the agency was being whittled down so that it seemed to spend most of its time keeping itself alive. Model Cities was a bureaucratic maze, a classic study of inefficiency. And BIA, Agriculture, Farmers Home, et al., were functioning as the atrophied bureaucracies that made them a legend.

It was no doubt true that between 1965 and 1968 more funds than ever before had been made available for a variety of social service programs. But by 1968 it became just as apparent that there was a huge gap between the availability and the usability of resources. The nature of bureaucracies and the political machinations of local politicians served to divert these funds from the people they were intended to serve. By and large the strings were pulled by petty bureaucrats at the local level who sat on their brains and gave contracts, jobs, and favors to relatives and friends. It was not consistent with the interests of those who controlled the political or economic institutions to allow or encourage the proper development of mechanisms that could truly deliver services to low-income groups. Grant-in-aid programs made sense and neighborhood boards were the proper recipients, but only in rare circumstances did the process work. The mechanism was too fragile and those establishment forces that wanted it to fail had too many opportunities to trip up or short-circuit the delivery system. And they willingly exercised that prerogative, wherever possible.

In conclusion, Murray Kempton's perception of the reasons for the EDA giveaway in Oakland seemed to be equally true for other Federal Government programs to assist minorities economically—"to him who hath it shall be given." There were laws on the books and promises aplenty, but for the nation's poor and minority groups the name of the game was to run as fast as hell, in order to stay in place. Whether or not Richard Nixon would grasp the moment remains to be seen. . . .

7 GETTING IT TOGETHER—THE FIRST SIX MONTHS OF THE NIXON ADMINISTRATION

On January 23, 1969, Richard M. Nixon was finally faced with the task of putting his program to work. He was certainly well primed for the challenge. Probably no other President in our history had devoted more time to grooming himself for this role than Richard Nixon—as Vice President under President Eisenhower for eight years; as his party's standard-bearer in 1960, having lost by only the thinnest of margins to John F. Kennedy; and as the titular head of his party for the past eight years. The sixteen years of preparation prior to his election could well serve as a model for "Presidential" vocational training. The time and the opportunity had finally arrived for him to activate all the policies that he had planned and envisioned during his long and studied apprenticeship.

The first thing that a newly elected President does is to find people to work for him. There were about 2,150 political plums that Richard Nixon could hand out to loyal supporters in the winter of 1968–69. Consistent with the principles of modern business management that the Administration had pledged to bring to Washington, the jobs and the job seekers were put on a computer. But in spite of the fact that there were job seekers from state and local Republican Parties all over the country, the management experts had difficulty coming up with enough candidates. Finally, they resorted to sending out letters to everyone listed in Who's Who, with the result that prominent Democrats all over the country received "Dear Republican . . ." letters, soliciting their advice on candidates for the Administration's jobs.

The nature of the people chosen to run Federal programs is the best guide as to how the programs will operate and for whose benefit. In the case of Black Capitalism, there were four key selections which reflected the President's commitment to the program. They were the selections of: Maurice Stans to be Secretary of Commerce; Hilary Sandoval, Jr., as Administrator of the Small Business Administration, Thomas Roeser, Director of the yet to be created Office of Minority Enterprise, and Sam Wyly, as Chairman of the also new Advisory Council on Minority Enterprise. Two other people who also played a role in the history of Black Capitalism, more through what they did *not* do than what they did, were Donald Rumsfeld, Director of the Office of Economic Opportunity, and Daniel Patrick Moynihan, Nixon's Senior Advisor on Urban Affairs. With the exception of Sandoval, who was a Mexican-American, all of the above were white.

It was no surprise when the President-elect announced that Maurice Stans would be Secretary of Commerce. By all indications, Nixon had selected his kind of man, a successful businessman and well-connected political fund-raiser. All the newspaper profiles referred to the Secretary as a "doer," a "shaker," and an individual who was certainly well intentioned.*

Maurice Stans is the archetypical successful American. His father had been an immigrant Belgian house painter who had emigrated to Chicago. Young Stans began his career as an office boy in the small Chicago accounting firm of Alexander Grant and Co. in 1928. Within ten years he became executive partner of the firm and by 1955 he had led the firm to the position of being the nation's tenth largest. In the process he acquired expensive tastes for such things as big-game hunting in Africa, and a fortune sufficient to indulge them.

---

* The next day Russell Baker of the New York *Times* in a review of the TV "Special" in which the President announced his Cabinet choices, commented that "the Cabinet is comprised of George Romney and eleven guys named Clyde."

In 1958 he was appointed Director of the Federal Bureau of the Budget by Dwight Eisenhower, a post he held for two years. By 1968 Stans was sufficiently established in both Republican and New York financial circles to be chosen by Richard Nixon to handle his campaign finance committee. He raised the necessary millions for the campaign. As a result, Stans privately felt that he had every right to be Secretary of the Treasury. It would have been a fitting capstone to his career.

But the President-elect decided that Stans was not the man for the job. Nixon chose instead, affable, but as it turned out, somewhat inept, David Kennedy, a Chicago banker. The President's stated rationale was that his Treasury Secretary should be a banker, a principle that was temporary at best, since Kennedy's successor was an ex-Governor of Texas—chosen while many of his old political associates were being implicated in one of the biggest banking and political scandals in the state's scandal-ridden history. Nixon's talent scouts also told Stans that for political reasons they needed someone not so closely associated with New York. Why this was so was never made very clear to anyone, and certainly not to Maurice Stans.

But Stans could have wondered if somehow it did not have something to do with his own conservatism. He might have recalled that back in 1960 Vice President Nixon pleaded with Eisenhower and the Republican Treasury Secretary George Humphrey for an expansionary budget so that Nixon would not have to face John F. Kennedy with unemployment rising past 6 percent of the labor force. Stans, as Nixon surely would have remembered, was stoutly on the side of traditional Republican dogma. The New York *Times*, the day after Nixon appointed Stans to the Commerce post, stated that: "The new Secretary of Commerce is well-remembered throughout official Washington as a man who demands results and demands them fast. In his two years (1958–60) as Director of the Federal Bureau of the Budget under President Dwight D. Eisenhower, Mr. Stans dedicated himself single-mindedly to holding down government spending."

Perhaps the President imagined that there again might come a time when there would be a choice between upholding sacred Republican principles and protecting himself at the polls. A conservative Republican capable of making a trip to Red China and instituting government control of wages and prices would certainly not have been troubled at the prospect of unbalancing the budget. And when it came to that he certainly would want and need a flexible pragmatist, someone with a talent for spending. It was apparent that the President, in his years out of power, had acquired enough lessons in modern Keynesian economics to realize the shaky ground on which Republican dogma rested. Whatever the reasons, the President did not choose Stans and the lead story on the nation's financial pages were devoted to David Kennedy, not to a discontented Stans, who was given the Commerce Department.

Commerce, despite its being a cabinet office, was a graveyard. It was a collection of miscellaneous agencies, some of which, e.g., the Weather Bureau, the Census Bureau, the Patent Office, were extremely important to the everyday life of the nation, but none of which gave the Secretary of Commerce much of an opportunity for headlines. The last Secretary of Commerce to rise above the office was Herbert Hoover.

But Stans was an entrepreneur and if the President wouldn't give him the headlines, he would go after them himself. A week after he was appointed Secretary, Stans announced that the President "made it quite clear" that he wanted his Secretary of the Commerce to be a member of the select team that was to decide the nation's economic policy, which then consisted of the Secretary of the Treasury, the Chairman of the Federal Reserve Board, and the Chairman of the Council of Economic Advisors—the Troika. Now, said Stans, it was to become the Quadriad. "And would the Secretary of Labor also be invited?" asked the Press. "If," replied Secretary Stans, "*we* want him." According to Stans, this was to be a "first step in strengthening the voice of business in the government." Later Stans had to allow that there had been a misunderstanding; the President was talking about another, far less prestigious committee.

And as Maurice Stans was desperately casting about for a function through which he could recover from the disappointment of not getting Treasury, he came upon the idea of Black Capitalism as a means for establishing a nexus of power. By that time, the Black Capitalism program was more alive in the typewriters of the press than in the minds of the President and his chief aides.

The late Senator Everett Dirksen of Illinois summarily expressed the mood of the Administration during the course of a meeting with a group of black leaders who had come to get his support for programs for their constituents. In reply to their quest he suggested that a look at the voting pattern of November 1968 clearly showed that this Administration owed the blacks nothing. It was just about the same time that HEW Secretary Robert Finch, in an offhand remark, said that Nixon owed very little to blacks.

Indeed, for anyone who took the trouble to bother, an examination of Richard Nixon's statements over the previous year would reveal that he had with one exception (Black Capitalism) offered nothing to blacks (or any other minority group). A speechwriter on Nixon's staff recalls: "We had a few references to Black Capitalism in the speeches before the Convention, but only a few ever got through. After the deals with Thurmond and Tower at the Convention, and with Mitchell taking over the campaign, nothing got through. In fact, Mitchell told us that he didn't want references to blacks in the speeches at all unless it was absolutely necessary."

The fact that the press persisted in calling Black Capitalism Nixon's program for the blacks, illustrates how little there was for the blacks in the 1968 campaign. And the fact that Maurice Stans was able to take the responsibility for the program shows how little political potential the rest of the Cabinet thought the program had, and how desperate Stans was for public recognition.

Although he had taken the job of promoting minority enterprise to recoup his political fortunes after the loss of the Treasury post, Stans had no clear idea of what to do next. Both his conservative nature and his experience prevented him from suggesting a bold new program. His function as Director of the Bureau of the Budget under Eisenhower had fitted in perfectly with his temperament. His job was to cut budgets and be skeptical about the need for new Federal initiatives, and he did his job well. But now he was in a different ballgame. He had to create a program for a constituency toward whom the Administration was at best indifferent and at worst hostile. Moreover, it was a constituency about which Stans had little understanding and certainly no experience.

Inasmuch as there were no other claimants for the Black Capitalism effort, Stans was made Chairman of a Cabinet Subcommittee on Minority Enterprise. The purpose of this and similar subcommittees was to advise the President on how the campaign promises were to be handled. Also on the Subcommittee were Robert Finch, Secretary of Health, Education and Welfare; George Romney, Secretary of Housing and Urban Development, and John Volpe, Secretary of Transportation. These three had problems of their own and so the recommendations of the subcommittee reflected a combination of Stans's views and the political perceptions of the White House which at this point in time was beginning to be referred to by some blacks as "Uncle Strom's Cabin."

The Subcommittee recommended that a new office be set up under Stans in the Department of Commerce to handle the program. The new unit was to be called the Office of Minority Business Enterprise and headed by an assistant to the Secretary. The fact that the head of the office was to be *an assistant to* the Secretary, rather than an Assistant Secretary, underscored the tentative nature of the arrangement.

Whether or not Stans was qualified for his new assignment was beside the issue. As Secretary of Commerce he stood beside the President at a press conference on March 5, 1969, when *Executive Order 11458* was announced. Thus, with much fanfare the new agency, the Office of Minority Business Enterprise (OMBE), was finally created within the Department of Commerce.

On signing the Order, the President said, "I have often made the point that to foster the economic status and the pride of members of our minority groups, we must seek to involve them more fully in our private enterprise system . . . Involvement in business has always been a major route toward participation in the mainstream of American life. Our aim is to open that route to potentially successful persons who have not had access to it before." It was further stated by the President that the new agency would have the responsibility of overseeing and coordinating all existing Federal efforts—116 programs spread over 21 departments and agencies—which relate to business ownership efforts on behalf of Negroes, Indians, Puerto Ricans, Mexican-Americans and other minority groups.

In the words of the Presidential message, it was announced that OMBE was to be "the focal point of the Administration's efforts to assist the establishment of new minority enterprises and expansion of existing ones." However, there was little notice given to the fact that the Administration's new Black Capitalism hothouse *was not* to have any funds itself to give financial assistance to minority enterprises, but was to "coordinate" and "plan" with the other Federal agencies those programs that should be useful to minority enterprises and to "mobilize" the private sector to make its contribution. Thus it served the purpose of giving a great deal of prominence and glamour to Stans's leadership while avoiding a commitment to spend a nickel.

In real political terms what did all this mean? OMBE was given the responsibility for "advising," "encouraging," "mobilizing," "evaluating," "collecting" information and "coordinating" activities. Beyond all the flowery language of its mandate, it could neither *decide* nor *implement* on its own, nor was it empowered to make loans or grants. As a matter of fact, it didn't even have an administrative budget. Money was taken out of OEO—the antipoverty agency—to establish OMBE.

The Presidential message was the opening bar of a theme that was to dominate the Administration's entire program. Ironically enough, a major charge made by the Republicans against the Democrats during the campaign and one which Stans was to repeat after having been in office more than a year, was that Democrats overpublicized and overpromised on behalf of *their* domestic programs. If nothing else, the White House, through a rather contortive bit of political adroitness, had managed to fabricate an elaborate and well-publicized illusion on its own.

What was even more ironic was the fact that a Republican Administration, which came into office with the notion that it could organize the Federal Government on an efficient, businesslike basis, had established an organization charged with the responsibility for carrying out its major program for minorities that made no management sense. For the government agency that was by far the most important for minority businessmen, from a management standpoint, was the Small Business Administration.

In the mid-1960s Gene Foley, a political protégé of Hubert Humphrey who had been made SBA Administrator by Lyndon Johnson, started the first program to provide special help to black and brown businessmen. It was a small and completely inadequate effort, but it was a beginning. And, as was recounted earlier, in 1968, Howard Samuels, the New York millionaire turned Democratic politician, took over SBA and in the space of a few short months had, at the very least, created a consciousness among businessmen, blacks, and bureaucrats for his program called "compensatory capitalism." Samuels' program fell far short of the need, hobbled in part by the severe budgetary limitations placed on SBA by Lyndon Johnson's Bureau of the Budget, which was desperately battling a Vietnam-induced deficit of massive proportions. Nor was there any doubt that the agency's past performance was sluggish. But SBA *was where the money was!* Short of a major Executive reorganization, therefore, any Federal effort to assist minority entrepreneurs would have to rely primarily on SBA's system of loans, loan guarantees, lease guarantees, and various other aid programs. The organization plan split the leadership for Black Capitalism from the resources needed to make it work. It also assured mutual distrust and suspicion between OMBE and SBA.

Had the Administration been even moderately concerned with creating an effective program, there were three potential organizational alternatives that might have ensured a modicum of success. The *first* was to put the responsibility for the effort in the White House and to assign a Presidential assistant to run it, rather than an assistant to the Secretary of Commerce. The *second* would have been to create a separate agency with the authority to make loans and provide other types of supportive assistance to minority entrepreneurs. The *third* would have been to give the full responsibility for leadership of the program to the Chief Administrator of SBA who in turn would have had the backing of the President in initiating a complete overhaul and internal reorganization of the agency. For, nothing short of a total shake-up would have made SBA an effective instrument of minority capitalism.

According to Maurice Stans the first option was rejected because Nixon was antagonistic toward any enlargement of the Executive Office of the President. Given the great expansion of that office under Nixon that interpretation seems to be rather specious. Stans claims the second was rejected because the President didn't want more people reporting to him than there already were. Again, given the proliferation of assistants, counsels, and committees under the Nixon Administration, this explanation doesn't hold much water. The third alternative seemed to be effectively foreclosed with the selection of Hilary Sandoval as Chief Administrator of SBA.

According to Stans, his preference was to opt for second course. He originally conceived of a plan whereby *his* new agency would have complete authority over all minority capitalism programs, those in existence or in the planning stages. He envisioned that each and every Federal agency and department, with programs that might conceivably aid minority entrepreneurs, would transfer those existing programs, along with their projected ones, to Commerce. On February 24, 1969, a memorandum went out from the Bureau of the Budget to the heads of a number of Federal agencies asking them for comments on a draft Executive Order prepared in the Commerce Department. The draft was generally along the lines of the Order that was published on March 5, but with one important difference. The Commerce draft contained the following language:

"The head of each Federal department or agency having any functions or responsibilities relating to promotion of minority business enterprise shall, consistent with law, allocate or transfer to the Department of Commerce, such funds available to his department or agency as the Director of the Bureau of the Budget shall determine are appropriate for the Secretary of Commerce to carry out the functions assigned by this order."

The Director of the Bureau of the Budget, Robert Mayo, was an old Chicago friend of Stans's and so the arrangement implicit in the Commerce draft seemed like a cozy horse-trade. In theory at least it could have meant the transfer of responsibility of almost any Federal program to the Commerce Department by order of the Bureau of the Budget. The letter from the Bureau of the Budget to the Federal agencies in question closed with: "Since the order draft and the transmittal letter convey an intention that the proposed duties of the Secretary of Commerce will be carried out by funds to be transferred from other agencies having programs in the field, please advise whether your agency has specific authority to so transfer funds."

Following a common practice that had become tradition since

the Republicans had last controlled the White House (when Xerox machines were less accessible), copies of the Bureau of the Budget order were immediately leaked to the press. Several papers, including the New York *Times* and the Washington *Post*, carried stories of Stans's attempt to take over other agencies' programs. Since most of the other agencies were headed by individuals who had the capacity and inclination to keep Stans off their turf, speculation centered on a takeover of the Small Business Administration and/or the Office of Economic Opportunity. The latter was especially vulnerable since it was anticipated that the new Administration would phase out the already, semicastrated antipoverty program.

But the Administration decided, at least for the time being, that it did not want the onus of totally eliminating the "War on Poverty." It was in the process of seeking a Republican director for the program and a continuation of the agency's budget for another two years, so as to give itself some breathing time to decide on what to do with it. The Administration had also assured the Chairman of the House Education and Labor Committee, Democrat Carl Perkins of Kentucky, that it had no immediate plans to dismember OEO. A copy of the Commerce draft was bootlegged to Perkins and, at a meeting with OEO officials a few days later, an irate Perkins threw the document on the table and charged them with bad faith. It was this sort of amateurish maneuvering on the part of the Administration that ultimately served to stiffen the support of Congressional Democratic leadership, which decided to save OEO's funds.

Several Congressmen who handled the Small Business Administration program also protested to the White House. They reminded the Administration that SBA had the same kind of small town, "main street" merchants constituency that comprised a large segment of the bedrock Republican base in the country. So, shortly afterward, Stans was told that he would have to content himself with "coordinating and mobilizing," not spending, other agencies' funds.

For Stans, who had a reputation for being a tough, no-nonsense accountant in the Eisenhower Administration, where bureaucrats knew their place, the experience of being thwarted by middle-level officials in a discredited antipoverty agency must have been a difficult one to absorb. Unfortunately for Stans, it only foreshadowed many more difficulties to come. More unfortunately for the minority enterprise program, the episode revealed something else as well; that while Stans was vocalizing with fortissimo gusto at press conferences, the Administration did not seem to care, one way or the other, whether his program succeeded or failed.

John Mitchell's statement to the "liberal-type" Nixon speechwriters, that Nixon would wait until after the election to present his program for Black Capitalism, violated political common sense and Mitchell knew it. What a candidate delivers to a group with more votes than influence is always less than that which he promises. And if the blacks and other minorities were not worth making campaign commitments to before the election, why should the Administration be interested after the election? Promises yes, commitments no; such are the schoolboy maxims of cynical politicians. With the inner circles of the new Administration populated by people like Kevin Phillips—who predicted decades of Republican hegemony if they would follow a conservative image and reactionary policies—and Harry Dent, a former aide to Strom Thurmond who was chief political assistant to the President, this Administration was simply not concerned about anything more than saving its "honor" by living up to its token promise to do something for a handful of middle-class blacks.

Meanwhile, back at the White House, not one of the important Presidential assistants had the assignment of shepherding Black Capitalism. Leonard Garment, the "liberal" on the White House staff, was vaguely responsible for it, but he had little or no influence over the important decisions. Even Robert J. Brown, the White House "house" black, only took a marginal interest in the program. Most of the White House duties fell to one Bruce Rabb, a young lawyer who was Brown's assistant. If Brown had no clout, Rabb was hardly noticed.

There was one significant burst of innovation. Stans announced, soon after the Executive Order, that the Administration was dropping the slogan Black Capitalism in favor of the broader and more inclusive term "minority business enterprise."

Before making his decision as to who should run the Small Business Administration, the President first had to fire Howard Samuels, who was the Administrator of the SBA under Johnson;

for Samuels would not submit his resignation, as is normally the case with Federal administrators when a change of Administration occurs. Since Samuels had in August of 1968 initiated his new minority entrepreneurship program, he felt that he should continue to lead it. In the short period of time he was at SBA, Samuels *did* set some fires under a bureaucracy that was traditionally known for its catatonic indifference to minority groups. He also instituted a policy of making loans less on the basis of the equity which the entrepreneur puts into the business and more on the basis of creating opportunities for entrepreneurs with little equity.

Of the people who were given the responsibility for recruiting talent for the incoming Administration in late 1968, Hilary Sandoval was easily identified as unfit for the SBA job. He was, of course, a member of a minority group. He was Mexican-American, and the Mexican-Americans voted for Nixon in somewhat greater proportions than did the blacks. But there were other chicanos with better qualifications. The single advantage that Hilary Sandoval had going for him was that John Tower had promised him the job. The Mexican-American vote is important to all state-wide politicians in Texas, and Tower was no exception. He stuck with Richard Nixon in the critical hours of the Republican Convention in Miami when it looked for a while that the South would defect to Reagan. And on the basis of that debt he had promised his middle-class, Mexican-American supporters that one big job in Washington would be theirs if Nixon was elected.

It was a debt clearly recognized in the White House and when Tower showed up to collect, they paid him. There was hardly any consideration of what this might do to the minority capitalism program. A few younger Republicans who cared, mostly Ripon Society types, tried to head off the appointment. They appealed to Senator Jacob Javits and Charles Percy to use whatever influence they had, but a Percy plus a Javits did not equal one Tower in the White House scale of values, and both Javits and Percy knew it. So they did nothing.

"Neither Percy nor Javits came up with the names of anyone for the job," said a White House aide who was busy recruiting people for the Nixon Administration. "Erlichman said that they didn't want anyone from New York or Chicago, and maybe that discouraged the Senators. And then there was still Samuels, who wanted to stay in that job very badly. He had done a good job laying the groundwork for the program and clearly thought it had potential. The word we got was that he offered to pledge that he would not go back into New York politics for several years if they kept him on. At one point Nixon even toyed with the idea. He liked the notion of appointing a few middle-of-the-road Democrats to create a sense that the Administration was more interested in performance than politics. He had hired Moynihan and he almost made Scoop Jackson Secretary of Defense. But when it was raised with Rockefeller, Nelson said: 'No. No. No.' And that was the end of it."

Several other names were suggested from various GOP leaders around the country. They included two respected Republicans from Philadelphia, John Bunning of the First Pennsylvania Bank and Thatcher Longstretch of the Philadelphia Chamber of Commerce, who later ran for Mayor, but none had political backing comparable to Tower.

"There was a brief moment," recalls the recruiter, "when we thought we could kill it. A rumor was circulating that Sandoval had a shady business past. We sent a man down to Texas to see if there was a scandal there somewhere, but he couldn't find any. Incompetent, sure, but we couldn't prove that, and they, the White House, didn't care anyway. The only thing we might have done was to find another job for Hilary, and find someone better for the SBA job. But it would have meant finding another candidate with political backing that the White House was interested in, and then, of course, clearing it with Tower. But we couldn't even get beyond the first step."

"The irony," said another source, "was that we had a lot of people convinced that minority enterprise was a conservative program. Businessmen and politicians too. John Tower was all for it in theory. But every time they were faced with a choice between a good new conservative idea and the old politics, they chose the old politics."

For Richard Nixon the appointment of Sandoval ironically seemed to kill the proverbial "two birds with one stone." During the primaries he was very big on attacking smut. In addition, he promised, several times during the campaign, to rid the countryside of filth pushers. And more recently—at the time of the release of the President's Commission on the Study of Pornography—he exhibited a curious case of uptightness toward the subject, by almost totally denying the existence of the findings and recommendations of what most experts considered was an excellent report. Well, it just so happened that Sandoval, a wholesale distributor of magazines in West Texas, New Mexico, Arizona, and Colorado, had, prior to his appointment, been under heavy attack by the "Citizens Committee for Decent Literature" in El Paso for distributing sexy books and nudie magazines throughout those four states in the Southwest. In fact, columnists Rowland Evans, Jr., and Robert Novak reported that the local police in El Paso had hauled him in for questioning immediately before his departure for Washington. For a puerile President to have rewarded a businessman whose sole qualification for a sensitive post was party loyalty, while at the same time to have removed a distributor of sexy books from the market, was truly a noble accomplishment.

Joe Bernal, a Mexican-American State Senator from San Antonio (Texas has 1.6 million Mexican-Americans), at that time said that Sandoval had campaigned extremely hard for Nixon, particularly through his Spanish-language publications. Bernal also stated: "If he [the President] looked behind every cactus plant in the state of Texas he would be hard put to find a more conservative Mexican-American." With regard to the prospect of Sandoval continuing the progressive policies of his predecessor, another chicano who is an experienced observer of Southwest politics remarked: "Sandoval is what we call a 'tamale and bean' sort of guy. You make a deal for a steak and you get tamales and beans. He thinks that chicanos should be in the frozen taco business. And he probably thinks all blacks should own fried chicken stands."

Once Sandoval moved into the office, the first order of business was to purge the Agency of the people within SBA who had supported Samuels in his drive to shake up the "business-as-usual" bureaucracy. Sandoval immediately replaced them with party politicians such as David Martin of Houston, James Reed of Austin, Albert Fuentes, and Father Antonio Gonzalez—the latter a partisan political activist from Houston who was trying to build a political base in Washington for Sandoval and in the Mexican-American community in Texas for Nixon and the Republican

Party. One high official at the Agency said in an interview in mid-'69 that "this team could well set back the SBA program for ten years and Gonzalez could personally retard the doctrine of separation of Church and State for a lot longer than that." Within a year Fuentes, who was made Special Assistant to the Director, was indicted and convicted of conspiracy and sentenced to five years.

In recalling his efforts to break down prejudices and reverse the priorities of the Agency, Howard Samuels wrote in *The Saturday Review*† that "turning an agency around is far different from revitalizing a business. To start, it's harder to fire the 'plant manager.' My attempts to displace one area administrator demonstrates this. After a systematic study of results from various areas, it was found that New York, despite its relatively sophisticated black and Puerto Rican populations, ranked seventh out of the eight districts in SBA support for minority businessmen. The area administrator had little ability to deal with the program goals . . . Since civil service regulations made his removal impossible, I transferred him to Washington." Samuels accused the man of being "one of the worst" among the Agency's administrators and "particularly weak" in helping to gain loans for minority businessmen. In addition, the Director of New York City's Small Loan Development Corporation charged that the same administrator summed up the problems of the minority businessmen by stating at a Federal Executive Board meeting—before a group of officials from other agencies—that "the trouble with *those people* (meaning blacks) is that they just don't know how to handle money."

The Regional Administrator's name was Charles Kreiger, a good friend of Congressman John J. Rooney of Brooklyn. Since Rooney was Chairman of the House Appropriations Subcommittee that handled the SBA budget, as well as being an important New York Democrat, it took considerable courage on Samuels' part to oust Kreiger. Rooney screamed to the White House, but Samuels held on and got his way. And although getting rid of Kreiger did not make the New York office a model of concern for minority businessmen, it proved that even SBA was capable of being changed.

† August 23, 1969.

One would have thought that Sandoval would have been grateful to his predecessor for having taken the heat from a powerful Congressman in order to improve the program. It meant that Sandoval would not have to do it. But any illusions about the ability of Sandoval to make tough decisions for the good of the program were quickly dispelled. Shortly after he became Administrator, John Rooney called him up. And a few days later Charles Kreiger was back in his old New York office.

The liberal Republicans who had lost the battle for SBA and who were saddled with Stans had very little to be optimistic about but at least there was still some hope for beefing up OMBE, which after all was to be the focal point of the minority capitalism effort. When the directorship of OMBE went to Tom Roeser, a Republican from the Quaker Oats Company with strong credentials in the Party and a record for concern with minority problems, things began to look up.

Tom Roeser was head of the Public Affairs office of the Quaker Oats Company in Chicago. He was the corporation's Government man, taking care of Quaker Oats interests with the appropriate Federal agencies and the many state governments whose agricultural policies the company felt it must keep on good terms. Much of his life has been taken up with Republican politics. His boss, Robert D. Stuart, Jr., the President of Quaker Oats, was the Republican Committeeman from Illinois.

Roeser says he is a conservative Republican, and his corporate background, his activity in the Goldwater campaign of 1964, and his loyalty to Richard Nixon in Miami are proof of it. He believes that the country needs a strong Republican Party. And being a man of the urbane corporate world he thinks that the Republican Party should be modernized and professionalized. He counts it as one of his life's accomplishments that while he worked for the Republican Governor of Minnesota he was instrumental in getting that state's party to hire a full-time professional staff and to streamline its operations.

He is also quick to say that he is no intellectual, but that he knows something about politics, and what he knows tells him that the base of the Republican Party is too small. He acknowledges that the Party will have to expand in the South, but he thinks that as a major effort for expansion a Southern Strategy would be a disaster. Roeser particularly thinks the party is making a mistake in writing off the black community. "Oh I know we can't compete in the civil rights area with the Democrats," he says, "but the Democrats have gotten all they can out of that. We've lost all we are going to lose as a result of the Goldwater campaign and the southern strategy. There are new issues emerging—issues in which the Republican Party has as much if not more credibility than the Democrats. Black Capitalism, for example."

Roeser sees the Republican Party as the natural home for those who rise into the middle class and hold middle-class values, and the population groups that are likely to expand its representation into the middle class most rapidly in the next decade are blacks and other minorities. To Roeser, Black Capitalism was the Republican chance to get a foot in the door, to stake out an area of rising interest to the black community—getting them a piece of the action—one where the Democrats were not very credible and in fact were limited because of both the opposition of the labor unions and the natural antipathy of liberal-intellectuals to business. If the Republicans could gather a solid constituency in the black middle class they would reap a steadily expanding power base as the black middle class expanded through long-term economic progress. The major breakthrough of establishing the rights of blacks to jobs and voting had been made in the 1960s primarily by the Democrats. Now that those breakthroughs had been made, the black middle class could be expected to expand rapidly over the next few years—and it could be a natural Republican constituency.

Roeser's interest in the black community began when he was a special assistant for civil rights to Governor Elmer L. Andersen of Minnesota where he began his career; first as journalist and then as a Republican Party official. He traveled a great deal around the state talking to Indians and blacks, seeing how they lived, and gradually coming to see the reality of discrimination and poverty.

After coming to Chicago to work for Quaker Oats, Roeser tried in the mid-1960s to put some of his ideas about the potential of organizing for Republican political interests to work. He certainly didn't believe that "if you've seen one ghetto, you've seen them all." The work Tom Roeser had done for the GOP earned him a place on the list of the people the party could reward with the Washington jobs which were gained by Richard Nixon's victory. His position with a large business corporation plus a record of concern for minority problems made him a prime candidate for the job of director of the Black Capitalism program; that is, if the Administration did not feel it was compelled to put a black in charge of Black Capitalism—and it clearly did not. Roeser was invited to come to Washington shortly after the inauguration, was interviewed by some people at the White House, and then saw Maurice Stans. Stans gave him the nod and Roeser was hired.

At first glance Roeser and Stans seemed to fit each other's requirements: Stans wanted a public relations man and Roeser wanted to work for someone with clout at the White House and in the business community. But they misread one another's intentions. Roeser thought that Stans also wanted to build a major program for the blacks that would serve the long-term interests of the party. Stans thought that Roeser would be content to be his p.r. man. Within a year Stans would say of Roeser that he had no administrative talent whatsoever, while Roeser could later characterize Stans as a "relentless dullard" insensitive to politics.

In addition to establishing OMBE and officially designating Maurice Stans as Nixon's Black Capitalism chief, the Presidential order of March 5, 1969, also set up the Advisory Council on Minority Enterprise.

Stans's original conception of the Advisory Council was that it would be his show with the business community; a large committee of businessmen and bankers who would create an image of the concerned business establishment which among other things might eventually support Stans in his quest for the Treasury job. But in order for him to get the cream of the business community Stans needed the President's personal backing. Men who were important enough to get to see the President on their own would not be likely to give much of their time to a council called to advise the Secretary of Commerce. Besides, there already existed the Business Advisory Council to the Secretary whose responsibility covered giving advice on tariffs, trade policies, and patent policies as well as domestic economic programs in general, subjects much more important to the leadership of large corporations than minority enterprise.

Therefore, while the Executive Order establishing the Council provided that it should be advisory to the Secretary of Commerce, the members of the Council were to be *appointed by the President.* Initially, there was some difficulty in recruiting the top leaders of large corporations to sit on the Council. Many corporations wanted to give their names to the program but wanted to send second and third echelon people to the meetings. But Stans and Roeser persisted, telling the businessmen that their presence would help the Party. Most of the comments were similar to those of Lawrence Phillips of Phillips-Van Heusen Corp.: "I am not really interested, but if the President really wants me to do it, I'll do it."

Stans and Roeser succeeded in getting at least a respectable sprinkle of business leaders. To be sure it was not enough to "mobilize" the private sector, but it was sufficient to give the operation credibility. Among the big prizes were James Roche, Chairman of the Board of General Motors; Arthur Wood, President of Sears, Roebuck & Co.; Lester Burcham, Chairman of the F. W. Woolworth Company; Donald Graham, Chairman of the Board of the Continental Illinois National Bank and Trust Co. of Chicago; Walter Haas, President of Levi Strauss & Co.; Samuel Johnson, President of S. C. Johnson & Son; Paul Johnston, President of the Glen Alden Corp.; Willard Marriott, President of the Marriott Corporation; Donald Naughton, President of the Prudential Life Insurance Co.; Albert Meyer, Senior Vice President of the Bank of America; G. William Miller, President of Textron Inc.; Charles Goodman, President of Grand Union Company; Edward Rust, President of State Farm Life Insurance Company; Robert D. Stuart, Jr., President of Quaker Oats Co.; Richard Tullis, President of the Harris-Intertype Corporation; Kendrick Wilson, Chairman of the Board of Avco Corporation; and Sam Wyly, Chairman of the Board of University Computing Company.

The blacks on the original Council included: the Reverend Leon Sullivan of Philadelphia, Darwin Bolden, Director of the Interracial Council for Equal Business Opportunity; Berkeley Burrell, Director of the National Business League; Joseph Goodloe, President of the North Carolina Mutual Insurance Company, the largest black insurance company in the country; and John H. Johnson, President of Johnson Publishing Co.

The initial composition of the sixty-three-member Council was heavily white. Complaints from the minority members of the Council were summed up by a statement from the highly respected and dynamic Sullivan, who said that if there were not more minority people on the Board he would have to resign. Eventually the Council was enlarged to eighty-five.

Maurice Stans's choice for Chairman of the Council was Donald Graham of Continental Illinois Bank of Chicago. Graham was an old friend of Stans's whose bank had been involved in some modest efforts to finance small black businesses in Chicago. Graham could be counted on to be loyal to Stans and, because of his bank's record, presumably was acceptable to the moderate minority members of the Council. It was a matter of indifference to most of the white business members.

But the members of the Council and the Chairman were appointed by the President, who had his own ideas about the Council. When Stans went to San Clemente one afternoon to present his recommendations for the Council and the Chairmanship, Nixon told him that he wanted Sam Wyly as Chairman. To insure that there was no misunderstanding, Nixon asked Stans to call Roeser to tell him. After Stans got Roeser on the phone, Nixon took over. It was a brief but to the point conversation. Nixon ended with: "I know *you* can handle it, Tom."

It was a double blow to Stans. Not only did he lose direct control but from his point of view it fell into the hands of one of the least acceptable members of the Council.

In his early thirties, Sam Wyly had become something of a business phenomenon. In the space of several years he built a small lease time computer company into a multimillion-dollar organization. And in the tradition of young, quick-rich Texans, no sooner had he made his money than he jumped knee-deep into politics. The feeling in Texas was that he wanted to run for Governor. As a start, he raised more than 10 percent of candidate Nixon's campaign chest, during the campaign of 1968. In doing so he got into several jurisdictional disputes with Maurice Stans, who was finance Chairman of the entire campaign. In addition to the generation gap (more than twenty years), their separate styles, and the conflict between two strong-willed personalities, their rivalry represented the tension in Republican Party circles between the new oil and defense money men from the Southwest and the West and the Eastern and Midwestern establishment based on the older banks and large multinational corporations headquartered in New York and Chicago.

The differences between Stans and Wyly were apparent from the first meeting of the Council. Stans and Robert J. Brown, the black White House assistant, welcomed the group and spoke for minutes before the President showed up. Nixon made a brief earnest speech about how important it was to provide the disadvantaged with the opportunity to become businessmen and participate in the American economy as owners as well as employees. Then the President left and Wyly took over.

He immediately noted that he had sent out a telegram the day before to all members of the Council stating that members were not to send representatives, that if they wanted to remain on the Council, they would have to come themselves. Only those in a position to commit their organization to whatever policies the Council recommends were wanted, said Wyly. Arthur Wood, President of Sears, Roebuck & Co., then rose and said that he didn't agree to give up his day and come all the way to Washington just to "advise" and if that was the sole role of the Council then he didn't want to bother with it. Wyly assured him that the Council's mandate was wider than that and he announced that the Council's specific goal would be to prepare a report recommending a basic and comprehensive minority enterprise policy for the White House. He noted that the Council had been appointed by the President and that therefore the President was the person to whom the policy recommendations should be addressed. Thus, with one fell swoop, Wyly took control of the Council from Stans and compromised Stans's position as czar of Black Capitalism.

Standing on the balcony in the Treaty room of the Executive Office Building where the Council's meetings were held, one Federal bureaucrat turned to another and said: "You have just seen the beginning of a civil war. Stans will never put up with that."

Rumsfeld and Moynihan were, along with Finch, considered to be the "liberals" around Richard Nixon and might therefore have been expected to play important roles in the Black Capitalism effort. But they did not.

Donald Rumsfeld was a handsome young Congressman from

a suburban Chicago district who had voted against the antipoverty legislation and Office of Economic Opportunity appropriations. When it was announced that Rumsfeld had been appointed Director of the OEO it was assumed by weary and cynical antipoverty workers that it was the end for the Agency. It was widely believed that he had taken the job for a short time on the President's promise that if Rumsfeld did a good job of dismantling the OEO, Nixon would help him get the Republican nomination for the then Senator Dirksen's seat when Dirksen retired. Unfortunately for Rumsfeld, Senator Dirksen died shortly after he took the OEO job, too soon for the President to fulfill his promise. But Rumsfeld kept his part of the bargain and began to dismantle the antipoverty program. After about a year and a half, Nixon brought him into the White House and eventually made him Director of the Wage-Price Council's staff.

Rumsfeld was as indifferent to Black Capitalism as he was to the more conventional antipoverty programs. After taking over as head of the Advisory Council, Sam Wyly came to see Rumsfeld and ask his advice. Rumsfeld's first comment was: "Sam, why did you ever take a job like that?"

Moynihan was another Administration "liberal" who was indifferent to Black Capitalism. Presumably, Moynihan viewed it as an ineffective way to help the poor and one which required too much Federal interference with the private sector of the economy, a fear that is reflected in his book attacking the Community Action Program, *Maximum Feasible Misunderstanding*. Moynihan, it seems, was much more interested in the social significance of *white* businessmen than *black* ones. On March 26, 1969, he issued a plea to an estimated twenty thousand businessmen, who had gathered before screens in twenty-seven cities for a closed circuit performance. Moynihan stressed that the private sector and private volunteers could do more to fight poverty than the Federal Government because "the National Government is not very good at delivering services." It was the kind of cheer-leader speech that a President of the national Jaycees might have made to a group of on-the-make executives, ten years before.

8 | WATCHING IT FALL APART

"I never did go in for making love to dry loins."*

F. Scott Fitzgerald

Tom Roeser's first tasks as Director of OMBE were to staff up the new organization, to create the advisory council and to come up with a program.

He set to work immediately. Recognizing that there would be some resentment among minorities that he was a white, middle-western WASP, and that the blacks in particular felt left out since a Mexican-American was chosen at SBA, Roeser quickly selected a black man, Abe Venable, for his deputy. Venable was an articulate, ambitious career civil servant who knew the black business community and the Federal bureaucracy. Roeser's idea was to have himself handle the politicians and the white businessmen while Venable would deal with the Feds and the minorities. Like the combination of Roeser and Stans, it seemed like an ideal arrangement. Later Roeser was to say that the hiring of Abe Venable was "the biggest mistake I made." According to Roeser, the hiring of a black deputy was also as much a matter of

* F. Scott Fitzgerald, *Tender Is the Night; A Romance* (New York: Scribner & Sons, 1st ed., 1933), p. 329.

principle as of politics; he felt strongly that he should make the same kind of compensatory hiring practices in the Federal Government that he had come to believe were right for private business, particularly in a program that was designed to benefit minorities. Therefore, he made a conscious effort to hire minority people to staff the professional positions in OMBE.

The performance earned some credibility for the Agency among suspicious and skeptical minority groups, but Maurice Stans didn't like it. Rocco Siciliano, the Undersecretary of Commerce and a close friend of Stans from Chicago, told Roeser at a meeting in the spring of 1969 that Stans felt he had been hiring too many blacks. "This is basically a white man's program to help the minorities," Siciliano said. "The Secretary didn't have in mind that we'd have to hire a lot of them." Shortly thereafter Stans called Roeser into his office.

Knowing what was coming, Roeser asked Venable to go with him. He felt that Venable's presence would inhibit Stans in objecting to hiring blacks. But he overestimated Stans's sensitivity. Stans told them they were hiring too many blacks who were not qualified. Roeser argued that many were as qualified as any whites. And as for those who were not as qualified as available whites, upgrading minority people was the whole purpose of the program and that in order to reach the minority communities and be credible to them OMBE was going to have to practice what it preached.

Stans did not agree. If the program was going to be a success both in what it did and in the eyes of the President, they needed to have bright, articulate, qualified people dealing with outsiders. He also suggested that the existence of so many blacks in the program might embarrass him at the White House. Stans ended the meeting saying that he didn't like OMBE's personnel policies and that he expected Roeser and Venable to change them.

When he took the job, Tom Roeser had thought that he would have a fair amount of freedom. Beyond the platitudes of Nixon's "Bridges to Human Dignity" speech almost a year before, there was nothing very specific about Black Capitalism in either the campaign speeches or the minds of the people in the White House, etc. Furthermore, Maurice Stans had not been very specific in any of their initial conversations. Stans had said that he wanted to control other agency programs and that he wanted to get something going quickly, but he did not seem to have a clear notion as to what the program should look like. So Roeser began to plan for a program.

Those who worked closely with Roeser on the plan were Gary Baden, Director of OMBE's Government Programs Division, Walter Sorg, member of a successful printing family from Chicago and head of OMBE's private Sector Division, and Bill Geimer, also from Chicago. All were white.

The plan that they were to develop eventually was drawn from the swirl of ideas on the need for blacks and other minorities to have economic power that had arisen in the past few years. They include some of the ideas behind the Community Self-Determination Act, the notions for increasing flows of capital to inner cities of those who testified at Congressional Hearings on inner city credit held by Senator Proxmire in the fall of 1968, Howard Samuels Project OWN, and the specific experiences of people in banks, poverty programs, and other activities around the country who had attempted to spur minority entrepreneurship with varying degrees of success.

The plan that Roeser and his assistants came up with is described in several internal documents of various dates in the summer and fall of 1969. The most definitive of these documents is a draft called "National Strategy," dated August 25, 1969.

The tone of the strategy is captured in its brief explanation of the program's objective:

> A national program designed to eliminate this contradiction of our professed principles must have as its objective establishing for those heretofore excluded by their racial or ethnic origins of nothing less than full equality of access to business opportunities and resources.
>
> Certain parts of the overall program do not fall into the scope of a national minority business enterprise program. The historical deficiencies will be remedied only by time. Even a national commitment to a comprehensive minority business enterprise program will not itself solve the range of housing, education, and health problems which afflict these minorities. Nor will it alone erase the pervasive and subtle discrimination and hostility which envelops these Americans. Many years of complementary efforts are needed to achieve broadly the kind of society we profess to want.

However, the new program recommended here can have a profound effect on our national life. We can compensate in part for the past by a large-scale sharing of expertise with minority entrepreneurs and potential entrepreneurs, thus increasing the capacity of these communities to productively use capital. And we can simultaneously meet the capital needs of those who can now productively use but cannot obtain financing and opportunities.

By doing so we will contribute immeasurably toward the building of a strong natural economic foundation under these communities. We will contribute also to the demise of the economic colonialism of our minority communities which has helped to render them unstable. Most important, we will redeem this country's promise that all men have an equal right to own and to build.

The paper identifies the causes of a low degree of business ownership among minorities as: poverty, discrimination, and lack of a business tradition. It discusses the resources available to change the situation and why they have not been used. Federal agencies are accused of insensitivity, excessive bureaucracy, and disarray: "Federal agencies present a unified picture in only one respect: most demand of the applicant a number of confusing forms, burdensome paperwork, and much patience."

The private sector comes in for some interesting criticism from a corporate Republican:

> Banks' lending policies, for example, frequently reflect the personal bias of bankers rather than informed business judgment. One bad experience with a black borrower or in a Puerto Rican community may be generalized into a negative attitude toward all loans to blacks or in the Puerto Rican neighborhoods. Simplistic racial viewpoints or hostilities may subtly become unwritten policy.
>
> . . . The strongest deterrent to the deployment of private sector resources, however, is the profit motive. The American business enterprise has seldom accepted social obligation as part of its operating philosophy. Businesses exist to make the greatest possible profit for their owners, not to redress grievances. Profits have recently been high; money has been in short supply; and it is not surprising that business has not felt it necessary or desirable to seek gain through minority enterprise.

The paper then goes on to analyze the various alternative approaches to expanding the resources available to minority entrepreneurs and to using the resources more effectively. The general alternative approaches are said to be: (1) coordination and persuasion; (2) compulsion; (3) new institutions. Coordination and persuasion is judged as a useful but limited approach. Compulsion is discarded as politically unacceptable (although it is interesting that compulsion is rejected only for the present: "Until we are certain we cannot innovate a system which will mesh the traditional private and independent sector objectives with the objectives of minority enterprise development, we need not seriously consider compulsory solutions."). Ultimately, only a new institutional framework can solve the problem.

"From an institutional standpoint," stated the paper, "the problem is more a lack than a wrong." Thus the lack of minority business ownership is not a result of present institutions not doing their jobs, their job is something else, such as making profits. "Minority business development is not a widely accepted goal, nor are the institutions of the private and independent sector operating in conflict with that goal. They are simply ignoring it or unable to assist. The racial hostility or ignorance of individuals may color institutional reaction in certain situations, but the institutions *as institutions* are effectively achieving their goals which are valued by the society at large."

Thus a new institution is needed. Such an institution, "must represent a joint venture by all resource segments of our society . . . It must use the unique strengths of each sector to overcome the weaknesses of the others."

"Created by Executive and Congressional action and backed by Federal tax policy, it must be a full, unified, and visible national commitment, replacing most present Federal minority enterprise programs." In short, the Roeser paper called for the eventual abolition of Roeser's own office, and replacing it with the new institutional system which he called the Minority Enterprise Development Corporation (MEDCO).

The MEDCO plan would establish a national Minority Enterprise Development Corporation as a quasi-public *for-profit* corporation. Its fifteen incorporators would be chosen by the President with the advice and consent of the Senate. The paper suggested that three members be chosen from the Federal Government, three from the private sector, three from the independent sector (churches, foundations, etc.), and six from the minority community. After the first year of operation, local MEDCOs would elect twelve of the Board members with the President appointing the other three.

The national MEDCO would be authorized to sell nonvoting debentures or bonds, the interest and principal on which would be guaranteed by the Federal Government. These funds in turn would be lent to local MEDCOs, and used to invest in minority businesses in particularly impoverished rural areas where no local MEDCO was formed.

The local MEDCOs would be formed in cities and areas across the country. Local residents would subscribe to the voting stock of a MEDCO and the state government would be required to pledge an amount equal to one third of the private subscription. The state in turn would apply to the National MEDCO for disbursement of organizational and administration expenses and for certification of certain benefits. "Rates of return to both the private and independent shareholders and also to the state governments could be guaranteed by the Federal Government." To prevent domination by one set of interests, no private shareholder could own more than 10 percent of the outstanding shares at any one time.

"The heart of this new institutional system would of course be the local Minority Enterprise Development Corporation. Large amounts of capital would be available through the sale of the equity and debt instruments mentioned previously.

"Large amounts of expertise would also be available. Private institutions might 'invest' executives, lawyers, accountants, etc., on a full-time basis in return for tax credits pegged to the salaries of invested personnel. Manpower contributions from independent sector voluntary action programs might be elicited by Federal grants keyed to the value of the voluntary labor expended.

"Thus it would be uniquely possible to join dollars with expertise, and to send both into the field together."

It would also streamline and concentrate Federal Minority Enterprise efforts:

"Implementation of this or a similar program will clearly render unnecessary many of the Federal programs currently attempting to support minority enterprise. Superfluous Federal programs would be eliminated simultaneously with the creation of MEDCO. SBA, for example, would cease its minority enterprise programs and return to its original activities, EDA would do the same with respect to its technical assistance programs. OEO would be relieved of the burden of managing experimental business projects, although it could well continue research in this field. On the other hand, some Federal programs such as contract preference and the VISTA MBAs would retain their present direction after having been established as MEDCO resources. The only agency to entirely disappear as a result of MEDCO implementation would be the Office of Minority Enterprise—which would have outlived its usefulness."

The authors of the plan recognized that it would take a period of time to sell these ideas to the Administration as well as to a democratically controlled Congress. It was also possible that MEDCO would never be approved. The MEDCO plan was therefore designated as "Phase Two" of the National Strategy. Phase One was concerned with expanding and making much more effective the resources that existing institutions could make available for the minority enterprise program. A full explanation and cost estimates for Phase One are found in another document from the summer of 1969, entitled "PROPOSAL: National Program for Minority Enterprise."

The proposal began by stating that if minorities owned American business in proportion to their numbers in the population, they would have owned about one million businesses in 1968. Data available at that time suggested that the actual number fell somewhere between 150,000 and 220,000.† The proposal called for the publicly stated goal of having 400,000 minority businesses by 1980. Given the high current failure rate for existing minority small businesses, this meant creating *substantially in excess of 200,000 businesses* in the ten-year period. The proposal was independent of the MEDCO plan in that if the latter were not approved, the former could achieve its goals. On the other hand, it would build a foundation for the MEDCO plan and could therefore be considered as Phase One. Independent of MEDCO, the preliminary or alternative plan called for the gen-

† A tabulation of statistics by the Census Bureau released in 1971 revealed that there had been about 322,000 minority businesses in 1969.

eration of over nine billion dollars for minority enterprise between 1970 and 1980, over 90 percent of which would have been
in loans repayable to private banks and the Federal Government. The major provisions of the program were:

1. The generation of $8.6 billion in loans, 75 percent of which
would be made by private banks and guaranteed by the Federal Government, and 25 percent of which were to be direct Federal loans. Of
the total $4.6 billion were to come from the regular Small Business Ad-
ministration Program, $2.6 billion were to be generated by Small
Business Investment Companies, and $1.4 billion were to be generated
by other programs such as the Veterans and Indian Loan programs.

2. A program to support local organizations which would provide
financial and technical assistance to minority businesses. Over the ten-
year period, $270.21 million were to be spent in urban areas and $88.03
million in rural areas.

3. A program to provide business training for minority individuals
through an Institute for Minority Business Education, with a ten-year
cost of $412.98 million.

4. A system of management assistance to minority enterprises called
Volunteers in Business (VIB) made up of

—Vista Volunteers.

—A new university business school fellowship program for graduates
who would serve as full-time consultants to minority businesses for
two years.

—Business volunteers who would serve in their localities for one
year on a salary contributed by their companies. Total cost for the
program including maintenance of a national office run by OMBE
would be $117.75 million.

All this of course was *Roeser's* plan. Stans had said nothing
about his plan and so Roeser assumed he had the field to himself. On the twenty-seventh of May 1969, Roeser for the first
time realized that his ideas and Stans's were not running down
the same track. The occasion was the first meeting of representatives of the Federal agencies which were to assist OMBE
in developing its program. Called the Inter-Agency Committee
on Minority Business Enterprise, it was composed of representatives of the Departments of Defense, Justice, Interior, Agriculture, Labor, Housing and Urban Development, Transportation,
Health, Education and Welfare, the Small Business Administration, the Office of Economic Opportunity, the General Services

Administration and the Veterans Administration, and the Office of the President.

Roeser opened the meeting and quickly introduced Stans, whose function was to impress the bureaucrats with the importance of the program to the Administration. In the course of his talk to the agency people Stans began to reveal for the first time his own notion of a minority enterprise program.

First, Stans stated that the most important objective of the program was to create "success stories." These success stories would "create pride among the minority which, in turn, creates aspirations of those down the line . . . What the black people, the minority people, need more than anything else today is a modern Horatio Alger, the kind of a guy who will tell the story of how he succeeded and let everyone else believe that they can accomplish the same result. As time goes on, we are going to do everything we can to publicize the stories, not only like Johnson [John Johnson, publisher of *Ebony* Magazine and other "black" periodicals] in these magazines, and so forth, and the sausage maker, Parks, what he has done, but we want to talk about the little fellow down in North Carolina or somewhere who got the idea of a delivery service two years ago and how he has seventeen branches and forty-seven people working for him. This is the way we will build the pride of these people, and this is the way we will convince the young fellows coming up that they have a chance to do the same thing."

Stans then went on to caution that "we have to be realistic about it. We are not going to create overnight the manufacturing companies with five hundred employees. The American economy did not build that way. It started out at the corner grocery, and the delivery man—the group of people who cut lawns or perform services, and so forth, and I think we have to recognize that by and large a very high percentage of the things we do are going to be in the small 'ma-and-pa' area, the restaurant, the small motel, the small franchise operation, and things like that . . .

"I do not think that we should expect that there will be very many cases where people will come to us with an idea that they will employ a hundred or five hundred people and, in many cases, the risk of that sort of thing may not be one that we can afford to take."

Next Stans moved to the question of money. "Another thing we have to keep in mind," he said, "is that money is not the sole answer . . . More businesses have failed because of lack of ability, lack of comprehension of the problems of the business, than have failed because of lack of capital. I can assure you of that. And I speak from experience because I spent much of my background in business and public accounting dealing with small businesses, and it is very, very difficult to tell the one that is going to succeed from the one that is going to fail, so we are going to have a failure record and in providing for these people we have to evaluate not only the individual capability but the competence that they have at their command, and the other aspects of the technology of the business itself, marketing, selling, producing, advertising, accounting, finance. They are all aspects of the same problem, so that there is a lot more required than money."

Stans then turned to what he called "the program itself." He emphasized the need for coordination among Federal agencies and how important the private banking community was. He said: "I would rather see, and I think the President would much rather see, a private bank make a loan to a minority enterprise with a Government guarantee than for the Government to put out the money. This has a lot of advantages. One, it brings the private sector into the act, into participation. Secondly, it gives them the degree of responsibility, because if it is a 90 percent guarantee, they have a 10 percent stake in it. Thirdly, it takes away the pain that some people have of dealing with the Government. They would rather deal with the banks. And I think that there are a number of other advantages in private participation."

Stans described the program as having four "phases": Marshaling the Government's resources, marshaling the resources of the private sector, publicity and information, and the building up of OMBE. In commenting on the latter phase, he noted that there would be black people to deal with the black community. "And he [Roeser] will have a couple of Spanish-Americans and, perhaps, an Indian in his organization to deal with those, to carry out communication with those minority groups."

He ended his speech by telling the assembled bureaucrats of the President's interest. "The President has his eye on it," he said, "and he has been prodding me every few weeks: 'How are you coming?' and 'What's going on?' and so forth. And it has taken a long time to get to this point, but now we are at this point, I hope we can move quite rapidly."

There were a number of important differences between Stans's and Roeser's plans, both in emphasis and philosophy.

First, there was little sense of a hard commitment in Stans's speech. The line about the President's interest was gratuitous and few if any of the bureaucrats were inspired by it. Second, it was vague as to specific goals. Thirdly, there was Stans's emphasis on small businesses and small individual accomplishments, and in no way was there any sense of the need to assist group economic power in the minority communities. Fourth, there was no mention of the need to change institutions or of the obligations of financial institutions to treat everyone equal. Stans saw his role as trying to persuade private and public institutions to be more helpful to their less fortunate brethren. Finally, Stans's speech completely soft-pedaled the need for resources. The problem would be taken care of primarily through helping the minority entrepreneur be a better manager and to do his books a little more carefully.

Perhaps more revealing than anything was Stans's attitude toward minorities. For Stans, black skin or brown skin or red skin represented not a group that had been mistreated or discriminated against, but one which lacked skills and talents, and most of all middle-class attitudes. The only substantive issue that Stans dealt with was the need to give help to "these people" who couldn't manage their affairs. He saw nothing wrong with the policies of banks who refuse to make loans to blacks, or corporations who refuse to consider black suppliers or Government agencies like the Small Business Administration or the Agriculture Department with well-known histories of incompetence and discrimination against black businessmen and farmers. Racial problems are based on the deficiency that exists in the minority, not in the society.

As Stans saw the task, therefore, it was not to change anything, but to assist the less fortunate. Somehow the black businessman lacked both skills and motivation. To help him become more competent, Stans would get "the availability of perhaps a hundred men in various areas who could help to see that the records are set up and that tax reports are filed and small details that a small business should undertake are attended to." For motivation there would be Horatio Alger stories.

But to provide a scenario for black business success that is based upon the nineteenth-century model of the small shopkeeper is to ignore the fundamental realities of the twentieth-century economy. One of the basic characteristics of the post-World War II American economy is the systematic squeezing out of small retail businessmen. Large corporations and chains so dominate the retail sector of the economy as to make the opening up of individual small businesses an exceedingly risky proposition. Whatever reality there might once have been in the notion of the entrepreneur starting an unsophisticated business on a shoestring and rising to be a captain of industry has long since been obliterated by the postwar expansion of the national and multinational corporations. Small businesses do survive and some even prosper, but the majority succeed in highly specialized and highly skilled service operations and are run by people who have both capital and, more important, contacts that took years to build. Stans refused in his speech to recognize the importance of capital and the existence of those racial barriers which make it all but impossible for a black man ever to achieve the contacts and social relationships that lie at the heart of most of America's business successes.

One official who attended the meeting said to another as they walked out: "You would have a hell of a time selling economic development this way to the white community. What does this do for the minorities? I mean, is the purpose of economic development to create a few millionaires in whom all the rest of the peons will have pride?"

The interagency meeting showed Roeser that he and Stans were thinking along two different lines and that if he didn't get Stans to change his views Roeser would be in trouble. But soon after the meeting Stans left the country and Roeser had no opportunity to discuss the issue with him. So Roeser went on with the work of developing his plan and by August he had one.

When Stans came back from his trips overseas, Roeser was ready to brief him on the plan—and he was ready for disagreement. The massive Federal commitment and the reliance on local organization and control contrasted strongly with the low-key paternalistic approach Stans had taken at the interagency meeting in Washington before he left. What Roeser was not prepared for was a reaction that denied Roeser's right to make any plans at all.

After listening to Roeser outline his plan, Stans exploded. He told Roeser that what he had expected him to be doing was coming up with a public relations plan, not a program plan. "You were hired as a publicist not a businessman," he told Roeser. "I will do the thinking, you get out the press releases."

Roeser protested that there wasn't a program to sell. He emphasized that if the Republican Party wanted to establish a long-term base in the black community that they would have to come up with a meaningful commitment to overcome the black skepticism.

"How did Bobby Kennedy get all that good press and support among the blacks?" demanded Stans. "He never spent any money on them."

Roeser suggested that Kennedy had transmitted a sense of personal commitment.

"Bullshit," said the Secretary of Commerce.

It was of no use. Stans rejected the strategy and the entire notion of specific goals, community participation, and a large Federal commitment. He told Roeser to get to work developing a public relations campaign or his days on the job were numbered.

To Roeser, Stans's response was not only a personal repudiation, but an undercutting of the whole political strategy of broadening the Republican Party base among minorities. It was an issue that the party could not afford to let be decided by Maurice Stans.

So Roeser tried to get help. He went to Senators Percy and Javits. They were friendly and sympathetic but said that they couldn't help very much with the Administration. They just didn't have the influence. Roeser went to the Secretary of Labor, George Schultz, but Schultz didn't see that it was any of his business. He went to Daniel Patrick Moynihan, but Moynihan was all wrapped up in pushing through welfare reform and had the conventional social scientist's attitude that business in the ghetto was bunk anyway. He went to Don Rumsfeld, who had given up his safe Republican Congressional seat to run the Poverty Program for Nixon. Surely Rumsfeld would see the importance to the party of having a strong Black Capitalism program. Rumsfeld was sympathetic, but shrugged his shoulders and said that it was "Maury's problem" and that he could do nothing. Finally, Roeser went to the White House. He saw Leonard Garment, Presidential assistant in charge of minority relations. Roeser found that Garment was having similar problems in making the Administration sympathetic to minorities and had been mostly unsuccessful. He was no help.

Roeser tried but could not get to see John D. Erlichman, the President's chief assistant for domestic affairs. And he had no other access to the President. In fact, he was told, the President had very little interest in the program.

Throughout the summer the relationship between Roeser and Stans deteriorated rapidly. Complaints from blacks that OMBE hadn't done anything yet began to filter back to Stans, who in turn pestered Roeser with demands that the public relations campaign begin. But Roeser was busy trying to line up support in the party for his program, and ignored Stans's demands.

In September, Roeser testified before a Senate committee that a comprehensive plan was being prepared and would shortly be completed. By then he was convinced that he could not sell the Administration on the importance of a minority capitalism program from the inside. Either the Administration did not share his analysis of the importance of investing in the black vote for the future, or the Administration's interests were not the same as the long-term interests of the Republican Party. And so he decided to make an effort to put pressure on the Administration from the outside.

Roeser also learned in September that he was through. A meeting on the minority capitalism program had been held at the White House between Stans and John Erlichman. Roeser had not been invited. Erlichman knew that the program was in trouble. Newspaper stories complaining about inaction had appeared and the comments of a few interested Republicans had gotten to the White House. Erlichman asked Stans what he intended to do about it and Stans replied that Roeser had failed in his job to get good press for the program. Erlichman then suggested that Stans do what Howard Samuels had done, that he go on the road and make a tour of several cities outlining his program and drumming up support. Stans agreed. At no time during the meeting does it appear that the notion of a substantial money commitment to the program was seriously discussed. The decision to concentrate on a public relations program meant that Roeser, the public relations man, was out.

But Roeser made a last-ditch effort to put pressure on the Administration to change its mind. He tried to rally the black and other minority organizations around the country to his cause. After all, they had the most at stake and since they represented middle-class blacks, many of whom were Republicans and had some influential Republican friends, a public show of support for Roeser might get the Administration to change its mind in favor of what Roeser felt were the Party's own long-term interest. Even if he failed, reasoned Roeser, it would be important to show that there were people in the Republican Party who cared about developing a political base in the black community.

The effort culminated at the National Business League convention in Memphis in October 1969. Roser made a speech appealing for black support for the program. He told the assembled black businessmen that the hope for a meaningful program depended on them. Appropriately enough the major topic of conversation at the convention was not the Black Capitalism program, but the general attitude of the Administration toward blacks and the strength of the "southern strategy." In particular, people from the audience wanted to know, where did the Administration people who expressed their concern with Black Capitalism stand on Nixon attempts to appoint Judges Haynsworth and Carswell to the Supreme Court.

Abe Venable said that he was sure that everyone understood that he was a member of the Administration and as such he had to support the President's nominees. Arthur Fletcher, black Assistant Secretary of Labor, wriggled off the hook without taking any position. Roeser said he did not support the President on Haynsworth or Carswell.

Julian Bond and Jesse Jackson congratulated Roeser warmly on his speech. Berkeley Burrell, black President of the National Business Association, threw his arms around Roeser and the audience cheered. A number of black leaders told him how much they appreciated what he had done and how much they admired his courage. Shortly afterward, Tom Roeser was relieved as Director of OMBE and Abe Venable was put into his place.

When Roeser returned to Washington, Stans called him in. He forbade Roeser to make any public statements without clearing them with him. "You have been disloyal to the President," shouted Stans. "You're a Lib!"

In view of Philip Pruitt's resignation at SBA and the growing criticism of the program, it was important to avoid more bad press. Stans therefore told Roeser that he was going to kick him upstairs, giving him a position as assistant to the Secretary for long-range planning. And if Roeser did not accept the job, or if he made any critical public statements, Stans would see to it that Roeser could not go back to his job at Quaker Oats. He also said he would fire Bill Geimer, the most loyal of Roeser's assistants, and see to it that Geimer could not get another Government job. Roeser capitulated and accepted the new post. Abe Venable was named Acting Director and then full Director of OMBE. And not a word of protest was heard from Berkeley Burrell, who had thrown his arms around Tom Roeser in Memphis.

And with Roeser went the hope for an Administration commitment to minority enterprise of any scale. Although Roeser was still a high official in the Commerce Department and responsible for long-range planning, he was no longer considered in the planning of the minority enterprise program and was himself looking for a new job. His assistant, Bill Geimer, sent him a long memo detailing how the Administration could generate an investment pool of ten billion dollars for minority enterprise from the private sector through a system of relatively costless (if successful) guarantees. But the game was over. Stans commented on an NBC television program that the idea was "crackpot."

Shortly afterward, Tom Roeser was back at Quaker Oats.

Meanwhile, over at SBA, Sandoval was in trouble. He was caught between the old-line bureaucracy whose interests were in maintaining the Agency as it was—a service to white, small businessmen who had small-time political connections—and the newer people who had been brought in by Samuels to "turn the Agency around." Sandoval's weakness in standing up to pressure, as exemplified by the reappointment of Charles Krieger in New York, alienated the latter. The fact that he was a Mexican-American, however conservative in his political views, alienated the former.

Added to these troubles was a growing hostility between Mexican-Americans and blacks over the program. Many blacks felt that they had been deliberately slighted both in the appointments and in the thrust of the program. The public announcement that the Administration preferred the bureaucratic phrase "minority enterprise program" to the term Black Capitalism, despite the latter having been a theme in the campaign, seemed a slap at the blacks who only gave Nixon 10 percent of their vote while the Mexican-Americans gave him about 25 percent of theirs. Furthermore, looking to 1972, it was clear that the Administration needed more chicano strength to keep the State of California in the Nixon column and to pick up Texas.

For their part many Mexican-Americans had long felt that the antipoverty and model cities programs had slighted their interests in favor of the blacks. Because of the civil rights experience black organizations were stronger and in a better position to control the local patronage of the Great Society programs than were the Mexican-Americans. And as the chicanos began to organize, tensions between the two groups mounted—exacerbated by cutbacks in money which provided dwindling "crumbs" for them to fight over. In such cities as Los Angeles, San Francisco, Denver, and Houston with sizable populations of both minority groups, weapons were commonly seen at neighborhood meetings, and sometimes used. Having felt slighted in the past as well as outgunned, many Mexican-Americans were determined not to let the minority enterprise program become a black one too. Therefore, as bad as many would privately admit that Sandoval was, they were forced to support him to protect their interests vis-à-vis the blacks.

The immediate issue that Sandoval had to face was that despite the pledges of Stans and Nixon, the Bureau of the Budget was refusing to allow the Small Business Administration to ask for more money or even spend all that had been appropriated to it. The Nixon Administration was looking for ways to hold down spending on social programs to free its hand on defense spending and to reduce the budget deficit. Money for minority businesses seemed like low priority. Given that Stans had no responsibility for the SBA and given his own inclinations to budget cutting, he did little to change the Bureau's mind. Sandoval, having no prestige or influence at the White House and no experience in Washington, was at a loss.

In order to light a fire under Sandoval, the Black Advisory Committee to SBA, which had been formed under Howard Samuels, demanded that Sandoval secure funds for the program. After getting no response to his telegrams and letters, Mayor Richard Hatcher of Gary, Indiana, Chairman of the Advisory Committee, announced that the Committee was coming to Washington to hear Sandoval explain the steps he had taken to expand the Black Capitalism program. Sandoval not only did not receive them, he panicked and ordered all of the doors to the SBA locked so that the Committee could not meet. Then he himself left town, leaving behind front-page stories and an embarrassed White House.

Shortly after, Philip Pruitt, thirty-three-year-old black man from New York who had been appointed Assistant Director of SBA in charge of minority enterprise, resigned and publicly attacked the Administration for backing down on its commitments. Pruitt said that the Agency had set a goal of ten thousand loans for that year which it could not meet unless the Administration loosened up loan money for the program.

The Ripon Society then released a statement saying that Sandoval was "floundering" and called for his dismissal. The Society said that "Sandoval no longer commanded the respect of the white and black communities with whom he has to deal."

While the Ripon Society's views were not influential in Richard Nixon's White House, they were somewhat more important to liberal Senator Javits who was ranking Republican member of the Senate Select Committee on Small Business. Thus, when Chairman Senator Alan Bible of Nevada called for hearings on the SBA program in June 1969, Javits raised little objection.

A Special Report that had been prepared for the Republican members of the Committee before the hearings accused Sandoval of incompetence. It said that SBA's employees had received "essentially no direction from the administrative level" and that a "management gap" existed in the Agency.

As expected, the hearings were a disaster for Sandoval. Sandoval said that he hoped to quadruple SBA's lending program for minorities. When asked how he would do this if the Agency did not have funds, he replied that he was relying on the banking sector to provide the loans which SBA would guarantee. Senators Javits and Mark Hatfield, also a Republican, said that such a plan was unfeasible given the shortage of banks' funds and high interest rates which existed at the time.

Bible termed the Black Capitalism program "hifaluting and pontificating statements. Minority businessmen have to have hard dollars. It's fine to say, 'Little businessman, we're trying to help you,' but it won't do him any good if we can't get him any money."

Sandoval also admitted that he had done nothing to reclaim $34 million appropriated by Congress for low interest loans by SBA that had been frozen by the Administration. Bible said, "Why don't you simply get on the phone and call Mr. Mayo—he is the Director of the Budget—and see if you can't get X million dollars released?"

Sandoval thought that was a good idea.

Sandoval had little ability to stand up under such pressures. At one point, he became ill at the witness table and could not go on with his testimony. Finally, Javits and Bible agreed that there was nothing further to be gained by continuing the hearings and they were held over for two more months, until the Agency could "get itself together." Said Javits: "I am not happy with what I see. They [the Administration] are not happy. After sixty days we have a right to expect them to come in with a program. There is a need for six hundred thousand new minority businesses."

Sixty days later Roeser appeared before the Committee and laid out his plan, which was then rejected by Stans.

The morale in the Small Business Administration, which was "unbelievably low" according to several SBA employees when Sandoval took over, was further depressed by interference from Stans and the White House. One Donald Brewer, a protégé of Maurice Stans who had been ousted from his job at the Four Corners Regional Commission because he had alienated three of the governors of the four states the region covers, was given the job as Sandoval's Deputy Administrator at SBA at Stans's insistence. The White House then sent Story Zartman, a legal aide, over to SBA as General Counsel. Sandoval had no choice in either selection. Said one Republican close to the program at the time: "Stans sent Brewer in to watch Sandoval, and the White House sent in Zartman to watch them both."‡

Coming on the heels of Pruitt's resignation, Roeser's departure from OMBE touched off several critical news stories about the program. The New York *Times*, syndicated columnists Evans and Novak, and the Washington *Post* and Washington *Star* all ran stories suggesting that the Black Capitalism program was bogged down and the President's campaign promises were being sacrificed for the Southern Strategy. One of the more perceptive stories was written by Phillip Shandler in the Washington *Star* on November 28. Shandler wrote that the "promotion" of Tom Roeser "has chilled the concept of a comprehensive White House-directed, grass-roots-oriented plan for increasing business ownership among nonwhites in favor of a more laissez-faire,

‡ Peter M. Flanigan, who was in charge of patronage for the White House, had a particular aversion to Sandoval. The same Republican reports that as Sandoval was walking through a hall in the White House one day, Flanigan came up and took his arm with a friendly gesture. "You know, Hilary," Flanigan said with a smile, "you're really doing a lousy job. We're going to have to do something about you." Still smiling, he patted the bewildered and shaken Sandoval on the back and walked away.

middle-class effort to create 'black Horatio Algers,' in the words of Commerce Secretary Maurice H. Stans.

"In political terms, the course is seen by some nonconservatives as a reflection of the proposed 'Southern Strategy,' which would minimize the need of the Republican Party to consider minority sensibilities.

"There is a wider feeling, however, that the course simply is a manifestation of a GOP inclination for established ways."

The answer to such criticism was to be the road tour that Stans and John Erlichman had agreed to in September.

But before Maurice Stans went on the road he had to have something to sell. And so the OMBE staff gathered together all of the separated ideas that people had suggested over the past months, culled out those which were either too expensive or too radical, and called what was left a program.

A briefing paper for Stans's road tour prepared by the OMBE staff in September 1969 described the following four categories and associated activities as the program with which Stans would vindicate the Administration's Black Capitalism efforts:

I. *Opportunities*
  A. *Franchising.* To promote minority ownership of franchises. As a beginning 25 "established and reputable" franchisors would commit themselves to providing a *minimum* of 25 franchises to minority people in a two-year period in return for SBA assistance in financing.
  B. *Automobile dealerships.* The plan called for a goal of 100 dealerships for minorities over an unspecified time span.
  C. *Service station dealerships.* An effort to increase the number of minority people having gas station dealerships.
  D. *Business Opportunities Retailing Program.* A program to get various retail associations to assist minority entrepreneurs begin businesses in their trade. The program was modelled after one started by Howard Samuels and the Menswear Retailers Association.
  E. *The Turn-key Spin-off Program.* A program by which an existing large corporation would create a subsidiary and "spin" it off to a minority person or persons once the subsidiary was started.
  F. *Contract Preference Program.* A program to get more business contracts for minority firms. In the private sector the task was to try to convince major firms to do business with minority firms "at least as readily as with majority firms." In the public

sector, a Federal Task Force on procurement was established to get more Federal contracts to minority firms. A similar Task Force was set up to help gain Federally sponsored construction contracts and subcontracts for minority firms.

II. *Assistance and Education*
   A. *Federal Technical Assistance Program.* An attempt to utilize more efficiently several Federal programs which already provide assistance to minority enterprises. These programs include: SBA's SCORE program by which retired executives assist struggling small businesses, VISTA volunteers with business administration education who assist small businesses in ghetto and impoverished rural areas.
   B. *An Institute for Minority Business Education.* A grant to Howard University in the District of Columbia to train minority businessmen and do research on motivating them.
   C. *University Management Assistance Center.* An attempt, again through Howard University, to get University schools of business administration to assist minority businessmen.
   D. *National Economic Organization Service.* A program to help develop trade and industry associations among similar minority businesses for mutual support and efficiency. For example, to establish group purchasing, standardized accounting systems, group insurance, etc.

III. *Capital*
   A. *Federal Financial Assistance Program.* An attempt in an unspecified way to improve the availability of existing Federal loan and loan guarantee programs to minority entrepreneurs.
   B. *Federal Task Force on Capital Development.* A Task Force to review existing capital programs and to consider possible "approaches at the Federal, state and private levels."
   C. *Minority Enterprise, Small Business Investment Companies.* A program to get large corporations to establish Small Business Investment Companies which would lend money to minority small businesses. The Small Business Administration would lend the "MESBIC" two dollars for every one of their own.
   D. *Minority Banking Program.* A program to help in an unspecified manner existing minority-owned banks and savings and loan institutions.
   E. *Credit Guarantee Program.* A program to convince "individuals, corporations, foundations, and churches whose credit standing is sufficiently high to secure short-term and long-term loans to minority businessmen who would not otherwise qualify for loans." The program was to begin with a grant to the black National Bankers Association.

F. *Foundation for Equity Capital.* Establishment of a charitable foundation which would receive contributions from individuals and institutions to invest in minority enterprises.

IV. *Communication*

A. *National Information Center.* A computerized information system "regarding minority businesses and businessmen, community groups and community leaders, sources of technical and managerial assistance, business opportunities and markets, and financial mechanisms" to be set up in OMBE.

B. *Business Opportunity Centers.* Agencies set up in various cities across the country which would serve as sources of information on business opportunities for minority people, would engage in "initial screening . . . to determine the basic competence of business candidates" and would refer existing minority businessmen to sources of financial and management assistance.

Compared to the program Tom Roeser had come up with, the above was a loose, uncoordinated, and extremely modest package. Most of the twenty items were things to be explored and considered. The announcement of three Federal Task Forces could hardly bring a room of black capitalists to their feet with cheers. Nor could the generalized notions of providing them with more education and "motivation." Most of all there were no commitments. Word had begun to leak out that Roeser had recommended commitments to minority enterprise totaling billions of dollars in SBA loans and loan guarantees. The best that Stans could muster in the area of capital commitments was a Task Force that would consider some new approaches.

Some businessmen would have felt at this point that they had to improve the product. For Maurice Stans it was a merchandising problem. And to a large extent he solved it brilliantly. He couldn't compete with the image Roeser had conjured up of large Federal commitments, so he didn't talk money. He talked about the programs that conjured up the most specific images in people's minds: the franchises, the service stations, the automobile dealerships, and the one new program that he had to offer—the MESBIC—in such detail that his listeners overlooked the lack of a big commitment. And where they understood the deficiency, they mostly kept their mouths shut.

The typical pattern for his city tours was to begin with a

breakfast with any and all of the prominent bankers and businessmen who would show up. There he would discuss the need to develop Horatio Alger stories to motivate blacks into loyalty to the free enterprise system. The next step would be a larger meeting with whatever businessmen wanted to stay and a larger group of black business and community leaders. At this meeting Stans would explain the program with an emphasis on detail. There would be a few questions after which Stans would have to leave to prepare for a press conference. Abe Venable would then take over the program and introduce speakers from various Federal agencies who would speak briefly about what they had to offer minority entrepreneurs. Invariably the program ran late and so there was little time to question or go into detail about mobilization of Federal resources that OMBE claimed to be doing. Any questions of a specific nature, such as how a member of the audience might get a loan, were to be saved for later. The inquirer was told that he could meet later with the appropriate Government official, who of course left for lunch as soon as the meeting was over.

Stans proved to be able and deft. Critical questions about the programs detailed were either sidestepped or answered with Stans's assertion that as a successful businessman he could assure the questioner that the OMBE program was sound. And Venable was a convincing partner. When the issues of the Administration's intentions toward the black community were raised Venable said that the meeting wasn't called to discuss that and that it was pointless anyway. We are here, he would say, to get more black people into business and that's what he was doing and he would continue doing it as long as there was a chance that he could succeed. Sprinkled with allusions to black power and the need for black people to "get it together," Venable's pitch usually silenced the doubters. For good measure, Berkeley Burrell, of the National Business League, was on the podium with Venable and would jump to Venable's side. He was, he told the audience, a Republican because they were the people who understood business and he was a black businessman. Burrell had hugged Roeser for his statement on Haynsworth and Carswell, but the Department of Commerce had become the almost sole source of support for the National Business League and as a businessman Burrell knew he had to be on good terms with his financier.

But while Stans and Venable proved to be good salesmen, they could not have pulled it off nearly so well had their audience been a different one. Invitations were screened out by the OMBE staff and local Federal officials to avoid "militants," but there is no doubt that anyone even remotely connected with the local minority business community could have gotten into the larger morning meetings where Stans described the OMBE program. But as Franklin Frazier pointed out so well, the style of the black middle class is accommodation, not confrontation.

The differences between meetings with black communities held by OMBE and those held by OEO on antipoverty problems couldn't have been more striking. At the former the frustrations of the poor and their professional leadership poured out in shouts and demands. Such meetings were a continual effort to drag more concessions for the community out of the Government. Nothing like that occurred at the OMBE meetings. When a man did stand up and complain, no one followed up on it. Venable rode over him with an appeal to black unity and they went on to the next question. The black businessmen were primarily interested in their own businesses, in their own deals. There was little sense of community and they hesitated to bring out their own interests in a public forum. They certainly were not going to insult the potential financiers of their business dreams. No, they would wait until the parade-like presentations were over and then get one of those bureaucrats in the corner and try to make the deal.

But then, before the incipient black capitalist could move, the bureaucrats were off to the next meeting.

At a meeting before black businessmen in Harlem, Venable and Stans announced that they had three hundred franchise opportunities to give out. This time the blacks cornered Venable. On closer questioning he said that what he really meant was that he had a list of companies which said that they would be willing to give franchises to qualified blacks on an equal basis with qualified whites. Where was the list? It will be available at OMBE's Harlem office. Where was the office? We haven't opened it yet. Where will it be? We haven't decided yet.

Stans's city visits were a bureaucratic success; he got his name in the paper and the Administration got through the year without having to spend much money on Black Capitalism. But despite lack of confrontation, the minorities soon realized what the game was. Darwin Bolden of the ICBO says: "The Administration did not score well in the black community on Stans's city visits. They overpromised and didn't produce anything. In the end it made people even more frustrated."

Stans's hucksterism also had a frustrating effect on the OMBE bureaucracy. The staff swelled but there was nothing for them to do but run around Washington "coordinating." The mutterings grew to grumbles and the grumbles grew to loud complaints, often getting beyond the Commerce Department's wall and up the street to the White House.

On March 5, 1970, Stans held an all-day conference with members of the OMBE and SBA staff and a few selected bureaucrats from other agencies to review the achievements and goals of his program after its first year. Stans opened the meeting with a long talk on loyalty. He said he knew there were instances where OMBE staff members had gone outside the Agency to complain about the way OMBE was being run. And he knew who those staff members were. However, he was willing right then to "wipe the slate clean," as long as his staff and anyone else connected with the Administration recognized that the first virtue of a civil servant was loyalty to his superior. Stans then turned to the business at hand; he spent the next eight hours leading a discussion on how to improve the public reception of his city visits.

The episode did not endear Stans to the blacks on the staff, who more and more were being accused by their "brothers" of having sold out to the Republican Administration. Their plight was made worse by a series of embarrassing incidents. In February 1970 OMBE opened its first field office, in Washington, D.C. Shortly after it opened, the story broke out that the remodeling contract had gone to a white-owned suburban Maryland firm. "The reason we used them," said the Department of Commerce spokesman, "was because of their availability." He didn't know whether any of the 150 black contractors in Washington, D.C., had been asked about their availability.

Another gaff was a letter sent out by Venable recommending a shoeshine franchise by the name of "Shine Boy" as an opportunity for minority businessmen. The letter raised a storm among blacks. Darwin Bolden wrote Venable that soliciting for a firm with such a name was an insult to black people. Venable's response was to accuse a staff member of forging his name. Then when he determined that he himself had signed the letter, he castigated the staff member for not calling his attention to it.

Stans himself was the star of what was perhaps the worst OMBE performance in terms of its insensitivity to blacks. After returning from an African safari, Stans invited the entire Commerce Department to see a showing of the films he had taken on his trip. And there in full view of the employees, black and white, he showed films of black porters and gunbearers and referred to them as "boys."

Given Stans's crusty and arrogant personality it is unlikely if the criticism that resulted from the above affected him very much. His heart appeared to be in other places. In the spring of 1970, the *Wall Street Journal* reported:

> Mr. Stans seems to have consistently bested the State Department and other free trade advocates in his determination to restrict imports of Japanese textiles. Although Japan has rejected his demand for voluntary curbs, and critics say his approach has been heavy-handed and dictatorial, he is lavishly praised by the textile industry.
>
> "Secretary Stans has won the admiration of everyone in the industry for his knowledge and persistence," says Frederic Dent, Chairman of Mayflower Mills, Inc. Another textile executive rejoices: "For the first time we have an unqualified ally at the Commerce." The textile issue, moreover, is considered a key element in the Republicans' so-called "Southern Strategy" for future election victories.
>
> The Commerce Secretary also achieved at least a short-term success with his dissent from a Cabinet-level task force recommendation to abolish the oil import quota system in favor of tariffs, which probably would result in an increase in crude oil imports. President Nixon shelved this recommendation, and appointed a new oil policy committee to make a further study. Mr. Stans, one of the two dissenters from the task force recommendation, was named to the new committee.
>
> On behalf of another big industry, the Commerce Chief quickly squelched a suggestion by the Council of Economic Advisors to permit more steel imports, as a counter to rising domestic prices. Only if Mr. Stans leaves the Government would this be an "open issue" again, an Administration official said sadly.

The *Journal* pointed out that Stans's other accomplishments included overriding the Justice Department's opposition to a bill exempting newspapers from antitrust legislation and successfully opposing pro-consumer proposals coming from other parts of the Administration. Finally, there was Stans the pitchman again. The *Journal* continued:

> As a salesman for the Administration (179 public appearances and 36 press conferences around the country last year), Mr. Stans concentrates on Republican-oriented groups, he stresses the conservative themes of reducing the Federal role and cooperating with businessmen, and extols the free enterprise system. Mr. Stans once proposed the creation of an American Enterprise Institute.

Given Stans's enthusiasm for big business and his lack of identification with minorities, it is not surprising that the greatest challenge to the way he ran Black Capitalism came not from blacks, or the Spanish-speaking or any other minority, but from a successful white businessman like himself—Sam Wyly.

If there was any doubt after the first meeting that Wyly was in control of the Advisory Council, it was dispelled when Wyly had the Director of his own Wyly Foundation of Dallas, Alan Steelman, appointed as Director of the Council staff. By donating Steelman's salary rather than having him paid by the Department of Commerce, Wyly insured that Steelman would be independent of Stans. The office space for the Council staff was also donated by Wyly—at the Washington offices of his own University Computing Company.

Despite the mandate creating the Advisory Council which clearly made it advisory to the Secretary of Commerce, Wyly and Steelman from the beginning dealt directly with the White House, getting from them commitments for staff and whatever authorities they needed. In a letter to Wyly dated November 25, 1969, Stans made it clear that he expected the Council to put any ideas and proposals they came up with in the form of "legislative, administrative, or budgetary recommendations to the Secretary of Commerce." But by that time it was too late. Wyly and the Council had already agreed that their primary objective was to write a report for the President and there was little that Stans could do to stop them. As Steelman said later in an interview:

"It was our assumption that since the group was named by the President, its mission was to report to him."

One of Wyly's first acts was to increase the Council membership from sixty-three to eighty-five members. Since most of the additional members were minority group spokesmen, it assured that there would be a critical tone to the deliberations of the Council. Because the Council was so unwieldy and large, it was broken into a number of subcommittees dealing with various aspects of the problem of developing minority entrepreneurs. These included: financing, business opportunities, management and technical assistance, and an "expanded participation" subcommittee to discuss ways of making the benefits of capitalism more widespread to minority people. The Committee had a staff of twenty-one and a budget of about half a million dollars. It gave out contracts and hired consultants to write reports on various aspects of minority enterprise.

The staff produced its first draft in the fall of 1970. It contained ninety-four separate recommendations going from the encouragement of unspecified "corporations" to "prepare a list of items that can be readily purchased from minority suppliers" to a proposal of a 50 percent tax credit for nonminority firms to invest in minority businesses.

The draft recommended a "substantial Federal resource commitment" of $930 million, not including loan guarantees for the next three-year period. But it was not made clear whether this was to be additional money or was a total effort including monies already being spent. One of the staff members said at the time that this was to be "new" money. Maurice Stans said that the Government was already spending $300 million a year for minority capitalism and that therefore the Wyly Council recommendations were already being implemented. Stans's figure included loan guarantees but since the Administration did not make public figures on loan guarantees, it was not clear who was right. Another staff member was probably closer to the truth when he said that the recommendation was written so that the minorities and those sympathetic to their cause could interpret it as a new money commitment, while the more conservative businessmen could see it as a total figure.

But the most controversial recommendation of the draft report was the recommendation for a complete reorganization of the minority capitalism program. The Council recommended the creation of a new Agency, the Agency for Expanded Ownership.* (An alternative title offered by the Committee was: Domestic Economic Development Administration.) The new Agency would be formed by combining the Small Business Administration, the Economic Development Administration, OMBE and selected programs taken from the Office of Economic Opportunity and the Department of Agriculture. A major function of the new Agency would be to establish and operate one hundred new local delivery centers to provide "one-stop" packaging service to assist the minority businessman with financial management and technical help.

It is hard to separate the substantive issues of this proposal from the Stans-Wyly feud. Clearly the proposal was a direct and obvious slap at the Secretary of Commerce and his programs. And that is how it was interpreted in the press.

In the fall of 1970 stories appeared in the New York *Times*, the Washington *Post*, the Boston *Globe*, and a number of other newspapers about the split between the Council and the Secretary. At the same time it was also clear that a number of the more aggressive spokesmen for the black businessmen were unhappy about the Nixon program and were seeking to use the Committee as a lever to pry more resources out of the Administration.

Foremost among these black critics on the Committee was Darwin Bolden. In an interview in the *National Journal* of December 26, 1970, Bolden blasted OMBE and the Administration. He described OMBE as "one of the poorest managed Federal agencies I know." He said that many of the organizations that were claimed as part of the OMBE affiliate program had already been receiving funds from Federal agencies. "All of these organizations existed before OMBE came into the field," Bolden said. "They have been slightly enlarged. But if OMBE were to go out of business tomorrow, there would be no void . . . OMBE is a tragic failure . . . it cannot be saved." Finally, Bolden added:

* This title was a contribution of John McClaughry's.

"If no new substantive effort is taken, OMBE must be regarded as a copout."

For a while it looked as though Stans was in for a tough time. Criticism of his program and his crusty, unsympathetic public image was becoming more common. The mood had even seeped into the Commerce Department. In June 1970, Rocco Siciliano, the Under Secretary, admitted to the New York *Times* that the Black Capitalism program had fallen far short of its goals, although he blamed it on the economic recession. He also said that there were no plans to revise the OMBE structure. But by December, Siciliano was trying to prepare for the expected blow from the White House in favor of the Wyly proposal. Siciliano was quoted as saying that Stans was committed to the program "but we're not looking at it from a jurisdictional point of view." He went on: "I don't think OMBE organizationally is a static thing. It is not frozen in concrete."

But Stans would not budge. And the draft report remained on the President's desk. Officially, the President had not received it. Neither had Stans. In an interview in January 1971 Stans said he shouldn't discuss the report because it hadn't been given to him yet.

But Stans was busy. Several members of the Advisory Council who were close to the Secretary or opposed the recommended budget as extravagant took up his cause. Chad McClellan, a Los Angeles businessman, W. P. Gullander, President of the National Association of Manufacturers, and several others managed to delay the report for several months.

But Bolden and others of the Advisory Council also held out. And as long as Wyly supported their position, it was clear that the White House would not permit the release of the report. Finally, in order to break the impasse, John Erlichman, and Leonard Garment from the White House, met with the Executive Committee of the Council. It was the showdown. And Wyly backed down. After months of leading the attack on Stans, he suddenly took the side of the White House and urged his own committee to delete the recommendation for the new Agency which was particularly offensive to Stans. The Executive Committee still held out but soon agreed to a compromise. The report would be offered three alternative reorganizations, one of which was the new Agency for Expanded Ownership and the other two of which were agreeable to Stans.

The report was released in February 1971. McClelland wrote a dissenting opinion, objecting even to the mention of the new Agency as an alternative. Gullander also wrote a dissent, objecting to the cost of the recommendations.

But Stans still held on. The fact that the report was released didn't mean that the White House had to act. Months went by and still no word. It was four months before Government Printing Office got around to printing the report. The staff began to disband. Sam Wyly's computer company began to run into trouble, and he spent less and less time trying to get the White House to respond. There were rumors that the reason that he had backed down on the report was that he needed the Government to approve a merger and needed Stans to intervene for him.

And so the tide began to run the other way. The wage-price policy became the dominant issue for most businessmen on the Advisory Council. Their economic futures were at stake and they certainly were not going to waste their time helping black businessmen with their problems. And then the Administration began to prepare for the 1972 elections. Sam Wyly had raised 10 percent of the campaign treasury in 1968, but Stans had raised 90 percent. Several stories appeared that Stans would leave his post to take care of financing the campaign again. It was the right time for Nixon to give his old friend a victory.

And so he did. On October 13, 1971, the White House announced that it was asking Congress for a supplementary budget increase of $100 million over the next eighteen months, to be administered by the Office of Minority Business Enterprise in the Department of Commerce. More important, Nixon issued an executive order giving more authority to the Secretary of Commerce and placing the Advisory Council under the Secretary. Stans won, Wyly lost. And that was the end of it.

9

COMMUNITY DEVELOPMENT CORPORATIONS VS. THE WALL STREET WHEELER DEALERS

"The solution lies in ignoring the propaganda of black militants and in doggedly pursuing the route of clear logic and justice: the *forced* injection of credit, risk capital, and entrepreneurial skills into the ghetto economy."

THEODORE CROSS, *Black Capitalism*

The Community Self-Determination Act was aborted but the underlying ideas refused to die.

Maurice Stans felt that blacks and other minorities should be helped to set up small, marginal businesses in which they would have to struggle night and day to survive. But somehow this struggle would ennoble them and bring them into the "system"; if they were particularly hard-working and diligent, they would build their businesses into successful, capitalist enterprises. John McClaughry characterized this view as the "Andrew Carnegie model for minority economic development—start with a dime, borrow a dollar, rise early and work late, and build yourself a steel mill."

Many blacks, however, are not contented with this romanticized and outdated image of how economic power is obtained. Other paths, based on the massing of capital under group control, are also being explored. In the South and Southwest, poor black and chicano farmers are gathering together into cooperatives for mutual support and protection and for the pooling of bargaining power. In cities poor people's credit unions are being set up to help combat the loan sharks and other exploiters. And in a number of rural and urban communities a new form of collective enterprise, much like that which was envisaged in the Community Self-Determination Act, has begun to develop. Indeed, the fact that poor people had already established community development corporations in several parts of the country had itself been an inspiration for the proposed Act.

These "real life" community development corporations, as opposed to the ideal model of the Community Self-Determination Act, differed from place to place. Since there was no Government "program" for CDCs which demanded conformity, each of them developed out of the economics and politics of its local area. The common theme to all of them was control of the corporation by representatives of the depressed neighborhood or area and the selection and operation of business enterprises to gain maximum benefits for the community.

The way in which community residents control the CDC varies. CDCs in Durham, North Carolina, and in Philadelphia sell stock to members of the community who in turn elect a majority of the Board of Directors on a one-man one-vote basis. Other CDCs, for example in Rochester, New York, and in St. Louis, are controlled through elections at community conventions. Others involve combinations of the above.

The activities in which the CDCs are engaged are even more varied. In Cleveland and Philadelphia CDCs have built shopping centers; in Roanoke, Virginia, and Rochester CDCs are operating electronic assembly plants; in Hancock County, Georgia, and among the Lummi Indians in Washington State CDCs are operating fish farms; in Knox County, Kentucky, and in the Watts section of Los Angeles CDCs are successfully manufacturing toys, and CDCs in a number of cities and rural locations have built housing projects of all types.[1]

Community Development Corporations represent poor people trying to pool their talents and resources to create economic opportunities for themselves and their neighbors. They do not represent investors trying to maximize the return on their investments. There is thus a limit to the amount of funds that they can raise in their own communities or from outsiders for business ventures. Therefore, they have turned to the Federal Government, principally the Office of Economic Opportunity, for seed money. The Federal Model Cities program, the Ford Foundation, and church groups and other charitable institutions were also sources of capital for CDCs.

At the time the Nixon Administration came to power the OEO had already made a limited commitment to support CDCs. The appearance of Richard Nixon's interest in the Community Self-Determination Act suggested to many that the CDC program was one Poverty Program that was in line with the Administration's stated intention to give blacks and other minorities a "piece of the action." And in fact some sympathetic staffers working for the new Secretary of HEW, Robert Finch, managed to get "community business development" a high priority in Nixon's first statement on the future of the Poverty Program. Moreover, the House and Senate Committees that oversee the antipoverty programs were sufficiently impressed by the promise of CDCs that they specifically directed the Administration to encourage their formation and support them with funds from Title I-D, the amendment that had been sponsored by Senators Robert Kennedy and Javits for their program in Bedford-Stuyvesant, a forerunner of the CDC idea.

But it soon became clear that whatever interest the President might have had in black economic development, it was no match for other notions that claimed his attention, such as the Southern Strategy.

In April 1969, three months after the Nixon Administration had taken power, the Office of Economic Opportunity made a grant to the Foundation for Community Development, a nonprofit corporation in Durham, North Carolina. The grant was for the support of United Durham, a profit-making CDC which the Foundation for Community Development had helped establish. The announcement of the grant raised a political storm in North Carolina because of the presence on the staff of the Foundation of Howard Fuller, a black militant.

The Mayor of Durham and the Governor, both Democrats, denounced the grant as did the Durham newspapers. The Sunday Durham *Herald* ran a color cartoon on the front page showing Nixon handing a bagful of money to the notorious Howard

Fuller, boots up on the President's desk and a big cigar in his mouth—a southern caricature of a black capitalist. Harry Dent, Nixon's Presidential assistant for political affairs, showed the cartoon to Nixon, who, in Dent's words, "went through the roof."

"Oh, I understand all about that Black Capitalism stuff," said Dent to the OEO bureaucrat in charge of the Special Impact Program. "But now you have to understand that the South is very important to this Administration. I know that OEO money has been used to start riots and elect Democrats and it is going to stop. The President wants that grant killed."

The CDC in Durham had the involvement of a number of highly respected businessmen, black and white. Compared with some of the CDCs that were forming in the North and the West it was a conservative organization. When Ted Berry, then head of OEO's Community Action Program in Washington, asked John Wheeler, black President of The Mechanics and Farmers Bank in Durham, why there was so much hostility to the project, Wheeler replied: "Don't forget this is the South, Ted. They are just not going to let a bunch of black people get control of that kind of money."

The White House's only black staff aide was Robert J. Brown from North Carolina. While the grant was being considered he had told the bureaucrats at OEO that, speaking as a White House assistant, he wanted to see the grant funded. When the trouble started, however, it was Harry Dent who spoke for the President, not Robert Brown. Ted Berry, who is himself black, and others at OEO tried desperately to reach Brown, but he couldn't be found and refused to return the phone calls.

Despite the President's and Harry Dent's desires, however, the grant was not killed. The bureaucrats at OEO, most of whom had already decided that they couldn't remain in the Nixon Administration very long anyway, refused to budge, and the Republican administrators, who knew nothing about OEO law and procedures, couldn't find a way to break the grant agreement. Legally, the grant could not be terminated without specific "cause" that had to consist of more than the fact that the Republicans didn't like the people involved. On the other hand, the Administration would not release funds to a project that was so clearly in conflict with its Southern Strategy. Most important, the Foundation's black director, Nathan Garrett, is an extremely intelligent and patient man. He had the skill and dedication to his cause to outwait the opposition. Finally, after a year of negotiation, and as a result of the intervention of a white businessman, OEO permitted the release of funds for a specific business project on the condition that it not go through the controversial nonprofit organization.

The delay was costly. A site for the location of a modular housing business which was available at a reasonable cost had to be given up. Committed orders for two hundred units of housing were lost and a potential manager had to be kept off the payroll. It cost the organization about $20,000 of scarce foundation money just to negotiate with OEO.

Two other community-based programs were not so lucky. A project in Lee County, Georgia, which would have helped black sharecroppers settle on some land and start their own cooperative farm, was terminated by the Administration because of protests from local white *Democratic* leaders. Another project in South Texas, involving a group of poor Mexican-Americans, was killed for the same reasons. And neither OMBE nor Robert Brown nor anyone else in the bureaucratic complex of minority capitalism raised a question.

The CDC program was giving the Administration more trouble than it was worth. Don Rumsfeld, the former Republican Congressman whom Nixon chose to direct the shrinking of the Poverty Program, expressed the view a number of times that CDCs were in the hands of irresponsible elements, both in the communities and in his own agency (eventually he managed to get rid of most of the more aggressive poverty bureaucrats in OEO). Rumsfeld claimed that the trouble with the bureaucrat in charge of the CDC program was that he was "too close to the constituency." In the Defense Department or in the Agriculture Department this would have been a complement. But the constituency of OEO was not that of the Administration.

As it turned out, "irresponsible" was a code word for Black. "What do we do," Rumsfeld wanted to know over and over, "if the Black Panthers take over one of these corporations?" With the help of Theodore Cross, a Wall Street lawyer and author of a book called *Black Capitalism,* Rumsfeld attempted to take the money away from the community development corporations and give it to a new nonprofit corporation called the Opportunity Funding Corporation which would be controlled by a Board of Directors consisting of five white financiers, whom Cross kept referring to as "nimble." Rumsfeld and Cross's major concern it seemed was that the program be controlled from Washington. Local control and freedom from Government restraints it seems was all right for white businessmen, but someone had to watch over these blacks to make sure they don't misuse "our" money.*

If Maurice Stans was a strong believer in the Horatio Alger style of capitalist accumulation, Ted Cross was a strong believer in capitalism as practiced in the more arcane reaches of Wall Street. The secret of business success according to Cross was to be found behind the door marked "Leverage." Leverage, Mr. Cross told the bewildered antipoverty bureaucrats, was the magic formula that could make poor black people rich, if only they were taught how to use it.

In his book *Black Capitalism*, which was published shortly after the Nixon Administration came to power, Cross explains:

"Almost every issue of the *Wall Street Journal* reports examples of how the ownership of capital of great value is created practically overnight by the use of leverage combined with a minor stake of risk money. New security issues capitalizing earnings, or even losses, by the process of multiplication build new and fantastic value from the operation of a rather pedestrian business enterprise. Applying financial magic unknown to the slum economy, the market 'decides' that a company's annual earnings of fifty thousand dollars are worth one million dollars. This is the essential 'secret' of finance or leverage."[2]

The book reasons, accurately enough, that the ghetto is not a profitable place to do business. But nowhere is there much of an analysis of what the root cause of such unprofitability might be. Reading Cross's book or listening to him speak one had the feeling that the major problem was that black militants did not understand the need for profit and that they were hung up with the issue of who controls. Once the militants were made to understand the need for profitability they would support the

* Republicans in Washington were constantly referring to Federal funds as "our" money, as if Nixon's election transferred to them the ownership of the U.S. Treasury.

provision of tax credits and other incentives to outsiders for the good of those inside the ghetto.

Cross's solution, therefore, was to provide tax incentives to corporations and banks to encourage ghetto investments and a system of guarantees to take out the risk. In other words, it was a program where blacks would be helped by providing white corporations and banks with benefits that would, one hoped, "trickle down." Cross proposed that the money that OEO had intended to use to help CDCs be used instead to test his proposals.

The Republicans who took over the Office of Economic Opportunity loved it. And Stans and the White House staff were enthusiastic for this notion of using money destined for the poor to guarantee the profits of the Chase Manhattan Bank. Rumsfeld and Cross presented their program to the President at a full Cabinet meeting, after which they reported that the President himself strongly supported the logic.

The community development corporations were somewhat less enthusiastic. When they heard about the program they came to Washington in carloads to see Rumsfeld and Cross and to find out what had happened to the money that Congress had appropriated for their program. After several days of dodging the CDC representatives, Rumsfeld and Cross agreed to meet with them. Rumsfeld began the meeting by saying that his interest was in helping the CDCs succeed. The CDC leaders, bearded blacks in dashikis, Mexican-Americans from the Southwest, white mountain people from Appalachia, stated with somewhat exaggerated politeness that their interest was in seeing his program— the poverty program—survive. Rumsfeld then turned to Cross and asked him to work out the details with the CDC people and left the room.

Cross gamely tried to sell his trickle-down theories, but the CDCs were not buying. They asked how poor people were supposed to take advantage of this leverage if even the Small Business Administration, much less investment bankers, high-priced New York lawyers and mortgage brokers, and venture capitalists, refused to do business with them. Cross replied that the new program would pay the salaries of some Wall Street types who would intercede for the poor in the money markets. In order to get the best people, of course, they should understand that OEO would have to pay the salaries that these people were used to.

Then the CDC people wanted to know how they were supposed to get the initial capital with which to play this leverage game if OEO was going to take the grant money away from them? Cross replied that they could raise it among the poor. Moreover he told them that he knew that these people weren't as poor as some would have him believe.

At that point the meeting became chaos. The CDC people shouted that he didn't know what he was talking about and that he had come to "rip off" what little chance they had to give the poor some economic opportunities. Cross, at the breaking point, threw down his pencil and fled from the room.

Convinced that the CDC leaders were unreasonable and irresponsible, Cross and Rumsfeld called another meeting of minority leaders, *their* minority leaders. Another meeting was held at the offices of the Bureau of the Budget. But the CDC people had gotten to the "brothers" and the scene was repeated. This time there was a sit-in in protest against the Administration's intentions.

The CDCs also had help from the Congress. William Spring, a staff member of Senator Nelson's Subcommittee on Employment, Manpower and Poverty, organized House and Senate members to protest the diversion of funds away from the CDC for whose support the Congress had intended the program.

By now things had gotten out of hand, and even Rumsfeld was beginning to have second thoughts about Cross. Finally a compromise was reached. OEO agreed to keep assisting community development corporations, and to reduce the aid it was going to give to the Opportunity Funding Corporation. It also agreed to put some minority CDC people on the board of the OFC.

The Office of Minority Business Enterprise, which was responsible for coordinating programs from minority enterprise and advocating the minority cause before other Federal agencies, not only did not intervene on the CDC's behalf, but actually assisted Cross in trying to take the money away from the minority community organizations so that OMBE could claim a role in helping create a more responsible OEO program for minority capitalists.

10 | WHAT THEY DID, NOT WHAT THEY SAID

"Another important principle is that we should carry out this program without overpromising or raising false hopes."

RICHARD NIXON, *message to Congress on minority enterprise, October 13, 1971*

"Don't look at what we say, but what we do."

Attorney General JOHN N. MITCHELL

I. MOSTLY DEBITS

A. *MESBICs.*

In October 1969, Commerce Secretary Maurice Stans said that by the following June one hundred Minority Enterprise Small Business Investment Companies would be established. By June 1971 the number of MESBICs was eleven. In December 1971, more than two years after Stans's announcement, the Nixon Administration had agreed to support forty-one MESBICs.

The MESBIC program is a good point from which to evaluate the Nixon Administration's accomplishments in Black Capitalism because the program represents Nixon's only new and innovative effort in the field. Most of the ideas that Stans was to implement between 1969 and 1972 were already being implemented or at least considered by the Democrats when Nixon took office. A plan that Howard Samuels sent to Robert Finch eight days after the President's inauguration contained a series of proposals covering most of what was to become the new Administration's minority enterprise program.

MESBIC, however, was new. And it was Republican. It was the brainchild of a Republican businessman using a program that had been established by the Eisenhower Administration in 1958—the Small Business Investment Company (SBIC). MESBIC is the program which received the most support and attention from the Administration. And it is the program that most reflects the Nixon Administration's approach to providing minorities with a "piece of the action."

The Small Business Investment Act of 1958 authorizes SBA to license and support Small Business Investment Companies whose purpose it is to finance small businesses which have had difficulty obtaining capital. A Small Business Investment Company is capitalized by private investors at a minimum of $150,000. The granting of an SBIC license requires that the investors agree to certain restrictions on their investment activities (e.g. limitations on the proportion of their funds to be invested in one business or one industry) in return for which SBA will agree to lend twice the capitalization to the SBIC by purchasing the SBIC's debentures.

The SBIC may invest in small companies in any number of ways—by making loans, by making loans with rights to buy stock, and by buying stock in the company. Interest on loans can be as high as 15 percent per annum. Moreover, the law provides generous tax benefits for investors.

The program proved to be a disaster. By 1966 in response to the generous Federal financing arrangements and the tax subsidies, 686 Small Business Investment Companies had been formed. Over the next five years more than four hundred went out of business. Federal investigators found that the program was shot full of fraud as well as incompetence. A report made by the U.S. House of Representatives House Committee on Small Business in 1971 revealed that of 637 SBICs studies, 236 were in violation of the law. Several SBIC operators were imprisoned for willful fraud.

The history of the SBIC program also showed that in order to have any chance of success a legitimately run SBIC had to be capitalized at least at one million dollars, since only at that level and above could an SBIC expect to have enough earnings to pay for the staff to run it. In 1967 SBA released figures showing that the average returns on investment for all of the SBICs capitalized at less than $325,000 was −2.3 percent in 1966 and −3.0 percent in 1967.[1]

This bankrupt program, which had failed in the world of white capitalism, was chosen to be the chief instrument of assistance to black capitalists.

The MESBIC story begins with Robert Dehlendorf, President of Arcata National Corporation, a $200 million conglomerate in Menlo Park, California. After the assassination of Martin Luther King in the spring of 1968, Dehlendorf decided to do something to help the black ghetto in neighboring East Palo Alto. With the help of several Washington lawyers Dehlendorf hit upon the idea of starting an SBIC to assist black businesses.

Dehlendorf was a Republican and a substantial contributor to the party. During the campaign he met Maurice Stans, who was raising money for Nixon. According to Stans: "Dehlendorf in Palo Alto came to me during the campaign last year when I was raising money, and he said: 'I will help Nixon get elected President, but I want something in return.' He said: 'What I want to do is to be able to help the Nixon Administration in helping minority people get into business.' I said: 'You are in.'. . .

"Well, I did not see him again for six months or so, and in February he contacted me, and he said, 'What are you going to do about minority enterprise?' And I said, 'We are working on a program and we will have it soon.' So, we saw him in March, and he came down here to see me, and I said, 'What have you been doing in the meantime?' And he said: 'Well, I started out to see what I could do. I went to Washington, and I studied all the things that could be done to help minority people, and I decided to set up an SBIC, and I got my company to agree to put up 2 percent of its profits every year into capital of an SBIC.'

"So he said, 'For the first year, we put in $150,000 and we went to SBA and got a matching grant of $300,000. Then I hired a bright, young white boy, and I hired a bright, young colored boy, and I got them together and told them what I wanted to do and said go to work and see what you can do to help minority enterprise in East Palo Alto. They have been on it for seven

months now, and in that period of time, we have thirteen enterprises started and going and all doing well. We have five more
ready to go and forty-two more under investigation.'"

For Stans it was a natural. It was an idea that came from a
Republican businessman and it did not require the Nixon Administration to spend any political capital getting new authority
from Congress. It was also cheap.

The heart of the MESBIC's attraction is the 15 to 1 financial
leverage it is supposed to generate; for every one dollar invested
in the MESBIC, it was theoretically possible to attract fifteen
more into the program.

According to Pete Hansen, the Stanford MBA chosen to run
the Arcata MESBIC, the leverage works like this:

"First, the company forms an SBIC by placing $150,000 in a
bank account for a basic loan fund. After three fourths of the
loan fund is used up, the SBIC may apply for a $300,000 loan
from the SBA. The loan is at about a 7 percent rate of interest,
and is unsecured by anything but the original $150,000. In other
words, the company agrees that any losses up to $150,000 will
be from its own capital and any further losses will be from the
Government loan.

"If the company would like to leverage funds further, the loans
and investments can be subordinated to bank loans, usually with
90 percent guarantees from the SBA. Generally, 20 percent of the
loan package must be granted by the SBIC and subordinated to
the bank loan. Maximum bank loan potential is therefore $1,800,-
000. Of this amount, the bank actually risks $180,000. The other
$1,620,000 is guaranteed by the SBA." Thus:

Company's SBIC	$ 150,000	paid in capital
Plus	300,000	unsecured note from SBA
Subtotal	450,000	
Bank loans	1,800,000	(90 percent or 1,620,000 SBA guaranteed)
Total	$2,250,000[2]	

The Administration pushed the program hard, particularly
since the Arcata Company's initial experience seemed to sub-
stantiate its potential. In the spring and summer of 1970, stories
appeared in a number of business magazines praising the
MESBIC program as an example of what concerned business-

men could do to alleviate social problems within the natural confines of the business system. The only sour note was heard from an article in the *Harvard Business Review* by Professors Richard Rosenbloom and John Shank who doubted that the MESBICs could attain the leverage being claimed and that small businesses could be successfully operated with such a large debt burden. But even Rosenbloom and Shank had to admit that Arcata seemed to be doing well. "Although it is too early to place much emphasis on observed results," they wrote, "the company's losses so far have been under 2 percent, and most of the businesses funded appear to be thriving or at least surviving."

A year later an examination of the Arcata MESBIC showed that of fifty minority businesses receiving loans, twenty-five had already failed, sixteen were in serious trouble, and nine were still surviving. And the Arcata MESBIC was bankrupt.

What happened? First of all, as Rosenbloom and Shank pointed out, the program was based on almost 100 percent debt financing of the minority businesses. "No matter what color the owner," they wrote, "successful businesses just do not get started with debt financing alone. Interest and principal payments on the full investment base would be an oppressive cash flow problem for a new business. To make matters worse, there would be no 'equity cushion' to absorb the inevitable, unforeseen setbacks and extra expenses associated with the start-up period. New businesses require a significant equity interest if they are to have any real chance of succeeding."

Thus the MESBIC was an unsound business proposition from the start. If white businesses couldn't be successful this way, how could one expect black businesses to make it?

Secondly, there was an insufficient appreciation of the economics of the ghetto. Small businesses simply could not survive in a depressed, crime-ridden market. Alone and small, unable to absorb the slightest loss from poor management and low-productivity workers, much less from a robbery, the model of individual, small entrepreneurship was not sufficient foundation for economic development.

The MESBIC solution assumes that the problem lies not in the economic environment but in the skills and capacity of individual blacks and chicanos. The answer was therefore to provide "technical assistance." So Arcata National rounded up a "white boy" and a "black boy" to teach minority businessmen how to run their businesses.

It is therefore little wonder that Stans could not live up to his prediction of establishing one hundred MESBICs by the end of June 1970. The wonder is that he managed to set up forty-two, two and one half years later. To be sure, from the beginning he had told businessmen that they should not expect a large profit from their investment in a MESBIC. The point was that they could do something to help preserve the business system and make a little too, or at least cover costs. But when the large corporations' financial analysts looked at the figures, they could see nothing but quick failure, even before the Arcata experience became known. Only if the parent company was willing to subsidize the program for a number of years would there even be any public relations benefit.

And in order to deliver forty-two MESBICs in two and one half years, OMBE had to water down its initial program design so much that the program became a formless mixture of financial objectives. At the beginning MESBICs were to be sponsored by established business corporations:

    1. to obtain the required private financing,
    2. to assure that MESBIC would have access to recognized business competence,
    3. to assure that a corporate "parent" would make an extra effort to make the program successful since their name was publicly associated with the MESBIC.

After failing to get very many business sponsors, however, the criteria were loosened. First, it was agreed to allow corporations to pool capital in order to raise the initial investment, thus deleting the visibility from the program. Of the forty-two MESBICs licensed as of November 15, 1971, only ten sponsors were at all identified by the name of the MESBIC.

An examination of the MESBICs also revealed that the motives for MESBIC sponsorship were not as altruistic as might be expected. For example, MESBICs were set up by at least two oil companies to finance their franchises in inner-city areas. And in Alaska, a consortium of oil companies set up a MESBIC which will serve double duty. It will undercut Alaskan native opposition to the oil pipeline which will cut the state in two and it will provide capital to help the oil companies finance and profit from the small service and supply businesses needed to support the pipeline construction.

Moreover, OMBE officials have admitted confidentially that the motivation behind several proposed MESBICs is for manufacturers to set up minority subcontractors to whom they could subcontract out work at non-union wages under the umbrella of a Government-endorsed and financed program.

In these cases the highly touted leverage of the MESBICs therefore becomes a device not so much to be used by the minority community, but by white capitalists to further their own market designs.

In all cases, the leverage benefits of the MESBIC go not to the minority entrepreneur, but to the owners of the MESBICs, the large white-owned corporations. If there is a 15 to 1 ratio to be had, it is the corporations who get it, and corporations can well afford to invest $150,000 to set up fifteen times that amount in franchise outlets, or to be able to reduce the effective labor cost of their goods.

And who pays for the leverage? Without a careful reading one would think from the Administration literature that the Government is the one whose money is leveraged and that it is the businessmen and bankers who are providing the leverage. But in fact, of the $2,250,000 of capital which could be generated by the MESBIC program, $1,920,000 is provided by Federal loans or loan guarantees, $150,000 by the original investors, and $180,000 by the banks. The latter, unless more than 92 percent of the original investments is completely unrecoverable (an extremely unlikely event), have their investment underwritten by the U.S. Government.

The MESBIC therefore becomes another in the long list of devices to enrich corporate America under the guise of helping the needy. The corporations sell their gasoline, the banks get their money back with a handsome profit, and the Federal Government ends up chasing down the poor black man to collect for everyone else.

B. *Franchising*

The OMBE franchising program might be called the program that wasn't. During the first year of Black Capitalism, franchising usually was cited first in the lists of new programs that the Administration claimed it was making available to minorities. Franchising was said to permit a relatively unskilled, inexperienced man to get into business under the protective wing of an established business corporation and it was stressed in all of the city visits that Stans made in the winter of 1969–70. The OMBE literature also gave great prominence to the franchising. And in testimony before Senator Harrison Williams' subcommittee of the Select Committee on Small Business which held hearings on the franchising industry in January 1970, Abe Venable, Director of OMBE, said: "I do think we will make going into business an achievable objective primarily through franchising."

The Administration called franchising its "25 × 25 × 2 program." The brochure unveiling "25 × 25 × 2" announced: "Franchisors are invited to Washington in groups of twenty-five to meet with Secretary Stans and Administrator Sandoval to receive a full briefing on the program. Franchisors will be requested to commit themselves to minority franchising and to pledge their best efforts to provide twenty-five franchise opportunities to minority persons over the next two years."

The brochure explained how the program would work. The franchisors would make their commitments and complete a questionnaire (standard Form 891). The franchisors would also identify the areas which they had earmarked for minority ownership. The Small Business Administration would then help the franchisor search for a minority person to invest in the franchise. If the identified minority candidate could not make a down payment, the SBA would help him get a loan. After the loan was made, more forms were to be filled out.

Like the MESBIC program, however, the franchising scheme that the Administration was promoting for blacks and other minorities had been less than a bargain in the white community. In 1969 the Federal Trade Commission issued a series of bulle-

tins warning people about the pitfalls of franchising. In the same
year New York Attorney General Louis Lefkowitz began a well-
publicized crackdown on the franchising industry. *Parade* Magazine in their issue of June 15, 1969, ran an article entitled:
"Franchise Frauds: How to Lose your Life Savings Without
Really Trying."

In a memorandum to Attorney General Lefkowitz dated January 7, 1970, and made public shortly afterwards, David Clurman
of the New York State Law Department listed the following points
as reflecting the operations of franchisors in the State of New
York:

A. Franchising companies are in many instances fly-by-night operations often with nothing more substantial than fancy multicolored
brochures.

B. Companies are created solely to profit from the sale of franchises
and not from their operations; the knowledge and background necessary to set up a successful operation is often lacking; in many cases the
promised support from the franchisor is either not forthcoming or
worthless.

C. Citizens of this state are surrendering their life savings to buy
worthless franchises.

D. Criminal elements and high pressure salesmen have infiltrated
into the franchise business.

E. Franchise purchasers are not given sufficient information upon
which they can make an intelligent evaluation of their purchase. In
many cases information is either half true or blatantly false.

David Clurman concluded: "There is substantial need for
minimum legislation to protect the public, particularly *lower and
middle income persons* who are being duped with respect to franchise offerings" (emphasis added).

There is no record of any official in the Black Capitalism program making any public reference to the need for protection of
minority people from franchisors.

But certainly only a small part of the industry could be accused of shady dealings. Both Stans and Venable said they were
primarily concerned with providing opportunities for minorities
to get franchises from the "reputable" franchisors, the larger,
more stable operators.

Testifying before Senator Williams' hearings on franchising,

Harold Brown, attorney and franchising expert, cited a number of reputable firms as having a history of illegal or exploitative practices:

"As for specific companies . . . it is interesting to note that some are now being challenged by the FTC or are being sued by franchisees in treble damage actions under the Antitrust Laws and, although it would not be proper to predict the results, the mere existence of such substantial claims would appear necessary information, particularly for prospective franchisees. Included in such companies are *Shell Oil Company, Shakey's* and *Chicken Delight.*

"Other major franchisors have also been hailed into court by their franchisees, including *Denny's Restaurant, Ford Motor Company, Sonoco Oil Company* and other major oil companies."

Brown went on to name *McDonald's, Howard Johnson, International House of Pancakes, Lum's,* and *A to Z Rentals* among others as having engaged in exploitative practices vis-à-vis franchisees.

But for the pitchmen of Black Capitalism such considerations were minor flaws in an otherwise near-perfect picture of business success. The Nixon Administration official who was most enthusiastic about franchising seems to have been Donald Brewer, deputy administrator of the Small Business Administration. Before Senator Williams' subcommittee Brewer sang long praises to franchising. Franchising was a "dramatic success story." It provided the "economic and business advantages inherent to large business"; it offered "ease of entry into the mainstream of the business community" and for people who have been deprived of the opportunity to own their own business, "franchising may well be their shining opportunity and, possibly, their port of last hope." Brewer concluded with a ringing endorsement: "We therefore believe the Federal Government should do everything appropriate to assist those Americans who have the necessary spirit and enterprise to operate a successful franchise establishment."

The only rights Mr. Brewer seemed to be concerned with were those of the franchisors. He said that "the Federal Government must be careful that it does not overprotect the franchisee by depriving the franchisor of the tools to maintain his goodwill and the public's acceptance of his product or service. The Government must recognize that the man who becomes a franchisee must sacrifice a part of his business freedom and must accept some control over his business conduct." Thus the first duty of the Government, according to Brewer, was not to protect the small businessman who borrows its money, but the franchise company that collects the proceeds of the loans. And who are these franchisors that the *Small* Business Administration is so concerned with protecting? They include:

- —Gulf Oil, Shell, Standard of New Jersey, Texaco
- —General Foods, owner of Burger Chef
- —United Fruit, owner of A & W Root Beer and Baskin-Robbins Ice Cream
- —Pillsbury, owner of Burger King
- —Great Western United, owner of Shakey's Pizza
- —Consolidated Foods, owners of Chicken Delight

At times it was hard to tell to what extent Brewer was representing the Government and to what extent he was representing the franchise industry. Again, before Senator Williams' subcommittee:

"Mr. Brewer: 'The value of franchising to the small business entrepreneur and to the American economy is also demonstrated by the record of business successes and failures. Franchises have a remarkably good chance to survive and prosper in our increasingly competitive economy.'

"Senator Williams: 'May I just interrupt there? Whose statistics do you rely on for these statements, yours?'

"Mr. Brewer: 'Ours and Mr. Atkinson's, to some degree, which we will cover here on the record . . . I wish to offer for the record a series of charts prepared by J. F. Atkinson regarding the mortality rate of franchised businesses as compared with that of independently owned businesses. Mr. Atkinson prepared these charts as part of a study on marketing for his master's degree from the Graduate School of Business, Northwestern University of Chicago.'"

And who was Mr. Atkinson? At the time of his testimony Mr. Atkinson was Director of Corporate Planning for *Telequick*, a franchisor of television repair services. His statistics were provided to him by the International Franchise Association, which also published his study. The study itself was attacked by Attorney Brown as based on "some incredible statistical acrobatics."

And who was Mr. Brewer? Let him answer for himself: "From 1963 to 1968, I was President of a concern that for thirty-two years successfully engaged in selling tires and related equipment through several hundred franchisees."

Thus, the OMBE program consisted in large part of promoting the franchise business to minority entrepreneurs. It also provided a special effort to arrange financing, but on terms that simply added to the debt burden of the franchisee, ultimately reducing his ability to succeed. Whether by design or not, it was a program eminently suited to generating sales to the franchisor at the expense of the minority franchisee. The down payment went to the franchisor for his fee. Therefore, whether or not the franchise was successful, the franchisor already had made his money. If the business succeeded, the franchisor of course made money. If it failed, the franchisor stepped in and reclaimed the franchise, selling it to someone else. But the black or Mexican-American who was lured into one of these deals had to pay off the SBA, win, lose, or draw.

The heart of the program was a promise by SBA to consider a loan.

Fortunately for the minority community, the program didn't go very far, although figures indicating success were tossed around with an abandon which put Johnson Administration bureaucrats to shame. In January 1970, Abe Venable claimed that talks with thirty-three franchisors had produced "seven hundred and fifty specific franchise opportunities."[3] At the same time the irrepressible Mr. Brewer estimated that minorities would own five thousand new franchises within two years.

Six months later, Walter Sorg, who headed OMBE's franchising program, told columnist Jack Anderson that two thousand franchises had been placed in the past year. When Anderson checked with some of the franchisors in the Chicago area he found that "most had committed no specific number of franchises. Some weren't planning offerings in the Chicago area at all and had no idea of how their names got on the list."[4]

Shortly afterwards, the OMBE quietly laid the franchising program to rest, although the Agency was not above claiming credit for any and all franchises given to minorities while Richard Nixon was in the White House. In a statement of program accomplishments made in October 1971, OMBE stated that the number of minority-owned franchises increased from 405 in 1969 to 1184 in 1971. When asked where the figures came from, William Rock of OMBE's information office said that they came from the individual franchisors. Was there any way to verify the figures? No. How many was OMBE responsible for? There was no way of knowing.

II. Some Credits, if You Can Find Them

A. *Loans and Loan Guarantees*

The inflated promises and claims of the Administration's Black Capitalism bureaucrats tend to obscure even those areas where real, if limited, accomplishments were made. Deliberately or not, the Administration surrounded the Black Capitalism program with a statistical fog through which it is almost impossible to navigate with any certainty.

In October 1971 the Secretary of Commerce claimed that the "Minority Enterprise Program has grown from an estimated $100 million in Fiscal Year 1968 to $566 million in Fiscal Year 1971. This is an increase of 566 percent." The fiscal year 1968, however, does not include the effect of Democrat Howard Samuels' program on the Small Business Administration which began in Fiscal Year 1969. Of the accomplishments since 1969 Stans said: "Federal grants loans and loan guarantees grew from an estimated $200 million in Fiscal Year 1969 to $425 million in Fiscal Year 1971—an increase of 212.5 percent."

The Secretary's language if not the figures was somewhat inflated. Although $425 million is 212 percent of $200 million, the increase is 112 percent, not 212 percent. But that is a quibble. Presumably the Secretary had let his accountant skills wither somewhat since he took command of the Commerce Department and one shouldn't tax him too hard for the oversight.

But what of the figures themselves? Particularly that "estimate" of $200 million for 1969. When asked for the data that made up those figures, the Administration statisticians admitted that they really had little idea of how it was arrived at. "They didn't keep very good figures in those days," said Bill Rock, OMBE Information Director. Although the figures were good enough to claim a rate of increase past the decimal point.

After some probing it turns out that the only figures available for any meaningful comparisons are those reported by the Small Business Administration for its loans and loan guarantees.

The number and dollar amounts of the loans and loan guarantees made by the Small Business Administration Fiscal Year 1969 and Fiscal Year 1971 are shown below. Disaster loans, displacement loans, and Local Development Corporation loans have been eliminated from the table.*

	Fiscal Year 1969			*Fiscal Year 1971*		
	number	dollar amounts		number	dollar amounts	
"7a" program						
all borrowers	9,494	543.7	million	13,754	923.1	million
minority	1,124	49.0	"	2,123	121.4	"
"EOL" program						
all borrowers	4,229	51.3	"	6,789	92.8	"
minority	2,922	36.8	"	5,451	75.7	"
Total						
all borrowers	13,723	595.0	"	20,543	1015.9	"
minority	4,046	85.8	"	7,574	197.1	"

(NOTE: The "7a" program is the regular SBA loan and guarantee program for small businessmen. The "EOL" program is a liberalized program for disadvantaged borrowers with a maximum of $25,000 per loan.)

Between Fiscal Year 1969 and 1971 the number of minority loans made under the two major SBA programs, 7a and Economic Opportunity Loans, rose from 4,046 to 7,574. The dollar

* Disaster loans are given to victims of natural disasters such as hurricanes, floods, etc. Displacement loans are those given to small businessmen displaced by Federal programs such as highways and urban renewal. Since these loans fluctuate because of circumstances having little to do with the development of minority enterprise, they are eliminated from the calculation. Local Development Corporations (LDC) loans are given to corporations made up of citizens from a given community usually for the purpose of relending the money to private firms willing to locate in their community. The problem statistically is that the SBA declared such loans "minority loans" if only a majority of one business that the LDC supported was minority-owned. Since an LDC can make loans to as many as five private firms, a loan could be classified as a minority loan if only a fraction more than 10 percent of the proceeds went to a minority firm. SBA officials have declared that the figures for LDC minority loans are "extremely weak."

amount of the loans rose from $85.8 million to $197.1 million, an increase of 130 percent. In 1969 minority loans were 14 percent of the total amount of dollars being lent under these programs. In 1971 they were 19 percent.

In terms of the problem it barely touched the surface. The number of minority loans made in 1971 was only 2 percent of the estimated number of minority businesses existing in 1969. If one adds the potential entrepreneurs to the universe of need, the Administration's efforts become minuscule.

The old Republican theme of doing for the poor by doing for the rich is woven throughout the program. Of the total dollars claimed as going to minority entrepreneurs, only one third, $60 million, was provided in direct funds to the minority business. The other two thirds was in the form of guarantees, whereby the SBA guarantees a loan made by a bank to a minority business *at bank rates.* For the minority entrepreneur the difference between a direct loan and an SBA guaranteed loan is the difference between roughly 5½ percent and 8½ percent, enough to spell the difference between success and failure for most small businesses. But for the Administration, a guarantee means that it can take the credit for having made a loan without having to spend any money right away. For the banking community there is even more gain. It takes the SBA out of the loan business where to some extent it might be competing with banks and, more important, it is a good deal. On a five-year loan with a 90 percent SBA guarantee, the bank gets back its entire 10 percent exposure in thirteen months! Everything after that is pure earnings. Not only do guarantees offer private banks a way to get in on business they would not otherwise make, but it gives them a better deal than the typical loans they make.

The banks therefore cannot lose. And the Small Business Administration takes what losses it sustains out of the public treasury several years after the loan is made. It is the minority borrower who is stuck. The minority borrower whose head has been filled with visions of business success, but, as Rosenbloom and Shank point out, whose debt burden is so great thanks to the high interest rates he is being charged that he cannot make a go of it.

In Fiscal Year 1969 the loss ratio† on Economic Opportunity Loans made by the Small Business Administration was 14.6 percent. In 1970 it was 21 percent. In 1971 it was 29 percent and according to SBA technicians still rising! Three out of ten loans made to people classified as disadvantaged were failing, and who knows how many more were on the rocks.

Poor people who begged and scraped and borrowed a few dollars to go into a business about which they knew nothing were suddenly responsible for paying off a loan that a bank would never have made them had it not been for the Federal Government agreeing to make good on the bank's losses. But who was making good on the black man's losses?

B. *Procurement and Deposits*

In the fall of 1969 Secretary Stans said that the Nixon Administration intended to provide minority businesses with $100 million in Federal procurement contracts by the end of June 1970. The commitment was later revised to $120 million by June 1971. By June 1971 the Administration had provided contracts in the order of $66 million to minority-owned firms.

Although it fell short of the professed goal, the $66 million represented some achievement. It is impossible to get reliable figures for years before 1970, but one can safely assume that the $66 million was substantially ahead of whatever the figure might have been for the Johnson Administration. The accomplishment seems to have been a result of the personal interest and dedication of Robert Kunsig, Director of the General Services Administration, who was one of the few people connected with the program to have a will to produce something of value for the minorities.

Using an obscure section of the Small Business Act which allows the Small Business Administration itself to become a Federal contractor and subcontract the job out to a business firm of its choice at a negotiated price, the program provided direct sales and benefits to a number of minority firms. Although there is some indication that some of these minority firms were organ-

† Loans charged off plus the loss estimate applied to the current SBA portfolio.

ized by whites in order to gain the Government contracts,‡ there is no reason to believe that the bulk of this procurement did not go to legitimate minority-owned businesses. However, the Administration's accomplishment in procurement can hardly be called a major success. Sixty-six million dollars represents less than one tenth of 1 percent of the total Federal purchases of $76 billion in 1971.

Some progress was also made with a program to provide minority-owned banks with more deposits. The few minority-owned banks in existence are marginal enterprises both in the sense of being able to survive as a business and in the sense of servicing their minority communities. Andrew Brimmer, a black economist and member of the Federal Reserve Board touched off a controversy in 1969 by concluding in his survey of black banks that their high costs of operation and their lack of access to large deposits made black banks more "ornamental" than useful as instruments of minority economic development.

Black bankers however were among the strongest black supporters of the Administration's program and a highly visible ornament to its success. Therefore, in October 1969 the Administration announced that it had launched a program to supply deposits to the thirty-five minority banks in the country. The first Federal effort was initiated by the Post Office Department, which announced that it was depositing $75 million in black banks throughout the country. The $75 million however turned out to be about $150,000 in cash which the Post Office churned over and over among the minority banks. Explained one business-man person close to the program: "It was like me saying I'll lend you $365,000 for the next year and then lending you a dollar every morning and taking it back again every night."

Don Sneed, President of Unity Bank in the Roxbury section of Boston, told how the Post Office refused even to bring the money down to the bank. "They expected us to hire a security service to collect deposits that we couldn't even make any money on." After a number of irate complaints and a threat by the black bankers to attack the Nixon program publicly, the Post Office pro-

‡ One Government official told one of the authors that he personally knew of several of these minority fronts, although he would not name them.

gram was discontinued and the bankers were promised that more valuable deposits would be made available.

Primarily a result of the work of Sam Beard, a dynamic young consultant from New York hired by OMBE to assist the program, a substantial increase in deposits to minority banks seem to have been made by large corporations. From October 1970 to October 1971 minority banks reported an increase in deposits of over $150 million, of which the Administration claims it is responsible for about $50 million.[5]

III. The Affiliate Program: A Leaf From the Book by LBJ

On October 13, 1971, the President announced a renewed Administration commitment to minority enterprise. To implement the commitment he requested $100 million to be spent on minority enterprise programs over the succeeding eighteen months. An immediate supplemental budget of $40 million was to be used between January and June 1972 and an additional $60 million for the following fiscal year.

The newspaper accounts, while noting that the President's request was far short of the recommendations of the President's own advisory council, nevertheless conjured up the image of more money flowing into the hands of needy minority businessmen. This was inaccurate. The new money was not intended to go directly to minority businessmen. Instead it was to go for "an expanded program of technical assistance and management services."

According to the President: "Approximately 10 percent of these new funds would be used at the national level— to strengthen minority business and trade organizations, to generate broad private programs of marketing and financial assistance, to develop training programs, and to foster other national efforts. The remaining 90 percent of the new money would be spent on the local level—supporting a variety of efforts to identify, train, advise, or assist minority businessmen and to put them in touch with one another and with nonminority businessmen who can provide them with additional help."

With his usual businesslike approach and with a straight face, Secretary Stans elaborated before the House Appropriations subcommittee how the Administration proposed to spend the $40 million.

The chief problem for minority businessmen, according to the Secretary's statement, is that they lack counseling. "In the last four or five years," said the Secretary, "as governments and private lending institutions have received more and more applications for minority business financing, they have become increasingly unable to give minority businessmen the hours of counseling that are often necessary to formulate business plans, fill out complicated applications, and secure outside advice."

The answer? Local Business Development Organizations, or "BDOs" to use the Secretary's shorthand. A BDO is an organization with eleven professionals and an annual budget of $250,000. It has an "outreach function"—speaking at conferences and seminars, meeting with persons who have a tentative interest in business, and in other ways making known the kinds of services and resources that are available to qualified applicants. BDOs also have a data collection function, and they have a "packaging" function "to assist the entrepreneur in preparing a plan for his business." Finally the BDO has a "management assistance" function.

The Secretary said that the Administration would spend more than $24 million on BDOs.

And $2 million on Contractor's Assistance Centers.

And $1.5 million on minority business and trade associations.

And $800,000 on National Business Development Organizations (NBDOs).

All in all the Secretary said he planned to establish or support 171 organizations in at least fifty state urban and rural areas.

But that was not all.

Another $3.8 million was to be spent on Business Resource Centers (BRCs). What is a BRC? Let the Secretary explain:

> The need for a vehicle such as the Business Resource Center and the productivity of the projects which BRC will undertake both are well established. In Los Angeles, the five MESBICs, nine banks, and five Business Development Organizations that have long been central parts of the Los Angeles local minority enterprise program recently decided to jointly sponsor an organization called MECLA, which is the forerunner to the BRC. The MECLA concept is simple: all of the

organizations who sponsor it have need for specialized management and technical assistance for their clients on a regular basis; each to some extent furnishes the assistance from its own staff or uses volunteers from the private sector. But none has enough staff, contacts, or time to be able to obtain the kind of assistance that every client needs all of the time. By merging their requirements, they are able to call on a central staff (MECLA) of full-time experienced professional specialists who can usually respond immediately to requests that otherwise would take wasteful time and effort to fill.

Thus if nineteen institutions in Los Angeles cannot do the job they are being paid for, add another.

After that enlightening statement, Stans went on with the rest of his program:

Private resource programs, intermediate organizations between national organizations and local organizations whose job was to "mobilize" everyone else would get $600,000.

Contractors give technical assistance to BDOs who themselves were supposed to give technical assistance would get $780,000.

Business management development programs to give more training and technical assistance to whomever is left get $1,400,000.

States would get $2,100,000 to start setting up their own OMBEs. The presumed goal here was to reproduce all of the above in fifty states.

And finally Stans said he needed one million dollars to experiment to see if there were more programs that he hadn't thought of yet.

Supervising all of this were 309 employees supported by an administrative budget of $5,597,000.

And not one thin dime for a black businessman!

Stans approvingly quotes the figure that it cost only $4,400 for each "BDO" to service a minority businessman for a year. But a study of the MESBIC program made by his own staff says that a minority businessman on the average can scrape up only $4,000 to go into business![6] Thus the bureaucracy Nixon created to assist minority businesses cost more than the minority businessmen needed to start up the business. One wonders what the effect would have been if OMBE had chosen to assist the small businessman by sending him the check for what it would have cost to help him.

As one official who requested anonymity said: "What with BDOs, MESBICs, BRCs, MECLAs, State OMBEs and all the rest we need to hire each black businessman a secretary just to keep his technical assistors off his back. When is he ever going to have time to run his business?"

In terms of getting help to minority businessmen the new program* was ridiculous. Organizations piled on top of organizations and a top-heavy bureaucracy to administer it all. It was an amazing performance for a conservative investment banker with a reputation for being tightfisted with the Government's money—at least where social programs were concerned.

But for a member of Richard Nixon's re-election team it was not at all surprising, and Lyndon Baines Johnson and the Democratic Pros who used the model cities and antipoverty programs in the same way would not have raised an eyebrow—except perhaps for the hypocrisy of the Republican strategy.

For the surest way of providing that people have a stake in your re-election is to make their jobs depend on it. Phase II of the OMBE program was a thinly disguised effort to buy off important portions of the minority leadership all over the country. The people who get jobs at BDOs and similar kinds of community organizations tend to be among the most educated, most vocal, and most politically active people in the neighborhood.

Certainly the President could not have expected that he would get a majority of the minority vote, but the provision of steady jobs to twenty-five hundred to three thousand educated politically active people in the ghettos and barrios at the very least has the potential for neutralizing politically hostile areas.

One might have thought that for the sake of appearances the Administration would have allocated some part of the budget to the minority businessmen in whose name they were spending the money (even the Democrats tried to spread it around). But no, the program was the same businesslike approach to life that has always characterized clear-thinking Republicans.

Said Stans to the appropriations committee:

* Taking a cue from the Administration's national economic policies, the Secretary called this the Phase II OMBE program.

"Before turning to specific program request, it may be helpful to recapitulate the approach taken by this administration toward minority enterprise. The essence of our approach has been one of cautious expansion. This has been exemplified by our practice of testing programs before launching them on a national scale, and by our refusal to ask for new funds unless there were assurances that they could be spent effectively."

IV. ONE THING THEY DID NOT DO

The industry with the largest number of minority entrepreneurs is farming. The most recent Census of Agriculture reported that there were two hundred thousand farms operated by nonwhites in the United States in 1964. This was more than the total number of retail establishments owned by minorities in 1969.

The bulk of the minority farming industry is concentrated in some hundred thousand black-operated farms, primarily in the South. Most of the black farmers are tenants or sharecroppers who work on leased land owned by others. Tenant farmers and sharecroppers take all of the risks of entrepreneurship and have none of the advantages of ownership. They endure lives of hard work and suffering and are among the most exploited class in America.

American agriculture is perhaps the best example of the comment of Michael Harrington that America is a land of socialism for the rich and free enterprise for the poor.[7] For the past half century the U.S. Department of Agriculture has been dedicated to the growth and expansion of large-scale corporately owned American farming. The Department provides large farmers with fixed and operating capital, it supports their markets, it absorbs their research and development costs, and gives them continual technical assistance. It even pays them not to produce. If ever there was a socialized industry in America, it is in agriculture. But not for small farmers. And least of all for the blacks.

The black man sees very little of this aid. Department of Agriculture programs are run by highly politicized state and local government systems which reinforce local bias against blacks. The U.S. Civil Rights Commission in 1965 released a detailed study of the operations of the Agriculture Department which showed that the Department was riddled with discriminatory practices in its programs and personnel policies.[8]

One of the results is that black farmers in the South have been losing their land at an alarming rate over the past two decades. In 1950 there were about a half million black farms as compared to slightly under a hundred thousand today.

It is part of conventional economic wisdom that black farmers have declined because they are likely to be small and therefore not as competitive as large farms. Recent studies however suggest that this is not necessarily the case. A report by the University of Texas on the relationship between farm size and the displacement of black families in the South concludes that the fact that so many blacks owning relatively large farms have been forced off the land suggests that it is the lack of capital rather than the small size of the farms that is destroying the black agriculture in the South.[9] The large investments by the Department of Agriculture in developing new machinery and techniques make survival in farming dependent upon being able to acquire new equipment and technical aid. White farmers are given both financial and technical assistance through the local banks and the programs of the Department of Agriculture. Black farmers are not and thus they cannot compete.

As part of that short-lived burst of liberalism in the U.S. Congress in 1964–65, the Economic Opportunity Act, which authorized the War on Poverty, contained provisions to provide some financing for the poor farmers who otherwise could not "qualify" for regular loans made by the Farmers Home Administration, an agency of the Agriculture Department. And as part of the compromises that diluted somewhat the effect of that burst of liberalism, the Farmers Home Administration was given the responsibility for running it.

The program, called the Economic Opportunity Rural Loan Program, was predictably not administered in the spirit of the legislation. For the first few years few of the loans even went to blacks. Even the conservative General Accounting Office condemned the Agriculture Department for failing to make loans to those who needed them most, and for giving more technical assistance to rich and middle-class farmers than to poor ones.

Even when loans were made they sometimes increased the

black farmers' problems rather than solved them. Loan applications were processed by local three-man committees, one of the members of which was usually the local white farm machinery dealer. When the black farmer would apply for a loan, the farm machinery dealer would try to talk him into using the loan for whatever piece of equipment he had in stock. It was often made very clear to the farmer that he would not get the loan unless he bought the machine, whether he needed it or not. If the black farmer "bit," the Farmers Home Administration would make him a loan with the proceeds going to pay off the machinery dealer. If, as frequently happened, the machinery was not suited to the farmer's needs, it would not generate enough income to pay for the loan. But the black farmer was still liable for the repayment to the Federal Government, with the result in some cases that the farmer went bankrupt and, if he had title to it, lost his farm.

Despite the complaints of a few Southern Civil Rights groups and a few antipoverty bureaucrats† the Department of Agriculture continued to mishandle the program. Nevertheless some money was going to poor farmers who otherwise would not get anything. And at the same time the revolving loan fund set up to finance the program grew to about one hundred million dollars by 1971.

That year, facing a huge Federal deficit, the Nixon Administration feverishly began looking for places to cut the budget and decided that the Rural Loan Program was such a place. So the budget for Fiscal Year 1972 provided that the program would be discontinued and *the loan fund be turned back to the Treasury*. Representatives of black organizations and others protested to the Administration and to Congress. The operation of the program was bad enough, but to take the fund that had been set up to aid poor farmers and use it to solve the Nixon Administration's budget problems was outrageous. As one witness before the Senate subcommittee on Employment, Manpower and

† One of the Republican rationales for cutting OEO's budget was that the job of OEO was to get *other* agencies to change their programs to better serve the poor. But when people in OEO asked Donald Rumsfeld to try to change the Department of Agriculture's program he replied that he didn't think it proper for OEO to get into questions of loans and other "banking" issues.

Poverty pointed out: "In 1967, 817 large farms in the State of Mississippi received an average of more than $45,000 each in subsidies. If the present Administration plan is adopted a poor farmer in the same state will not even be able to get a loan. Moreover, the money that those poor farmers are paying back on former loans will be used to subsidize large corporate plantations."

Finally, in response to these pleas, Senators Kennedy and Javits introduced legislation to save the loan fund for the poor farmers and to reorganize the program, taking it out of the hands of the Department of Agriculture. The plan was made part of a package of antipoverty legislation which included a new life for the OEO and a bill providing expanded child care services. The package passed both houses of Congress but was vetoed by the President in December 1971. Among the objections the White House had to the bill was that it prevented other agencies, like the Department of Agriculture, from running some of the antipoverty programs.

One of the stated primary purposes for OMBE was to be an advocate for minority businessmen within the U.S. Government. Yet there is no record, on paper or in the memory of people in OMBE or the Bureau of the Budget, of any attempt by OMBE to raise the cause of the minority farmer. Despite the fact that farming was the industry with the largest number of black capitalists and was also most susceptible to Government suasion, Maurice Stans took little notice of it. It was, however, brought to his attention at least once. At the meeting of Federal officials on the OMBE program in March 1970 one bureaucrat asked about black farmers. Stans said that he thought the Department of Agriculture had that situation well in hand.

11 | CORPORATE AND GOVERNMENT LIBERALISM REVISITED

By early 1972 it had become apparent that the Nixon Administration had no comprehensive strategy for fostering minority economic development. It was also apparent that most Federal programs designed to serve this end were either bogged down in internal bureaucratic conflicts or beset by budgetary problems. Moreover, private-sector efforts were grinding virtually to a halt. In spite of President Nixon's near-fanatical faith in the "free enterprise system," which he called the "greatest instrument of change and of progress the world has ever known," the "system" had in fact proved to be of little help to minority and low-income Americans. The promises and pledges that were made by leaders of corporate America in 1965–68 were not matched by performance. By early 1972, after four years of "policy by press release" and hastily conceived crash programs, the results of private sector efforts could be summed up thus:

(1) There was no overall, coherent private sector strategy;

(2) Corporate involvement in and financial institution support of economic development had been largely devoted to advertising and public relations;

(3) Private sector coalitions and volunteer advisory/support groups had been overpublicized and underproductive;

(4) Business leaders had yet to perceive the full dimensions of economic development as a multifaceted, community issue;

(5) The business establishment was still unwilling to encourage the development of new institutions (such as CDCs) for the minority (poor) community that might one day demand interaction on the basis of real equality.

(6) Time was running out. Those minority and community leaders who were at least willing to give the private sector a chance—as Max Ways said back in 1968, "Business is the one important segment of society Negroes today do not regard with suspicion"—were becoming more distrustful of the business community and were under increasing pressures from their own constituencies to deliver concrete projects.

In essence then, the desire for corporate deliverance—prominent in the period of 1967–69—was being dashed by the painful experiences of '69, '70, and '71. This disappointment was compounded by raised expectations fueled by overly enthusiastic corporate public relations departments. It was an aspect of the whole effort that was both unnecessary and revealing. There were many examples of the duplicitous nature of myth-building, but one, in particular, stands out. It was symbolic of the emptiness of the promises.

This high point for corporate machismo came in early 1969 when H. R. Romnes, the Chairman of the Board of AT&T, took time out from a busy schedule to speak out on the achievements of the private sector on a prime-time television program.

His corporation presumably thought the subject important enough to pay for both the commercial time and the preparation of four spot commercials extolling the virtues of corporate America. (In retrospect, they were much more convincing than the earlier Nixon campaign spots.) The manner in which they were presented demonstrates that private industry would not be cheap about its desire to create an image of the private sector's "grave" concern about social problems and its role in actively providing a solution.

The public relations gambit occurred on an hour and a half national network show on April 17, 1969. It was part of an NBC *White Paper* series, "The Ordeal of the American City." This particular show was entitled "Confrontation." The subject matter was the problems of San Francisco, and the show depicted, in a rather heavy-handed manner—by means of action shots, films, narratives, and interviews—how the faculty and student strikers at San Francisco State College contributed, specifically, to the deterioration of San Francisco and, generally, to the overall urban crisis. Lest viewers be left with a picture of unmitigated discouragement, however, the sponsors provided "commercials," *not* promoting the delights of their products, but reporting on their own sense of responsibility as representatives of the private sector in bringing the benefits of free enterprise to black (chicano, Indian) America.

The show opened with a face shot of Mr. Romnes, who righteously announced that it was more important to relinquish his company's valuable commercial time to demonstrate what industry was doing to save the ghettos and to aid minority groups.*

There were four "American dream" commercials. Each depicted for the home viewers how a once jobless and young black (then Indian, then Mexican-American) dropout had been given a new lease on life by the sponsoring corporation's commitment!

The commercials went something like this:

In Portland, Oregon, there was the Albina Corporation. They're *doing* this and that and creating black capitalists and jobs and it's really a helluva operation. One cat is rapping at the camera from behind a welder's mask about how he's gonna own the business soon . . . with a little more help from "the man" . . .

In Philadelphia there's this Project-In whereby a group of Negro youngsters were entreated to some uplifting words as to how one day, they too could . . . become "captains of industry" with just a little hard work, savings, and some practice. It all seemed so simple, the old Andrew Carnegie pitch; it was geared to turn the kids on.

And in New Mexico, industry (in this case Dreyer Pickles) was doing all those wonderful things and, oh boy, aren't they making the Injuns happy. They even dragged out the Chief of the Isleta tribe to say a few words for Dreyer Pickles. It really warmed one's heart to know that something was happening, that industry really cared.

Finally, there was a commercial on Coors Beer and all that it was doing for the chicanos.

* Apparently Mr. Romnes opened all of the segments of the four-part series in the same manner.

It just happens, however, that the facts were a little different. Albina Corporation was started with a $300,000 OEO grant and was then on its second round. It obtained a lease-guarantee purchase-back from SBA and a forty-to-fifty-man MA-3 training contract from Department of Labor. It might possibly be owned by the blacks by 1977. Yes, one individual, Mr. L. J. Niedermeyer, was helpful. No, industry did not lift a finger—the Federal Government put in every red cent. Albina is now out of business.

The "Philadelphia story" was absurd: the industry didn't organize the program; blacks did.

And out in badlands of New Mexico, the Isleta Indians have been negotiating for forty years and still don't own the factory.

The commercial on Coors Beer was the real payoff. It is an exemplary performance of the sleight-of-hand blarney that private industry feeds the American people. The Chairman of the Board of AT&T need not have divested their corporations of $50,000 (pro-rated) worth of advertising on the NBC "Free Enterprise Doing Their Thing" extravaganza on behalf of Coors. For Coors may "brew their beer with pure mountain water"† but they certainly didn't mix their lily-white staff with chicanos.

At the very same time that industry was singing its misleading and expensive commercials to the suburban TV-viewing, white audiences, Coors was being boycotted by the same people it claimed to help, because it had maintained a discriminatory hiring policy. With regard to the company's doing its bit re economic development of ghettos or helping minority entrepreneurs —at the time of that show *they hadn't invested one head off a glass of brew.*

Just to keep the record straight for AT&T, NBC, and the advertising agency that prepared the commercial, it was reported that Coors gave about $1,200 in 1968 to a teen-age educational project (a pittance of a tax deduction). To have taken a $50,000‡ TV commercial to tell about a $1,200 contribution to a bilingual reading program is an obscene gesture, typical of the "colonial welfare" mentality of American industry.

These compelling and uplifting presentations of the American

† As their billboard advertising—throughout the West—proclaims!
‡ It is estimated that the four shows cost AT&T and its Bell subsidiaries in excess of $1,000,000.

corporate helping hand gave new hope and confidence to millions of viewers. Indeed, the companies found this so important an achievement that the investment in dollars on the show, unfortunately, seemed to have left virtually nothing for the actual economic assistance programs being displayed. Viewers were discretely spared the disappointing contrast between image and reality. They never learned that the corporate sponsors of the television show were not *actually* involved in economic development.

If commercials are deceptive about what companies have achieved in the battle against underarm perspiration, there might even be a lawsuit. But the divergence between p.r. and substance in ads* (and programs) on poverty and consumerism is so endemic that substantial achievement to back up claims is treated not only as secondary but almost as out of the question as if the only problem were to stay one promise ahead of the hopes one has betrayed.

These themes have tended to create the impression that the "laissez faire" wheels of American corporate ingenuity are in full motion, spinning off all sorts of beneficial programs around the country. For the TV-viewing, suburban "silent majority" this has served merely to reinforce the suspicion that ". . . too much was already being done for *those* people." For the corporate liberals of American industry the sweet lullabies of free-enterprise benevolence were both reassuring and self-seductive. For the forty-five million or so black, Mexican-American, Puerto Rican, Indian, and white poor—who have become used to a mixed bag of other promising and catchy tunes in the past five years—there has been a good deal of choreography, but . . . *not much music!*

The mystique of private-enterprise "volunteerism" had not only become central to the policy of the Administration but it was

* There have also been many specific instances where corporations have exercised negative "influence" over the media. Two examples that come to mind are when the Lipton Soup Co. canceled its advertising in the Cleveland *Plain Dealer* after a consumer article on salmonella in soup and when Publix and the Winn-Dixie Food stores stopped advertising, after a critical article about supermarkets, in the Miami *News*.

As one public affairs TV executive said, "Those guys can lean on you so hard that they make your teeth rattle."[1]

widely accepted in the business community, which is said to be given to hardheadedness.

It should be recalled that Nixon interlaced his expansive references to the role of the private sector with strong allusions to "the spirit of volunteerism." Needless to say, this spirit was *contrived* and *self-serving*.

Consistent with his stated belief in volunteerism, the President pledged:

> "As one of the first tasks of the New Administration . . . I intend to set up a national clearinghouse for information on voluntary activities—on what's been tried, what the difficulties have been and what the solutions are. By setting up a comprehensive, computerized data bank, the Government can make it possible for groups or individuals anywhere in the country to discover at once what the experience of . . .
>
> "But I intend to go beyond making information available. I will expect Federal departments concerned with social problems all to be actively dedicated to the stimulation of new voluntary efforts—and I will expect the Secretaries of these departments to make this a personal responsibility."

He further stated that

> "private enterprise, far more effectively than the Government, can provide the jobs, train the unemployed, build the homes, offer the new opportunities which will produce progress—not promises—in solving the problems of America."

Thus it was easy to comprehend how the President, Stans, Moynihan, Sandoval, Romney, Rumsfeld, and other high Administration officials made a fetish out of "entrepreneurial noblesse oblige."

The thrust of Nixon's social strategy (urban/minority) was based on two premises—black capitalism and corporate volunteerism—and these premises rested on the assumption that corporate America could and would deliver the goods. As time wore on and the facts began to accumulate it was increasingly obvious that he was striking out on both counts—assumption and premises.

The concept of Corporate Volunteerism was nearly a total disaster. Sure there were some corporations who attempted to rally support for social programs (as was mentioned in Chapter 6); but the vast majority of corporations did nothing more than appoint an Urban Affairs officer or Community Relations Director who had no power and little money. More often than not when the corporation was under pressure, it referred minority/community problems to the new executive, who doled out, piecemeal—$250 to $1,000 donations, here and there—contributions for charity affairs, swimming pools, baseball bats, jazz mobiles, and street theater. But lunches in exquisite dining rooms on the top floor of corporate edifices were mainly a seduction game, and one that was time-consuming. It was certainly no substitute for rolling up the sleeves and sitting down for some hard long-range planning. The coffers of establishment minority organizations like the Urban League, the NAACP, and the SCLC swelled with guilt money for about two years. But even those symbolic gestures began to diminish by 1970.

By 1971, 99 percent of America still hadn't even heard of the National Center for Voluntary Action, the organization that Nixon set up to "enlist those millions of Americans who stand ready to serve and help, if only they knew what to do and how." If the National Center has undertaken any major project on behalf of low-income or minority groups it must have been the most well-kept secret in the country.

Even the conservative *Wall Street Journal,* a strong supporter of the President's initial dramatic appeals to corporate volunteerism, admitted that the response was nonexistent.

It said:

> Not many people have heard of Horace Sheldon. But the very fact of his anonymity tells something important about the Nixon Administration.
> Mr. Sheldon is President of the National Center for Voluntary Action. Voluntary Action was candidate Richard M. Nixon's pet program to help solve the nation's social problems . . .
> Now, two years later, those millions of Americans still don't know what to do and how. Nor do they know Mr. Sheldon, because he is only an "interim" President; he was lent to the NCVA by Ford Motor Co. as a substitute for former football coach Charles (Bud) Wilkinson, who quit abruptly after seven months at the helm to return to Oklahoma and politics.
> Though Mr. Sheldon is optimistic about the voluntary program's fu-

ture, he does concede, in masterful understatement, that "we have not been able to treat very many of the nation's social problems up to now." Thus even its friends conclude that Voluntary Action has been stillborn . . .

. . . the record also contains those items that have disappeared or been de-emphasized. What happened? Though the reason differs in each case, the general explanation—as is not uncommon in the early years of a new President—lies in a combination of organizational inexperience, outright ineptitude, conscious or unconscious neglect and second thoughts.[2]

Why—in spite of the growing body of experience and expertise—is there such a lack of creative imagination on the part of establishment leadership within the Administration and in the private sector? Richard Nixon, Maurice Stans, Hilary Sandoval, Jr., Donald Rumsfeld, George Romney, David Rockefeller, James Roche, Harold Geneen, George Moore, and H. R. Romnes are, to the man, successful business and professional men who have assumed public responsibility and leadership roles. They have committed themselves (at least verbally) to the general economic betterment of the poor and/or minority groups. Yet, collectively, they were unable to perceive that in any way the subjects of their attention might have something to contribute. Why? It is reasonable to assume that they simply do not want any program which would put political or economic power in the hands of the poor to succeed.†

Moving beyond the question of motivation, then, it also seems possible that the personal styles and backgrounds of these individuals would render them both insensitive and unequal to their tasks, in spite of the sincerity of their intentions. For, not one of them comprehends how a poor community is organized. Not one of them has a perceptual framework upon which to make a rational judgment. And ultimately more damning, they all *listen* to information and data which reinforces their own limited conceptual views rather than *hearing* critical intelligence which

† Harold Lasswell provides further valuable insights into the political motivation of leadership. He suggests that a craving for deference is "displaced upon public objects (persons and practices connected with the power process)." He concludes that the drive for power, inherent in the political personality, is grounded in: (1) private motives, (2) displaced on public objects, and (3) rationalized in the "public interest."[3]

relates to the reality of a way of life that is alien to their common experience. If each one has his own preconceived notions about how to get things done—which may work for political parties, corporate law firms, banks, Pepsi-Cola, General Motors, ITT, American Motors, AT&T, or Chase Manhattan Bank, but not one of them seems to behave as though a lesser human being (i.e., minority or poor-community leaders) might provide some correct answers or be on the right track. Furthermore, the establishment leaders seem to be caught in a double bind; for not only do they take the wrong tack but they also fail to realize how pitiful their attempts are because they are inclined to be extremely self-righteous and/or hopelessly rigid. These are problems peculiar to the mentality of a ruling elite, infatuated with its own charitability.

A former Secretary of Commerce once wrote:

> . . . The vast repetitive operations are dulling the human mind . . . The aggregation of great wealth with its power to economic domination presents social and economic ills which we are constantly struggling to remedy.

And a former President of the United States stated that the

> American people from bitter experience have a rightful fear that great business units might be used to dominate our industrial life and by illegal and unethical practices destroy equality of opportunity.

That President was not LBJ, JFK, FDR, or HST; the Secretary of Commerce was not a radical populist. In fact, they were one in the same person, Herbert Hoover. It is ironic that so many establishment "liberal" columnists liken Nixon to Hoover, thus displaying the mind of the knee-jerk liberal who hasn't learned anything new since the end of the New Deal. Hoover had many shortcomings, but he maneuvered beyond belief to keep that which belonged to the public out of the hands of private industry. Instead of rereading their own warmed-over press releases or the Nielsen ratings, Nixon and his Cabinet would do well to read Hoover's book *American Individualism*. Hoover's failures and shortcomings were economic in nature, but even he gave up believing in the "trickle-down theory." He, in fact, was a strong advocate of public control over the private sector and believed that the control should be in the interest of the community development, social and economic.

What is especially tragic is that those who were proclaiming the loudest to have the most interest in promoting social and economic development—and are in the best position to really get something done—seem to have totally overlooked the gut of this crucial issue. For—at a minimum—in order to insure the success of *any* economic development project, the painful experiences of the past several years have clearly demonstrated that there must be well-defined mechanisms to provide for community involvement. (Most sharp-eyed leaders of minority and poor communities have acquired enough smarts to know that in the absence of these mechanisms, the rich and upper-middle class will continue to grow wealthier, the middle class will become squeezed further, and the poor will continue to expend their energies fighting for the crumbs.) Yet, there was not one individual among the top echelon of establishment (Government or business) decision-makers who had exhibited either the slightest comprehension of or the slightest sympathy for the drive for economic development and political equality as it exists in America today.

The characteristics of the white establishment's reaction to the drive for community economic development has been marked by an unwillingness to make a high risk loan in a significantly higher risk area, the unwillingness to invest significant capital in an inflation-glutted economy, the desire to promote corner candy stores with microbes of capital in an economy heavily populated by successful new business concentrated in technical industries and sophisticated services.

They conveniently forget that American industry was heavily subsidized in the nineteenth and twentieth centuries by Federal, state, and local government. They forget that several industries such as the railroads, shipbuilding and aerospace are heavily financed by Government spending. They forget about the oil tax-depletion allowance. They willy-nilly ignore the fact that many other industries are propped up, supported, protected by insuperable tariff barriers and often totally financed by the Government. How many corporations are being exclusively subsidized by the Pentagon? The challenge of community economic development is not *whether* national policy can create private wealth; the defense budget *has been* demonstrating this capacity quite adequately. *In the last twenty-five years multibillion-dollar corporations have been created out of whole cloth by the grace of Government.* This exotic notion of socialism for the rich and capitalism for the poor must be dispelled.

Consistent with its summary of "volunteerism" the *Wall Street Journal* continues by saying:

> Voluntary Action's stillborn state contains many of these elements. From the official kick-off in Mr. Nixon's inaugural address, the program has been hampered by changing direction and personnel. Max Fisher, the Detroit financier and friend of Urban Secretary George Romney, and Robert Shea of the American Red Cross masterminded the early organizational effort. It was thought that Mr. Fisher would assume command of the national center upon its establishment, but he didn't. Mr. Shea bowed out, too. An arduous search for a prominent President failed to turn up anybody. So Mr. Nixon's friend, Mr. Wilkinson, was tapped.
>
> "Look," says a disappointed spokesman for the U.S. Chamber of Commerce, which embraced the voluntary plan eagerly at its inception, "it really hasn't gotten off the ground yet. Ineptness has characterized the program from the start. And Bud Wilkinson didn't exactly help matters." This dismay is shared by others in the world of voluntarism.
>
> Much of Voluntary Action's appeal to President Nixon rested in his view that it could serve as a substitute for costly Federal aid programs. Black capitalism held the same allure. "The ghettos of our cities will be remade, lastingly remade, when the people in them have the will, the power, the resources and the skills to remake them," he said during the 1968 campaign. "They won't be remade by Government billions."[4]

The results were becoming painfully obvious to all but a semiliterate Cinderella, yet spokesmen for the private sector kept up the rhetorical charade while their Governmental apologists looked for other excuses, wherever they could find them.

James Roche, the Chairman of General Motors Corporation, is probably the single most powerful businessman in the country.‡ He said of Black Capitalism, "It is for us who have worked within and gained from the free enterprise system, to help others to share in it. It is us, who most cherish the freedom in free enterprise, to assure that it is freely open to everyone."[6] And so it goes . . . From 1961 to 1970 General Motors received over $4 billion from the Federal Government in defense contracts alone. He wasn't talking about free enterprise; he meant to say "corporate socialism."

Another spokesman for corporate America took a more pragmatic approach—the best defense being an offense. *Barron's National Business & Financial Weekly* pulled out an old chestnut and blamed the urban/black crisis on the universities and those people who were "wrongly" educated. In a front-page editorial Barron's told businessmen and corporations to stop supporting the *real culprits.** It said:

> The cadres marching on American business have trained at Berkeley, Wisconsin, Cornell, and hundreds of other schools. The propaganda which has set them in motion has been going on a lot longer. Isn't it incredible that American businessmen and financiers are still so naïve as to think they are being charitable when they support institutions and individuals who, measure by measure, move us all closer to the end of the capitalist system?[7]

Meanwhile, back in Washington, Secretary Stans was blaming the poor performance of corporations—among the group being General Motors, which had initially welched on a MESBIC com-

‡ In his capacity as chairman of General Motors he controls $24 billion each year in gross sales, giving him an annual budget bigger than any state in the country and every country in the world except the United States and the Soviet Union. General Motors employs 800,000 people, the largest employer in the country except the Federal Government. General Motors sells cars to more than three million people through more than thirteen thousand dealers (of whom ten are nonwhite). Its customers buy cars, purchase tires, buy gas and oil, and drive on highways. General Motors has nearly a million and a half shareholders who get a small chunk of the profits each year. It has $8 billion of cash surplus on deposit at some 380 banks around the world. General Motors annually provides some $250 million of advertising revenue to hundreds of television and radio stations, as well as to newspapers and magazines. It is a major client for many law firms around the country and a large source of scholarship and research money for many of our universities.[5]

* Italics added.

mitment—on the sluggishness of the overall economy. "I think we've made extraordinary progress, considering the state of the economy," said Under Secretary of Commerce Rocco C. Siciliano. "It's hard to imbue businessmen with social consciousness when business is bad."[8] But excuses and apologies could not explain away the failures, for they were becoming a matter of record. The fall-back myth was that the private sector needed prosperity to acquire a social conscience. But, this was based on the premise that in 1968 and 1969 there was solid accomplishment and that one must expect a slight retreat in 1970. The truth of the matter is that very little was accomplished in 1968 and 1969, and still less was happening in 1970. It also reveals the cynicism of the whole assumption that corporate America will take an interest in minority groups, public good, and community betterment only when profits are up. The facts of life were that the corporations had beat a hasty retreat when economic conditions weren't so bad.

What did this general retrenchment mean to the minority community? How did it affect job-training efforts, "corporate spin-offs," loans to minority businessmen, contracts for medium-sized minority companies, new markets in housing, and other programs that were discussed in Chapter 6? What were the reactions of various industries such as banking and life insurance?

By 1970 the manpower and job-training efforts of the private sector were in total disrepute. Programs such as those sponsored by the National Alliance of Businessmen had just about lost their last ounce of credibility. Hard-core were trained by corporations at Federal expense, not for jobs, but to move on to yet other job-training programs.

"Many companies," according to Whitney Young, Jr., "limit their concern to press releases, empty speeches, or less. I remember listening," he said, "to the head of a major corporation brag about all his firm was doing. After some close questioning, I found the sum total of these grand efforts added up to less than two dozen summer jobs for black youths in only three of the sixty cities in which that company operates."[9]

By early 1971 there was hardly a whisper about new corporate "spinoffs," and some of the well-publicized ones that were started back in 1967 and 1968 had collapsed. Such was the fate of the E.G.&G. operation in Roxbury, the Avco plant in Dorchester, and the Crown Zellerbach effort in San Francisco. And those that hadn't folded were, with rare exception, teetering on the brink.

Banking policies, which were traditionally bad, had become worse. Most banks simply refused to change their rigid management and inflexible loan policies. The criteria and procedures for loans were still rigged to keep potential minority entrepreneurs running around the revolving doors at the entrance of the banks. Discriminatory practices of the past hardened as money became tighter. Circumstances became *so* outrageous that a member of the *U.S. Federal Reserve*'s Board of Governors, Sherman J. Maisel, finally blasted the banking community in a speech before the National Conference of Christians and Jews in Omaha, Nebraska. Maisel said that by ignoring the problems of the ghetto —by refusing to grant loans to inner-city projects—the banking community had "helped create major social and economic problems of crime, decay, and segregation."[10]

Maisel went right down the line in spelling out how the discriminatory practices of the major lending institutions of our nation were in fact endangering our urban centers. He pointed out how banks used different risk factors in determining how loans are given, according to color. Maisel further accused the banking community of acute myopia. He stated that, "As a result, banks may allocate their resources so as to endanger their own long-term profitability, and also to reduce far below optimum the use of their communities' human and economic resources."[11] This damning and open indictment of the banking industry finally echoed what minorities and community spokesmen had been saying for years. But this time the charge was made by a member of the nation's highest regulatory body for the industry.

Most industry officials and economists agree that the record boom in housing that occurred in 1971 will continue in 1972. The most optimistic experts believe that housing starts will rise about 12 percent in 1972 compared with the 37 percent increase in 1971. This means that more money for housing is, and will be, available. It also means a healthy growth for the construction industry and for contractors. This rosy picture for white builders and contractors will doubtless have little effect on the minority contractors, however. For them the outlook is bleak.

The future of minority-group contractors in the United States is very uncertain at best, according to a report by the *Race Relations Information Center* (Nashville, Tennessee). Among the points made in the report:

1. In many cities, the once-lucrative single-family dwelling business is giving way to large apartment complexes and subdivisions that are "out of reach of minority contractors." The large commercial construction work has never been open to minority firms.

2. With nearly $100 billion projected to be spent this year on construction, minority-group contractors, most of whom are black, are expected to earn less than $500,000—only one half of 1 percent of the total.

3. Of the estimated 870,000 construction firms in the United States, fewer than 8,000 are minority-group firms.

4. Only 5 percent of the nation's minority construction firms are capable of handling jobs in excess of $200,000 because of problems ranging from capacity to bonding.

Noting that the number of minority contractors is declining, that the nonprofit housing corporations have not generated much work, that the Federal Government's efforts have been anemic, and that private agencies have not been able to fund programs significantly, the report says that minority contractors see at least two alternatives left if they are to overcome the obstacles the white-controlled construction industry has placed in their paths:

*joint ventures with those white contractors who want to help their black counterparts. These are few but are growing in number. Joint ventures will provide the white contractor with the entree needed to build in the inner-city ghettos, as well as help the minority contractor establish himself as a viable entity.

*mergers with other firms. Through mergers and formations of consortiums (in Boston, for example) black contractors are able to pool their resources, management know-how, and building capacity. This type of project would provide the same, if not better, advantages as a joint venture.[12]

By the end of 1971 it had also become clear that the life insurance industry was ready to throw in the towel. The urban investment program of the industry had always been hailed by corporate boosters as the single-most concrete example of private-sector commitment. However, it was reported that the decision to discontinue the program was reached at a meeting of representatives of seventy-nine life and health insurance companies on October 10 and 11 in Harrison, New York. The top executives at the private confab discussed a wide range of social issues confronting the industry and concluded that the industry as a whole would no longer continue to make the kinds of investments in socially oriented programs that they had made in the past.[13]

As corporate America backed off from its commitment, what happened to the little guy—the one who thought he had a chance to open a new business or who decided to expand an existing one—the minority capitalist, who was going to ride the waves of corporate and political rhetoric?

One doesn't have to be a devotee of the *Wall Street Journal* or *Barron's* to know that a recession for the nation meant a depression for the ghetto. It meant that unemployment rates for blacks (and other minorities) began to soar. So much so that the Nixon Administration made the decision in November 1971 to stop making public the percentage of jobless teenage blacks— which by that time had risen to 43 percent in most urban centers. One of the monthly chores of the U.S. Labor Department of Vital Statistics had been to make such figures available to the American people.

If things were bad for the last-to-get-hired-first-to-be-fired, they were worse for aspiring entrepreneurs who believed all the blarney that passed for campaign pledges during the '68 campaign. Many of the new businessmen, with small capital, jumped smack into retail businesses in the ghetto. And they were hit the hardest by unemployment and declining buying power. To make matters worse, the banks cut off additional capital because of tight-money conditions just when the new entrepreneurs needed it most. Their plight—in most cases, a fight for survival—was summed up by Bert Mitchell of Lucas Tucker and Company, a black accounting firm in New York: "The people least likely to succeed in business were trying to make it at a time when seasoned businessmen were having trouble."[14]

How did the media treat this mass retrenchment? Dispensing news and truth is a tenuous business nowadays. Our national and local media keepers have lately run into some delicate problems when it comes to covering the seesawing fortunes of economic development issues particularly as it relates to "corporate responsibility."

One of the best indicators of trends, for example, is the New

York *Times* and its coverage of black economic development. Dependent on corporate and Government press handouts, the *Times* had for three years been carrying stories wearily quoting corporate or Government officials who went on about the value of this or that program and the numbers of dollars that would be released to insure the success of the endeavor. It would seem that even the goodwill of the *Times* has run out, for on January 12, 1972, in an annual special section devoted to a "National Economic Survey," the subject of the "black American economy" has been dropped to page 16 and was entitled, "Blacks, Looking at Economy, Voice Despair." It was a short two-column article that conveyed a lackluster message of failure.

If the gloomy mood of the piece was not enough to demonstrate that the media—at least the *Times*—were down on the private-sector-playing-saviour routine, the placement of the story cinched it. The article had been placed eight pages behind a more pressing analysis of other "burning" issues. The page 8 story had an eye-catching headline: "In the World's Richest Nation, Ongoing Problems." The three most important problems that the *Times* saw fit to print were "Despite Need, Few Want to be Maids or Butlers," "The High Cost of Medicine," and "Out-of-Work Executives,"—in that order.

Just as the corporate community has downgraded its "social conscience" priorities so has the *Times* in its coverage. There was an ironic note in the "Maids and Butlers" piece that punctuates the reversal of priorities. It read:

> "Help we can get, but good help is another thing—it's hard to find," said . . . one of the owners of Flatiron Home Service, Inc. "We find that people don't *give a damn.*"[15]

If the private sector had backed off, what could be said of foundations and nonprofit organizations? By 1971 most of the large foundations (with the exception of Ford) had done very little to help minority economic development.† Total giving, in all fields, for the approximately twenty-six thousand private foundations was estimated at 1.5 billion dollars.

According to the latest survey conducted by the Foundation

_____
† See Appendix for a list of major U.S. foundations.

Center, grants of $10,000 or more were given in the following fields:

Education	$281 million
Welfare	$136 million
Health	$121 million
Science	$ 93 million
International Activities	$ 59 million
Humanities	$ 52 million
Religion	$ 51 million

Thus, the burden of providing capital grants, soft loans, and technical assistance fell to smaller foundations (mostly religious) and other nonprofit organizations. Among them were: the Presbyterian Economic Development Corp. (PEDCO); the Interreligious Foundation for Community Organization and the Interchurch Center; the Cooperative Fund (sponsored by the Taconic Foundation and several smaller foundations); and Capital Formation.

Those nonprofit organizations (the amount of funds which they had at their disposal was minuscule) which provided technical assistance were: The Inter-Racial Council for Business Opportunity, Capital Formation, the Black Economic Union, the Southwest Council of La Raza, the National Council for Equal Business Opportunity and the Federation of Southern Cooperatives.

Of those establishment organizations that were set up nationally to help minority groups, the Urban Coalition was the most prominent. During its first year of operation a task force of the Coalition defined urban economic development as one of its major strategies. It is generally accepted that Coalition operations have been failures. Perhaps the best way to sum up the performance of the organization is to quote a former Associate Director of their Washington operation. Malcolm Kovacs had concluded that: "The Urban Coalition in practice has been an effort with little to show for it except to have diverted white and black liberals from the hard political job which they have had to do in a world where businessmen are more often enemies than allies."

THE GOVERNMENT AND CORPORATE AMERICA

If the minority entrepreneur and low-income communities were taking it on the chin in 1971, big business was, on the other hand, certainly enjoying unprecedented benefits, subsidies, and windfalls. Not only were dividends, interest, and profits exempted from wage-price controls‡ but President Nixon recommended to Congress new tax laws that were geared to reward industry with lavish giveaways. Rather than deal with the urgent public needs and a more equitable distribution of the tax burden, the President instead requested enormous tax benefits for business. In addition to the 7 percent investment credit the Administration proposed and got, it pushed through a fat 20 percent accelerated depreciation write-off of business outlays for machinery and equipment. Nixon said that the write-offs were "a reform to create jobs and growth." This is pure hogwash and the benefits may well be passed along to stockholders in the form of higher dividends.

These tidy bonuses add up to a tax giveaway to the nation's largest and wealthiest corporations and unincorporated businesses. In effect, the Federal tax structure, which already unduly favors big business, thus was becoming more inequitable. As part of the tax bonanza package, the Administration also gave U.S. corporations the legal right to set up "DISCs"—Domestic International Sales Corporations. Thus companies establishing dummy DISCs could indefinitely defer payment of taxes on half of any income these sales units earn. The tax package for this year alone provides corporations with a $7 billion subsidy. As a direct result of Administration decisions a massive shift away from progressive taxing has occurred. By fiscal 1973, regressive social insurance taxes will account for twice as much raised by the corporate income tax (a progressive source of revenue). Budgets and tax

‡ The wage-price controls instituted by the President look more like psychological pump-priming for the poor and middle class, while for big business they represent a form of financial pump-priming designed to inject healthy benefits for corporate economies.

laws are dull as dishwater, but that's where the big money is divvied up.

As a result of the new tax cuts, corporations stand to save $25.8 billion over the next three years. Furthermore, it is estimated that the depreciation gimmick will wipe out $37 billion worth of business tax revenue over the next decade—monies that could well be spent to reverse the social decay of our urban centers and provide the necessary social services to alleviate poverty.[16] Dr. Martin Luther King, Jr. once said, "only a tragic death wish can prevent this country from reordering its priorities." And the Nixon Administration and the private sector seem hell-bent on fulfilling his prediction. The nation's "fiscal dividend," out of which was to be paid the cost of social programs and human services, has been effectively wiped out by the dissipation of tax revenues!

Indications are that the Administration is preparing to propose more legislation that will be favorable to the position of large corporations particularly as they affect antitrust policies. And Administration efforts will become a lot easier since Richard W. McLaren has departed from the Justice Department's Anti-Trust Division. It is known in Washington that McLaren's views on antitrust enforcement have placed him in direct conflict with Secretary Stans,* Mitchell, members of the White House staff, the President, and commissioners of regulatory agencies. Mc-Laren insisted on bringing antitrust cases to court that the others opposed for political or economic reasons. For example, McLaren did not endear himself to the White House when he sought to oppose the merging of Warner-Lambert with Parke Davis. The former Chairman of Warner-Lambert was Elmer Bobst, Nixon's long-time friend and a heavy campaign contributor. Bobst was credited with bringing Nixon to Mitchell's Wall Street law firm. The same firm represented Warner-Lambert in the merger and Nixon and Mitchell were incensed over McLaren's efforts at taking his job seriously. They finally got him out of their hair by convincing him to accept an appointment as Federal judge in Chicago, replacing Julius Hoffman. In effect then, the Admin-

* Since Stans had been planning to resign from Commerce and did, in fact, in January 1972, it is understandable that he would want to be on good terms with those firms who will be filling the GOP campaign war chest.

istration has no *anti*trust policy. Both the antitrust division of the Justice Department and the FTC are politically controlled and subject to the political whims of Nixon and Mitchell.

For those of stout heart who might still maintain any lingering doubts about either the politicizing of the Justice Department or the abusive and flagrant ways that corporate America exercises its power to corrode our legal system, the circumstances surrounding the International Telephone and Telegraph Corporation scandal which burst into the headlines in March of 1972 should serve to dispel such naïve notions. Yes, Virginia, there is a Santa Claus! At least for the corporate giants, and apparently Santa slides down the chimney at the antitrust division of the U.S. Justice Department whenever he is needed. Though deliberate collusion has yet to be proved, the ITT case is a singular example of improper, corporate/government coziness.†

Whether or not there are criminal indictments, whether or not there were any actual violations of the law, or whether or not the full truth is ever known about the whole sordid mess is beside the point. What is clear is that the "law 'n' order" tough guys of the Nixon Administration got caught aiding and abetting influence peddlers, and they got caught with their pants down. These are the same hardliners who have advocated: wiretapping, bugging, mass arrests of peace demonstrators, preventive detention, and a wide variety of other "no nonsense" policies. But when it came to enforcing antitrust laws they seem to have behaved like pantywaisted cream puffs. It is also worth pondering that specific "contracts" or "deals," which were so vigorously denied by high officials of the Government and ITT, *were never really,* in fact, alleged as part of the formal "arrangement" but *merely implied.* What is especially illuminating about the ITT affair, then, is not the specifics of one isolated scandal, because the *system* doesn't work that way . . . on the basis of a defined predetermined quid for an agreed upon quo.

† ITT, apparently unsatisfied with merely perverting justice in the U.S., was instrumental in attempting to overthrow the Allende government in Chile, according to a column by Jack Anderson (March 21, 1971). Anderson reported that one of the unshredded memos linked an ITT director, John McCone (himself a former CIA head) and ITT V.P. William Merriam with William V. Broe (CIA, Latin-American Division) in a bizarre plot to plan an uprising in Chile.

The ITT affair is a familiar and obvious scenario to anyone who has carefully observed the machinations of Government bureaucracies. Of fundamental importance is that an incestuous relationship exists between big corporations and Government that is permanent, ongoing, and open-ended. As Mitchell, Acting Attorney General Richard G. Kleindienst, and other officials said, the deal (the out-of-court settlement) was handled in a perfectly normal and usual manner. Day in and day out favors are "bought" or exchanged between the wealthy "biggies" and politicians in Government, and the guilt cuts both ways. The chips are not necessarily raked in, for example, like after a hand of poker. Markers may be held for days, months, or years, but they *are held* in general anticipation of some future "call" on delivery. It's one big snugly profitable and accepted working relationship that protects the privileged in the private sector on the one hand, and fattens up the coffers of the campaign war chests of pliant politicians desirous of perpetuating their own power on the other.

Some of the details of the ITT scandal do offer valuable insights into the character and/or judgment of high officials—present and former—of this Administration. It also provides some instructive information about how the American *realpolitik* functions. Whether or not Harold Geneen promised to foot the bill for the Republican presidential convention is beside the point. For ITT, $400,000 is like sending a box of candy to your girl friend for Valentine's day. It's a way to keep on gracious terms with the people who control the Justice Department, and Geneen would have done the same for the Democrats, as long as the object of his "affection" was willing and able.

The initial allegations of skullduggery in high places began to surface when syndicated columnist Jack Anderson published what he maintained was a memorandum written by ITT's high-powered, Washington lobbyist, Dita D. Beard. The purported memo discussed the possibility that ITT's contribution toward the Republican National Convention would be of considerable help to the company in its efforts to achieve a desired settlement of pending antitrust cases. The alleged memo reads as follows:

Washington Office

1707 L Street, N.W.
Washington, D.C. 20036
Tel. (202) 296-6000

To:　　W. R. Merriam　　　　　　　*Date:* June 25, 1971

From:　　D. D. Beard

Subject:　San Diego Convention

　　I just had a long talk with EJG. I'm so sorry that we got that call from the White House. I thought you and I had agreed very thoroughly that under no circumstances would anyone in this office discuss with anyone our participation in the Convention, including me. Other than permitting John Mitchell, Ed Reinecke, Bob Haldeman and Nixon (besides Wilson, of course) no one has known from whom that 400 thousand committment had come. You can't imagine how many queries I've had from "friends" about this situation and I have in each and every case denied knowledge of any kind. It would be wise for all of us here to continue to do that, regardless of from whom any questions come; White House or whoever. John Mitchell has certainly kept it on the higher level only, we should be able to do the same.

　　I was afraid the discussion about the three hundred/four hundred thousand committment would come up soon. If you remember, I suggested that we all stay out of that, other than the fact that I told you I had heard Hal up the original amount.

　　Now I understand from Ned that both he and you are upset about the decision to make it four hundred in services. Believe me, this is not what Hal said. Just after I talked with Ned, Wilson called me, to report on his meeting with Hal. Hal at no time told Wilson that our donation would be in services ONLY. In fact, quite the contrary. There would be very little cash involved, but certainly some. I am convinced, because of several conversations with Louie re Mitchell, that our noble committment has gone a long way toward our negotiations on the mergers eventually coming out as Hal wants them. Certainly the President has told Mitchell to see that things are worked out fairly. It is still only McLaren's mickey-mouse we are suffering.

　　We all know Hal and his big mouth! But this is one time he cannot tell you and Ned one thing and Wilson (and me) another!

　　I hope, dear Bill, that all of this can be reconciled -- between Hal and Wilson -- if all of us in this office remain totally ignorant of any committment ITT has made to anyone. If it gets too much publicity, you can believe our negotiations with Justice will wind up shot down. Mitchell is definitely helping us, but cannot let it be known. Please destroy this, huh?

●

A photocopy of the memorandum purportedly written by I.T.T. lobbyist Dita D. Beard, which kicked off the controversy surrounding the dropping of antitrust actions against the conglomerate by the Nixon Administration. Others mentioned in the memo are: W. R. Merriam—head of I.T.T.'s Washington office; EJG and Ned—E. J. Gerrity, head of I.T.T. public relations; John Mitchell—the then Attorney General; Ed Reinecke—Lieutenant Governor of California; Bob Haldeman—assistant to President Nixon; Wilson—Congressman Bob Wilson, Republican of California; Hal—Harold S. Geneen, president of I.T.T.; Louie—former Republican Gov. Louie R. Nunn of Kentucky; McLaren—Richard W. McLaren, former head of the Justice Department's Antitrust Division.[19]

Immediately following the publication of the memo, which hit Washington like a bombshell, Mrs. Beard disappeared. The cast of characters implicated by the memo was most intriguing. They included: Mitchell; Kleindienst (at that time Attorney General Designate); McLaren; former Governor Louie B. Nunn of Kentucky; Richard J. Ramsden, a former White House aide and partner in the Wall Street Management investment firm of Brokaw, Schaenen, Clancy & Co.; Peter M. Flanigan, a former investment banker who is an assistant to President Nixon and viewed by many as the principal White House contact with the business community; Lieutenant Governor Ed Reinecke of California; Representative Bob Wilson, a Republican from the San Diego area; Nixon himself; and several officials of ITT, including Harold Geneen (its President) and Felix G. Rohatyn, a director of the company, among others.‡

Within three weeks the furor created by the memorandum had generated a series of charges, counter-charges, denials, counter-denials, evidence and "newly found" counter-evidence, some of which was extremely bizarre in nature. It became a sort of high-stakes game of "can you top this?" Most certainly the testimony of high Government and ITT officials before the Senate Judiciary Committee served to tax the credibility of the Government's position as well as the propriety of the company's actions. (It received the kind of press coverage that is *usually* reserved for a black who mismanages $2,500 of antipoverty funds.)

Certain facts in the case are beyond dispute. They are: ITT was involved in litigation of three antitrust suits; it obtained a more favorable settlement than competent Justice Department officials had initially indicated—certainly more favorable than Government economists and independent legal experts expected; and, during the same period that negotiations were in progress, ITT pledged to contribute at least $200,000 in cash and a guarantee of $400,000 through a subsidiary, the Sheraton Corporation, to help finance the 1972 GOP Convention in San Diego. The

‡ On May 16, 1972, the Washington *Post* revealed that Rohatyn became the sole trustee for Stans's successor as Secretary of Commerce, Peter G. Peterson. When Peterson left the White House his position was filled by Flanigan. The unusual agreement between Peterson and Rohatyn occurred just about the same time that Kleindienst and Flanigan were meeting with Rohatyn to discuss the ITT mergers.

commitment was announced publicly eight days before the favorable decision.

Beyond that there were serious conflicts with regard to interpretations of facts, intentions, roles, and truths, some of which seemed downright fishy. Items for consideration are:

—John Mitchell initially stated that he had absolutely no knowledge of the case, did not participate in the decision, and knew nothing about the gift to the Republican Convention. Mitchell later disclosed that he met with an ITT director, Rohatyn—in two separate meetings—in his office on April 29, 1970, the same day that Rohatyn made a presentation, two floors below, at the antitrust division. It was that particular presentation and a special report prepared by Ramsden that got ITT the favorable decision. Among those present at the meeting was Flanigan.

When questioned about the public statements by Reinecke that he told Mitchell about the Sheraton pledge, Mitchell replied that he could have forgotten the remark because "it made no impression on me, *I having no interest in it.*"* He said that he learned later that "the Republican National Committee, *or whatever committee makes these decisions,*† had picked San Diego." Mr. Mitchell *is* the President's chief political strategist and had just resigned his post in order to become campaign manager. One can only presume that he might have had some slight concern since Mr. Nixon *was* anxious to have the convention in San Diego and was interested in the arrangements.

Mitchell also disclosed during his testimony that he discussed the Government's antitrust policies with Geneen for some thirty-five minutes during a meeting on August 4, 1970. The meeting took place at Mitchell's office, and he said that he had made Mr. Geneen promise not to discuss the ITT cases (scout's honor?). Mitchell stated that the session was "an entirely theoretical discussion." He did not indicate whether or not he told Geneen "in effect, to shove off," as he did Mrs. Beard—who had the same theoretical bent—at a Kentucky Derby party.

We are led to believe then that the widely accepted image of John Mitchell as a shrewd, tough-minded, calculating, political strategist is false; that he is, instead, a sort of bungling, naïve,

* Italics added.
† Italics added.

mushhead who is given to theoretical discussions and forgetfulness when decisive action and bold initiatives are called for. . . .

—Richard Kleindienst originally said in a letter to Democratic National Chairman Larry O'Brien that "the settlement between the Department of Justice and ITT was handled and negotiated exclusively by Assistant Attorney General Richard W. McLaren . . ."

Kleindienst later admitted in Senate testimony that he arranged and attended a meeting in the spring of 1970 between ITT corporate officials and Government lawyers that led to the antitrust decision. He also disclosed that he met privately four other times with Rohatyn. It is unclear as to how much of the discussion focused on theoretical problems and how much on specific problems. If nothing else, the high echelon of the Justice Department suffers from an appalling semantic gap.

Kleindienst further stated that he "set in motion a series of events by which Mr. McLaren became persuaded that he ought to come off his position." There seems to have been a problem with the definition of the word "exclusively." Perhaps one's participation becomes inclusive when you meet with someone more than five times? Nonetheless, *it was* established that McLaren had not been convinced of ITT's "financial hardship" until he was introduced to Rohatyn at Kleindienst's urging. It would seem that Mitchell instructed Kleindienst to manage the show, in spite of the disingenious disclaimers.

—McLaren, the Government's chief trust buster, apparently, fought hard against the ITT-Hartford merger, that is, until he was introduced to Rohatyn and read an "independent" report that he claimed he had requested from Ramsden. McLaren also maintained that he was under *no* political pressure from the White House, although at first he couldn't recall who recommended Ramsden to him. The argument that seemed to sway his judgment was, in effect, the proposition that there would be a "negative ripple" effect on the stock market and the nation's economy if ITT didn't get a favorable decision. It's rather incredible that McLaren never considered that possibility until Rohatyn's presentation and the Ramsden report.

In an exchange with Senator Ted Kennedy, McLaren was still unclear as to how he located Ramsden.

KENNEDY: Why would the White House recommend a financial expert in a case?

MC LAREN: Because I asked them.

KENNEDY: To recommend a financial expert?

MC LAREN: Yes . . .

KENNEDY: Who in the White House?

MC LAREN: Probably Peter Flanigan. But I may have gotten the suggestion of Mr. Ramsden from Mr. McLaury . . . Either Flanigan or McLaury, I would say. I have no specific recollection.

Two days later in an interview, Ramsden stated that he had dealt entirely with Flanigan and that he had not even seen McLaren. He further stated that Flanigan knew him when they both worked together at Dillon, Read & Company, a brokerage firm. Ramsden said in the interview that "Peter Flanigan contacted me and I returned the report to him. . . . Flanigan relayed the questions to me that I was supposed to focus on." It was not mentioned that Flanigan's former employers made $600,000 on the Grinnell merger, one of the cases in litigation.

Both Kleindienst and McLaren denied that they had any knowledge of the ITT contribution until they read it in the newspapers in late November or December. Yet Senator Kennedy introduced a letter addressed to Kleindienst from Reuben B. Robertson, Jr., an associate of Ralph Nader, informing him of the shady link. Kennedy also produced a response from McLaren, a letter which was written in September, denying the connection on behalf of Kleindienst. . . . With lawyers like this the client (in this case the American people) might be justified in demanding a refund.

—Flanigan, who is known to some White House observers as "Mr. Fixit" was cited by Senator Thomas Eagleton of Missouri in a Senate speech as the "real missing witness" in the ITT case. Eagleton said that Flanigan should be hauled before Congress to answer questions regarding White House favors to large corporations.

Eagleton stated that there is mounting evidence that "shows Peter Flanigan to be no mere patcher of plaster, no apprentice applier of Band-Aids. Rather, there is reason to believe that he is the mastermind, . . . in the wake of a White House ordered cave-in to some giant corporation."

The Senator cited cases of White House pressure involving Flanigan in circumstances favoring the Anaconda Company; Armco Steel Corporation (which was dumping highly toxic chemicals into the Houston Ship Channel); Dillon, Read; and Texas Eastern Transmission Company. On the same day of the Eagleton charges against Flanigan an "independent" rebuttal was made by Senator Norris Cotton of New Hampshire. Senator Cotton stated later that Flanigan called earlier in the morning of the same day and said that his staff wanted to respond to the Eagleton speech. Cotton added that "they got some information together for me, and the boys from downtown came up with it." Flanigan is protected from testifying by executive immunity.

—Senator Robert Dole of Kansas, the chairman of the Republican National Committee, initiated a counterattack on March 10—during the second week of the hearings—against the Democrats by charging "improper activities involving the Democratic National Convention involving vast sums of money improperly received from big business."

This major "disclosure" related to the fact that the Democrats hadn't paid their telephone bill to AT&T for the last convention in Chicago and were still in arrears to "Ma Bell." It was rather ill-conceived for Mr. Dole to have mentioned AT&T, that is, unless he has a short memory. For the last major controversy over the settlement of an antitrust case also involved AT&T and a Republican Attorney General back in 1958. And that case, also, centered on an internal company memorandum. T. Brooke Price, the general counsel of AT&T, reported on a private meeting he allegedly had with Herbert Brownell in an isolated cottage at White Sulphur Springs, West Virginia.

According to the memo Mr. Price received "a little friendly tip" from Mr. Brownell about settling a suit that had been brought against the company during the Truman Administration. The contents of the memo were aired before the House Antitrust Subcommittee. In essence, the suggestion by Brownell was that AT&T should allow itself to be enjoined from doing certain things that it could cease doing "with no real injury to our business," Price recalled. The company would not have to divest itself of its manufacturing subsidiary, Western Electric.

If Mr. Dole wanted to throw around ridiculous countercharges to take the heat off the ITT hearings, perhaps he might also want to respond to yet unanswered questions regarding the activities of the Republican Party, former Attorney General Brownell, and AT&T.

—Other pertinent information which came out during the testimony related to officers of ITT selling stock (illegal "insiders" sale) immediately after key meetings with Federal officials; the Justice Department attorney, Charles D. Mahaffie, Jr., who was responsible for jurisdiction over two of the three cases against ITT, refusing to sign the consent agreements settling them; the President of ITT admitting that all of Mrs. Beard's files were shredded; the reappearance of Mrs. Beard in a Denver hospital with a heart condition that supposedly blocked her rational thought processes; the family doctor who was caring for her, who himself had been under investigation by the Justice Department, whose wife was about to be indicted and who purportedly was on the ITT payroll at one time; the eventual denial by Mrs. Beard of authorship of the memo—eighteen days after its publication; and the spectacle of ITT finding the "real" memo three days after that.

As Art Hoppe the columnist wrote in discussing a mythical case (involving International Peanuts & Popcorn) entitled "The Great IPP Scandal:"

> So the scandal, of course, involves the management of IPP. Imagine a huge corporation that would hire drunken crackpots, alienate San Diego and pay $400,000 for what the Republicans wanted to give them for nothing.
> It's unbelievable.

In reviewing the statements of Government officials and their reaction to the demands of conflicting interests—justice and politics—one is struck by the strained credibility of their statements.

It would appear that a good deal more than the ITT files got shredded in the whole affair—most prominently, the truth.‡

For those who were becoming more cynical about the way this Administration manipulates the system and its institutions the contagion must surely have spread when *Life* Magazine rocked official Washington and the Nixon Administration with new charges of impropriety, right on the heels of the ITT fiasco. On March 19 *Life* charged that the Administration "tampered with justice" in blocking legal action against C. Arnholt Smith, a multimillionaire political supporter and friend of Nixon from San Diego, and several of his associates.

Life charged that the Administration "squelched" an investigation into an allegedly illegal contribution to Mr. Nixon's 1968 presidential campaign; "shut off" a probe into the possibility that the contribution was part of a larger scheme to illegally channel "many thousands" of dollars to political candidates, principally Mr. Nixon, in 1968; refused to allow an Internal Revenue Service agent—a key witness—to testify against the ex-Mayor of San Diego, Frank Curran; and postponed a tax evasion indictment against John Alessio, another Smith associate, who owns a bookmaking operation in Mexico and has interest in horse and dog tracks, among other investments.

The activities of Mr. Smith, his friends, and colleagues are not well known publicly, but they belong to an exclusive club of California businessmen who provide one of the most bountiful sources of big campaign money for Nixon. The Lincoln Club of Orange County, California, is made up largely of millionaires who like to boast that Nixon wouldn't be in the White House today without *their* efforts and generosity. The club supposedly has 124 members who are carefully screened and selected, and the affairs of the organization are tightly controlled by a handful of Mr. Nixon's personal friends, including Smith, who sits on the board of directors. A good deal of secrecy surrounds the club,

‡ Another angle that was hardly mentioned during the hearings had to do with plain old profit motive. ITT is always looking for new markets. President Nixon wants to expand trade with Russia. In November of 1971 Stans made a highly publicized trip to Moscow. One month after the Stans visit, ITT opened its own trade discussions with Russia, supposedly with Administration blessings. Stans resigns to become GOP fund raiser and the moola rolls in—"From Moscow to San Diego, with Love."

which has no headquarters and only maintains a post office box in nearby Fullerton, California.

The President of the club is Arnold O. Beckman, and the man credited with being the moving force behind the activities of the organization is Herbert W. Kalmbach, Nixon's personal attorney on the West Coast. Another member is Donald Nixon, the President's brother, who is an employee of the Marriott Corporation. The club's membership is loaded with bankers, land developers, and real estate brokers; but they do make exceptions for special outsiders such as John Wayne. One source indicated that the organization makes huge unreported contributions to the Republicans' national campaign chest by individual members through Beckman or Kalmbach. The way this is done is that the individual donor is provided the names of several different committees in order to circumvent the $5,000 limit on individual contributions. One former member alleged last year that, on occasion, large sums had been delivered in cash, notably a suitcase containing $45,000 in fifty-dollar bills said to have been sent to Washington by an unidentified Newport Beach businessman in 1970.

Smith, whose conglomerate holdings include the United States National Bank, hotels, ships, the San Diego Padres, Air California, and a virtual monopoly of California taxicab franchises, is quite active in the club. (His former associate, ex-Mayor Frank Curran of San Diego was indicted on charges of accepting bribes to help secure a "hefty" fare increase for the Yellow Cab Company.) The San Diego multimillionaire supposedly raised more than a million dollars for the Nixon-Agnew ticket in 1968, including a contribution of a quarter of a million dollars of his own money. It was reported that on election night Smith sat with Nixon in the latter's New York hotel suite watching the election returns on television.

At the Lincoln Club's annual dinner on April 9, 1969, there was a belated celebration of Mr. Nixon's election, and the minutes of the meeting show that Mr. Beckman expansively stated, "We elected Richard Nixon President of the United States." Kalmbach, another power in the organization, was vice chairman of the Nixon-Agnew National Finance Committee under Maurice Stans in 1968. It is anticipated that he will assume the same post in the '72 "crusade," as Stans calls it. . . . Another businessman in Newport Beach said of Mr. Kalmbach, "If you have business with the Government and you want a lawyer, you go to Herb, but you can't talk with him for less than $10,000." Kalmbach is also Secretary of the Nixon Foundation and a close friend of Robert H. Finch, a presidential adviser.

According to the *Life* article a U.S. attorney, Harry Steward, who was responsible for investigating the Yellow Cab payola case, was himself investigated by the FBI. A report was filed with the Justice Department Criminal Division declaring that Steward had been "indiscreet" in the handling of the case. In February of 1971, Kleindienst announced, "There have been no wrong doings," and exonerated Steward.

When asked about this judgment, on March 19—the day the *Life* story broke—in an interview with Mike Wallace of CBS, Kleindienst replied, "I am no penny-ante two-bit little crook." Mr. Kleindienst may not be a crook, but the fellows that he seems to help are neither penny-ante nor two bit, and some of them tend to get in "compromising" circumstances.

Another example of Administration favoritism toward corporations—particularly those with defense contracts—was revealed by Clark Mollenhoff, a former White House aide, who reported in his "Watch on Washington" column that President Nixon supported the Air Force's effort to fire A. E. Fitzgerald, the Air Force analyst who blew the whistle on Lockheed. It was Fitzgerald who in 1968 revealed to Senator William Proxmire's subcommittee on economy in Government that there was a massive and wasteful $2 billion cost overrun on the C-5A air transport contract with Lockheed. Fitzgerald, for his patriotic act, was rewarded by being fired by the military in November of 1969.

His replacement was John J. Dymant, who was a partner in Arthur Young & Company, Lockheed's auditor. The firm was a co-defendant in a suit charging both companies (Lockheed and Young) with concealing the massive cost overruns. There were several complaints from Congress about the "incredible insensitivity" of the Air Force's hiring of Dymant as a consultant, but the Administration seems to know no shame.

Even more disturbing than the Fitzgerald case is a recent Task Force Report charging that the Federal Government was being "militarized," in that over 300,000 retired military personnel are occupying Federal civilian jobs under devious means. The report which was made available early in 1972 was prepared by the National Capital Area Department (NCAD) of the AFL-CIO American Federation of Government Employees (AFGE).

The Task Force Report was prepared for use and testimony before the House Civil Service Manpower subcommittee. It estimated that the retired military personnel drew an average civilian salary of $20,000 a year and an average retirement income of $12,000 annually. Thus, the NCAD charged that the American taxpayers are presently footing the bill for double salaries to the tune of an additional $3.6 billion each year. The Task Force Report attacked the "buddy system" and what it referred to as the "double dipper" pay arrangement whereby military brass used devious means to flout the merit system and get their friends on the payroll.

The report further charged that this arrangement was hampering Government efficiency and economy because it placed into key civilian positions ex-military types with "their obsolete thinking and archaic business practices." The Task Force made several specific recommendations to prevent further military takeover of non-defense agencies. And so it goes . . . Government by caricature.

In addition, the Civil Aeronautics Board (CAB) is supposedly preparing legislation to create an Aerospace Reconstruction Finance Corporation which will have the authority to lend up to one billion dollars to airlines and aerospace firms which might have financial troubles. And the President has already indicated that he intends to allocate more funds for "R&D" for corporations in the future.* All of this is, of course, in addition to the American taxpayers getting soaked in order to save Grumman, Penn Central, Lockheed, and the brokerage industry—which was propped up by a Federally financed Securities Industry Protection Corporation. In the past three years, under this Administration, the dangerous gap between the rich and poor has widened. The myth of free enterprise has become a joke and the American

* The President in his 1972 State of the Union Message asked for the $700 million of R&D incentive funds for corporations to help them do some "free enterprise" technological research and development; a hefty chunk of capital for an election year.

people literally have no one to protect them from the corporate free-loading that is encouraged by this Administration.†

Apparently the extent of the Administration's commitment toward minority economic development is not dissimilar from the quality of its commitment to solving the problems of hunger as well as other social problems. The following is the text of a White House meeting between the President and members of his Urban Affairs Council as quoted by Nick Kotz in his excellent book, *Let Them Eat Promises*.

> PRESIDENT NIXON: The most troublesome question is, how wide is the hunger problem in fact?
> SECRETARY OF AGRICULTURE CLIFFORD HARDIN: We know there are six million persons in families with less than $300 per capita income, 25 million with less than $3,000 family income, and probably one half have nutritional problems, give or take one or two million. We're absolutely convinced this is a serious problem . . .
> PRESIDENT NIXON: To what extent does our report respond to the Senate [McGovern] hearings?‡ . . .
> SECRETARY OF HEALTH, EDUCATION AND WELFARE ROBERT FINCH: Let's take the play away from the McGovern committee and send a couple of your guys [White House aides] in a helicopter to southern Virginia, for example.
> PRESIDENT NIXON: Good. . . . How soon do we have to move? This week?
> SECRETARY HARDIN: I have three speeches to give this week. . . . And what I need to do when I speak is to say that I'm speaking within the policy of this Administration.
> PRESIDENT NIXON: You can say that this Administration will have the first complete, far-reaching attack on the problem of hunger in history. Use all the rhetoric, so long as it doesn't cost money.[17]

It is a poignant and representative example of the Administration's attitude.

† Nixon's Supreme Court has already begun to hand down decisions which favor corporations. In one particular case (decided in January 1972), Reliance Electric Co. v. Emerson Electric, the Court decided that "insiders"— large stockholders—would not have to give up profits on "two step" transactions. This decision not only violates the spirit of Congressional and regulatory intent but it has been considered illegal and phony in the past. It could possibly mean another huge windfall for corporations in the future.

‡ President Nixon was referring to the hearings being held before the Senate Select Committee on Nutrition and Human Needs under the chairmanship of Senator George McGovern.

In summing up the role of the private sector in helping minorities during the years 1966 to 1971, it seems appropriate to quote from the last article written by Whitney Young, Jr., before his untimely death in Lagos, Nigeria. Mr. Young, among all the black leaders of the sixties, was the first to extend himself to the business community. As Executive Director of the Urban League he made every attempt to involve corporate America in a joint effort toward providing assistance to blacks. He wrote:

> The statements of concern and the rhetoric of "involvement in the community" that emanated from so many public relations departments of major corporations a few years ago seem to have given way, if not to a retreat, then to an orderly withdrawal, from the problems of society.
>
> In many quarters, the "great involvement" in the social arena is beginning to look like the "great copout." In fact, our business leaders sometimes act like restless college kids, flirting first with civil-rights action, then speaking up against the war, and, now, clutching the newfound environment issue to their collective bosoms.
>
> That sound, hard-headed businessmen are reflecting the same qualities they find so reprehensible in others—lack of staying power and dilettantism—is a rough charge, but a very deserving one for some inhabitants of executive suites.
>
> The period of corporate activism in social concerns coincided with two phenomena of great importance—a booming economy and the spread of urban rioting. On the one hand, companies were rolling in record-high profits; on the other, they perceived civil disorders as harming the good climate for business and as demanding responsible civic action from the corporate citizen.
>
> But when he's trying to help solve social problems four hundred years in the making, created by the racialist attitudes of companies and unions like his own, he suddenly expects fast returns and instant successes.
>
> It is beginning to look like business, in its attempt to become part of the solution, is once again becoming part of the problem.[18]

Thus, as the Nixon Administration has systematically subverted all social programs designed to help minority and poor people, corporate America has selfishly enhanced its own position by acquiring enormous new subsidies. While corporate leaders dillydally and talk out of both sides of their mouth about "corporate responsibility" they have done next to nothing with regard to solving major social problems. "Corporate volunteerism," which

President Nixon called for, turned out to be another empty p.r. slogan by a politician who didn't want to spend a nickel for concrete programs. Although a handful of businessmen stepped forward the efforts of those individuals were washed away by a sea of mediocre performance. While therapeutic for the business and political leaders rhetoric has little to do with breaking through the structure of deeply imbedded social and economic problems. At best it tends to create confusion and false illusions, at worst it compounds the misery of those caught in the trap of poverty by toying with their hopes and aspirations. The politics of perpetuating the inequities of distribution of income in America has been a dismal history of human greed, callousness, and institutional indifference. And in 1972 the character of both American corporate and political commitment was still business as usual.*

---

* On October 12, 1970, in Amarillo, Texas, Vice President Agnew said that a basic reason for unrest in the country was that Americans never had it so good. He emphasized that "the hidden cause of malaise in America is the success—the success of the American system. . . ."

In this Administration, as in the past, one of the chief assignments of the Vice President has been to concern himself with urban problems, particularly with regard to coordinating Federal, state, and local efforts. There has been a noticeable absence of mentioning Mr. Agnew, which is primarily due to the fact that it is difficult to discern any creative or positive action on his part. Suffice it to say that he has not progressed very far since his comment, "If you've seen one ghetto, you've seen them all." Mr. Agnew's political insights are nothing more than the kind of rhetoric prepared for cigarette commercials.

12 | CONCLUSION

This short, uninspiring history of the Nixon Administration's efforts at Black Capitalism raises several questions. The first is, what did it accomplish?

For minorities it accomplished very little. The programs consisted of some Federal contracts, a few more small loans for undercapitalized businesses, and gimmicks like the MESBIC, which probably helped white businesses more than it did minority ones. There was also the promise of a moderate-sized political pay-off for the deserving blacks and Spanish-speaking who were capable of public allegiance to Maurice Stans's "Andrew Carnegie" model of capitalist success.

A few minority businessmen prospered. And a few minority professionals took well-paying jobs in the Black Capitalism bureaucracy. But the amount of resources the Administration put up could not possibly have made a dent in the lack of capital ownership among minority people. It was a mockery of the President's own vow to give them "a piece of the action."

But what of the Administration's objectives? Surely this overpublicized anemic program could not have done much to serve its goals. The answer to that depends on what those goals were.

It is also important to separate the personal goals from the

Administration's objectives as a whole. It was John Mitchell who set the political parameters. Maurice Stans, who ran the program, had personal goals for higher office that were not the concern of Richard Nixon or John Erlichman, who told him how to run it. Within the framework set out by the White House, Stans was free to use the program to whatever advantage he could. But it was the White House who set the policy objectives. And Nixon's highest policy priority was to get re-elected.

One thing seems clear; the purpose of the Black Capitalism program was not to create a political foothold among the blacks. Roeser, McClaughry, and a number of others—not including Maurice Stans—had the dream of black voters marching into the Republican Party, but few in the White House lost any sleep over it. After a fleeting moment of concern in the "Bridges to Human Dignity" speech, the Nixon machine turned 180 degrees away from any concern with the black vote. When John Mitchell took over the campaign at the Republican Convention, speechwriters were ordered not even to mention blacks. One writer quotes Mitchell as saying, "As far as we are concerned blacks don't even exist."

After the election the Administration treated Black Capitalism with the same indifference it treated other areas of concern to minorities. Administration officials made it quite clear that they did not feel they owed anything to the blacks who had produced such lopsided majorities against them. Despite the fact that Black Capitalism was widely hailed in the press as a major domestic policy thrust of the new Administration, none of the more prestigious Cabinet secretaries wanted the action. George Romney, for example, with his business background and liberal record as Governor of Michigan, would have been a natural to run the program. But he turned it down. So did Robert Finch, who chose to involve himself with the seemingly un-Republican area of welfare reform rather than Black Capitalism. And only after Maurice Stans was rebuffed for the Secretary of the Treasury slot and was desperate for something else to do did he decide to pick up this program that no one else wanted. In an administration that was to backtrack on school integration, was to sack Leon Panetta and Commissioner James Allen for pushing civil rights and quality education, was to gut the War on Poverty, was to shilly-shally on its own welfare reform,* was to cut back on the food surplus program, and was to nominate Haynsworth, Carswell, and Rehnquist to the Supreme Court, there didn't seem to be much of a political career in pushing Black Capitalism—or Black anything.

But the President did support, or seemed to support, welfare reform—a program that would have made more of an immediate impact on the lives of the poor minorities than Black Capitalism. He sold the program in the most negative and destructive way; he demanded that welfare mothers be put to work and railed against the welfare "cheaters" when it was plain that the number of people on the welfare roles who were in fact able to work was less than 5 percent. Nevertheless Nixon did identify with the principles of a minimum guaranteed income which liberal Democrats had not had the courage to endorse.

Part of the reason for Nixon's welfare stand is undoubtedly found in the pervasive character of his chief domestic adviser of the first two years in the White House—Daniel P. Moynihan. Moynihan must be credited with selling a conservative President on accepting what on the surface appeared as a radical social innovation. The radical nature of this improved welfare program, however, is more apparent than real. It is realistically an instrument of control and coercion. It is not out of character for one so supportive of the virtues of private economic power as Moynihan to suggest that a social crisis be solved by improving the workings of society's Poor Laws. If the demands of the poor have to be met, how much easier to meet them by giving the destitute a little more money than to tinker with the distribution of power. As long as the poor remain supplicants by scraping some added crumbs from the tables of the rich, the corporate welfare state remains untouched and those who rule it retain their power. Furthermore the work requirements are arbitrary to the individuals and advantageous to the potential employers.

In principle, although hardly in practice, Black Capitalism was politically a far more radical idea than beefing up the welfare state. It was based on a class analysis of capitalism, and concluded that the way to political power for an unpopular and disenfran-

---

* Governor Ronald Reagan told reporters, after testifying against the Family Assistance Plan before the Senate Finance Committee, "Well, frankly, I don't think the President believes in it."

chised minority in a capitalistic democracy was to buy it. This was what Booker T. Washington had in mind and why the racist Thomas Dixon thought that Washington was a more dangerous man than his more radical contemporaries. And it is clearly the root idea behind the economic development activities of black community leaders all over the country.

The point was surely not lost on so acute an observer of the politics of class as Daniel Moynihan—nor so skilled a practitioner as Richard Nixon. So it was not surprising that when faced with the choice between trying to provide equality of opportunity and throwing a few more coins into the poor box, those two defenders of the long-term interests of business society chose to support charity.

The Administration's lack of enthusiasm for the program was also illustrated in its choice of people to run it. Maurice Stans was notoriously insensitive to the needs and feelings of minorities. According to Darwin Bolden: "Maurice Stans doesn't understand black or brown people or their aspirations, and I doubt that he ever will." A white man who works for Stans put it more bluntly: "The Secretary just does not believe that blacks are competent. That's why he believes in small business. They can't handle anything else."

The style and environment of OMBE also reflected these views. Aside from the largely figurehead Director's job, most of the top positions were held by whites. In the fall of 1971 the heads of three of four OMBE divisions were white. Three of four, including the one black Division Chief, were ex-Department of Defense employees who had no experience in minority business programs.

The programs were a dumping ground for defeated Republican politicians. Thomas Kleppe, who succeeded Hilary Sandoval at the SBA, was an ex-Congressman from North Dakota. John Altorfer, who ran OMBE as Stans's Special Assistant, was an Illinois Republican who was invited to Washington to keep him out of the Republican Governor Olgivie's hair. An article in a New York newspaper quotes Altorfer as saying: "I'm not sure how I got here, other than I've been a friend of Chuck Percy."[1]

Finally there was the lack of resources put into the program. When questioned about how the President's alleged commitment to the program squared with the paucity of funds he allocated to it, Maurice Stans refers to the "political realities." Such realities of course are rooted in the Administration's priorities which resulted in the total amount of loans made to minority businesses by the Federal Government in 1971 being less than that which the Federal Government guaranteed one white-owned firm—the Lockheed Aircraft Corporation—to save it from bankruptcy.†

The notion that the program was designed to help minorities does not stand up to the facts. There was neither the necessary political motivation, nor were there enough people who really cared about Black Capitalism to make it succeed.

Still there was a program. And there was an effort made to make it look like a success. If all the Administration cared about were southern voters they would not have made the effort. And yet if the black and other minorities were not the program's constituency, who was?

The only answer that makes sense is that the program was a sop, not to the blacks, but to a small but influential group of liberal Republican businessmen, who felt that they had to do something for the minority people. While their motivation varied many were responding to public demands that corporations take some responsibility for solving the crises of race and poverty.

As businessmen go they tended to be somewhat more liberal, although very Republican in their politics, and more sensitive than most to the growing complaints about the business system. They were people like James Roche, President of General Motors, a corporation under attack by Ralph Nader and other consumer advocates, Donald McNaughton, President of Prudential Insurance, whose financing of neighborhood-destroying urban renewal projects has been attacked by community organizations, Rodman Rockefeller, President of IBEC, an international holding

† When the Administration wanted resources for programs that it considered important there were no bounds to its imagination. For example, Secretary of Defense Melvin Laird conjured up images of our nation becoming paralyzed by electromagnetic pulses in order to extract an additional $254 million from Congress (The New York *Times*, January 26, 1972, p. 1). Mr. Laird, who has "enemy nuclear attacks" surgically implanted on his inner brain, will go to any length to get more funds for his constituents, the defense contractors.

company whose activities in Latin America have been criticized by religious and antiwar groups, and Albert Meyer, President of the Bank of America, whose branches have been stoned and burned by rioting students. All of the above were members of the Advisory Council on Minority Enterprise. Their spokesmen are men like Senator Charles Percy and Jacob Javits, strong on conventional civil rights and stronger on protecting the assets of American corporations.

Many of these men may have a sincere desire to help the less fortunate and a willingness to do something about it. Analysts of the corporative behavior have observed that men who reach the top of their business often broaden their concerns and become involved in charitable and even somewhat liberal causes to maintain the image of the corporation as a good citizen. But there is a limit to their charity and their liberalism.

John Kenneth Galbraith once wrote that liberal Republicans are the only people who believe that one can have social justice without paying for it. And in terms of Black Capitalism it was clear that corporations were not willing to put up any substantial money to see it work. Businessmen, liberal and conservative, are concerned with their own profits, with enlarging markets, and with justifying their own salaries. Nowhere in the system (domestic) are there incentives for them to create a business for someone else.‡

When Corporate America, not the blacks or other minorities, is viewed as the constituency for minority capitalism, then much of what the Administration did makes sense. Therefore:

—It was not necessary to spend a great deal of money because the corporations were interested in image, not performance. Several blacks who were on the National Advisory Council on Minority Enterprise have told how difficult it was to get the businessmen to recommend even modest levels of public spending. And when the Administration allocated even less money

‡ Unless it is when they go into joint ventures in foreign markets abroad, where the risk of loss due to political instability, riot, revolution, or expropriation has been largely lifted from the investor and shifted to the U.S. Government through the Overseas Private Investment Corp. (OPIC). "Our foreign aid program has become a spreading money tree under which the biggest American businesses find shelter when they invest abroad," said Senator Frank Church in a Senate speech, October 29, 1971.

than the Advisory Council asked for, the corporation executives looked quite liberal.

—It was not necessary to pay attention to getting dynamic minority leadership into the program. Stans's remark that he did not want a lot of minority people around OMBE because he wanted his staff to be able to deal with corporate executives is perfectly reasonable, if the latter are to be the principal constituency.*

—It was necessary to stress the private sector's contribution. Thus franchising and MESBICs and loan guarantees were the most important parts of the program. The only surprise was that Stans realized too late that the corporate sector was even less willing to put money into MESBICs than he thought.

—It was also necessary to stress volunteerism. Thus it had a ring of charity which ironically enough the corporate businessmen understood when it came to blacks. Moreover it also did not obligate anyone.

—It was not necessary to be concerned with problems of the Rural South. Blacks were concerned about them, but the corporations were feeling no political pressure from southern blacks and in any event would not have cared enough to make life uncomfortable to an Administration which was carefully cultivating white southern voters.

—Even the $100 million to the "Affiliates" makes sense in this light. The people who are most valuable to the liberal Republican business leadership are the minority political activists, the community leaders who form the organizations that receive the Federal grants. A black businessman has no time to be publicly appreciative of the bounty of the private business sector and little inclination if his business is failing. But the local leadership can appear on television and radio, can appear at seminars sponsored by the business school of the local university, and can generally spread the word that the American corporations really care about the blacks, and that Maurice Stans's business-

---

* Stans's decision is consistent with his past business associations. On January 4, 1972, his former business partner General Charles J. Hodge was indicted in Philadelphia with two other prominent corporate executives who "conspired in their corporate activities to divert in excess of $21 million from the treasury of the Penn Central for themselves and others."

like approach will bring the ghettos out of poverty. As an extra added attraction for the Administration, it keeps the leadership politically neutral, since people on the payroll of a Federal grantee are restricted in their ability to engage in politics.

To sum up, seeing the corporation leadership as the prime beneficiaries of the Black Capitalism program makes it clear that the program did not have to work to be a success. *It merely had to have the appearance of success.* The old shell game! Heads the corporation leadership wins, tails the minority groups lose.

In his high praise for the Arcata MESBIC, Stans referred constantly to the fact that Arcata got a twenty-four-year-old, "bright white boy" and a "bright black boy" to run the program. When Arcata flopped, Stans brought the "white boy" to Washington to run the national MESBIC program.† Aside from reflecting contempt for the practical needs of the minority businessmen, the incident reflects just how little Stans felt obligated to produce successful minority businesses. What program in which the Administration placed a high priority would have been entrusted to such inexperienced direction?

Some indication of the uses to which the Administration was putting the Black Capitalism program was the statement of Undersecretary of the Treasury Charles Walker before the House Banking and Currency Committee in 1970.

The Democratic members asked Walker about the huge "tax and loan" accounts that the Federal Government keeps, interest free, in the nation's banks. The accounts represent windfall earnings to banks at the rate of 6 to 8 percent of the deposits. Congressman Ruess, of Wisconsin, asked why the $5 to $10 billion couldn't be used as a fund to generate capital for inner-city projects.

Walker opposed the idea for a variety of vague reasons, and then pointed proudly to the Administration's commitment of depositing $35 million in minority banks around the country! Of course at no cost to the Government.

For the Administration therefore, as well as the businessmen involved with Black Capitalism, the program represented social justice for close to nothing. The latter could go back to New

---

† He has since resigned in disgust.

York and Detroit and Chicago and Los Angeles and tell the local newspapers how they supported programs to let every American have an equal chance at getting rich. And if the Administration failed to follow their recommendations or if the programs failed, one would have to chalk it up to the arrogance of big government, or the incompetence of minority people, but certainly big business had done its part.

At today's prices for social justice, Black Capitalism was a bargain. It was old Nixon with new tricks.‡

But what if the program had been operated with a black constituency in mind? What if Richard Nixon and Maurice Stans and the rest had been seriously concerned with putting blacks into business? What if they had provided more money for minority enterprises? Would the small business, "Andrew Carnegie" model have been sufficient to provide minorities with the economic power needed to break out of their poverty and despair?

The answer is no. And the reasons why illustrate again whose interests the program really serves.

First of all, establishing small business is a very risky proposition. All private and Government studies indicate that about two thirds of all businesses started to fail within the first five years. Failure rates for small businesses have been estimated as

‡ Late in December 1971, Herbert G. Klein, the President's Director of Communications, distributed a fifteen-thousand-word document entitled "Richard Nixon's Third Year." The White House claimed that the Nixon Presidency had produced "large conceptions, daring innovation, and substantial progress." Mr. Klein who has publicly proclaimed the Administration's dedication to truth more times than Judy Garland sang "Over the Rainbow" said that when the Democrats in Congress took the pulse of the nation during Christmas recess they would return to Washington eager to complete the President's agenda. The great successes ranged from a reduction of highway deaths, "very substantial good news" for farmers, and efforts to find a political solution to the India-Pakistan crisis. There was very little for minority groups to cheer about in the long list of claimed "achievements."

There is a story told by reporters who covered Nixon in the 1960 campaign which had to do with Klein. During the course of a question-and-answer period, after a speech in Philadelphia, one woman rose to her feet and said, "Mr. Nixon, if you were elected President would the fact that you were a Quaker affect your decision to 'push the button' if an atomic war was imminent?"

Without allowing Nixon to respond, Klein, who was sitting on the stage, jumped up and exclaimed, "Don't worry, madam, Mr. Nixon never let his religion get in his way."

high as 80 percent. In the past, because of their screening procedures, the loss rate on loans made by the Small Business Administration have been much below this figure, indicating that the SBA has been serving above-average small businessmen. But as Government has tried to make more minority loans, the failure rates have increased. As we have seen earlier, they rose from 15 percent in 1969 to 29 percent in 1971.

Small business is rapidly becoming a thing of the past in the United States. With the exception of some highly specialized operations, large corporations have come to dominate the economy. Even the retail grocery business, the mainstay of the "mom-and-pop" store, has become a property of the large chains and the conglomerates that own them. In many areas even chain stores stay open for even longer hours than did the neighborhood grocery store of the past. And where there is an after-hours business, that too is being absorbed by chains of mini-markets.

And small business in ghetto areas is riskiest of all. Incomes are low, crime is high, insurance is unavailable,* and the labor force is less productive. Small business is less efficient than large business and black businesses—which are the smallest—are the least efficient of all. Andrew Brimmer points out that the average white business is five times the size of the average black business and at least five times as efficient. Because he is inefficient, the small businessman cannot offer the prices or the quality that the supermarket can, even where the supermarket is some distance away. Poor people's time is not expensive, and so they will often travel some distance to save a few pennies. Thus competition from giant corporations and the social and economic determination in the inner cities make it well nigh impossible for any but the most talented and dedicated to survive.

A few do survive, some even prosper; but they are likely to be operating low overhead businesses and exploiting capital investments made decades ago and long since paid for. Under current conditions, attempts to create more small businessmen

---

* Although some recent steps have been taken to make insurance available to inner-city businesses, premiums are still very high and the program of pooled risks is not likely to reach nearly all that need it.

without regard to the social and economic and political environment in which they find themselves, are doomed to failure. A staff member of a Congressional Committee which oversees the Small Business Administration says: "The failure rates SBA is giving out now are just the tip of the iceberg. In another two years, if they ever get published they'll be up to 50 percent." Of course by that time Maurice Stans will have moved on to another job. And Richard Nixon will either be in his second term as President or he won't be. Either way it won't much matter.

Secondly, the Nixon-Stans model of minority entrepreneurship can at best help merely a handful of people. The notion that the problems of race and poverty can be solved by the creation of a few successful millionaires who will be a "pride to their race," is an absurdity.

Even if you discount the hidden political motives of the Nixon Administration, Black Capitalism is an insulting lie on its face. It presumes that what black men truly lack in this republic is the good old spirit of enterprise and the "pride" that comes only from a fellow black's fat bank account. Given the sight of a few black cats with wads, however, the ghetto dwellers will become inspired to do—what? Nothing, that's the point. Hopefully they will be content to remain in the ghetto pridefully; the owner of the laundromat is a black man.

Racial tensions are not reduced with every sale of Parks Sausages, or with the ascension of black people like Leon Sullivan to the Board of General Motors or Patricia Roberts Harris to the Board of Chase Manhattan Bank. Unless an economic development program does something for the masses of poor and near-poor people—those seventy-five million who comprise the underbelly of America—it is not worth the investment of public funds.

Finally, the Nixon-Stans model cannot work because it chooses not to recognize, for blacks, the interdependence of politics and economics. When it comes to enhancing their own (or family) economic self-interest they know only too well how the system "really" works. For example, the $205,000 loan to M. Donald Nixon and Mrs. Hannah Nixon from Howard Hughes, in order to set up "Nixonburger" stands. This loan was allegedly made in return for political favors for Hughes—and was never repaid, nor was the story denied. (A replay of the Nixon "slush fund" and the resulting "Checkers" speech.)

And Stans's role in the Penn Central disaster? How did he know that he had exactly 39,955 shares of Great Western when the distribution of shares to Glore Forgan & Co. happened after the "blind trust" had been set up? How would Stans have known of the split (10 for 1) if the Secretary had no idea, whatever, of his holdings? "Apparently that blind trust had eyes," said Senator Vance Hartke. The GOP Financial Chairman also had some part-interest in a manufacturing plant in Thailand (while Secretary) which is enhanced by AID support . . .

And the Wall Street law firm of Mudge, Rose, Guthrie & Alexander—Nixon and Mitchell's old firm—came under heavy fire for the cozy fashion in which it made substantial sums of money and acquired new contracts after its former partners came into office. On July 29, 1971, Congressman Morris K. Udall —a principal backer of the 1970 Postal Reorganization Act, under which the Post Office was made a quasi-independent Postal Service—charged that the firm stood to make "millions of dollars" as bond attorneys for the first issue of U.S. Postal Service Bonds. In criticizing the transaction, Udall stated that an unidentified Service official had said that firm "had to be hired." Representative Udall said, "Surely, somewhere among the 250,-000 lawyers in this country, there is someone else who can handle this. And surely, with all its other business this barefoot firm in New York can survive without this particular multimillion-dollar contract."

Other conflict of issue charges were raised with the acknowledgment that the firm had been selected as bond attorneys for the Washington (D.C.) Metropolitan Area Transit Authority's $2.5 billion subway. As luck would have it, the firm managed recently to acquire large parts of tax-exempt bond business from the states of Kentucky, Nebraska, New Jersey, and West Virginia (The New York *Times,* July 30, 1971).

And the corporations whose representatives sat around the table advising blacks to learn how to compete in a free market were themselves supported by huge subsidies. General Motors, whose wealth and power is based upon billions of Federal highway subsidies; Textron, many of whose contracts come from the Defense Department; Quaker Oats, whose Chairman is Republican Committeeman from Illinois and in whose interests, and the interests of other agribusiness, the Federal Government has been driving small farmers off the land for years while subsidizing large ones—all have become successful corporate entrepreneurs on the backs of the American taxpayers. If this is capitalism, then the road to economic development for minorities is most of all a political road. Only through the exercise of political power will blacks or any low-income group ever get a piece of that capitalism cum socialism which in America is reserved for the affluent. It is clear that the large investments that must be made in the inner city are not going to come from the private sector; they are going to come from the public treasury or they are not going to come at all.

This will require of course the reordering of priorities in the nation, which everyone talks about but no one ever does anything about. It can begin with the resources that already flow into the inner city but which are controlled for the benefit of the rich, not the poor. It can begin with Urban Renewal programs that are not designed for real estate speculators but for the people who live in urban areas.† It can begin by turning the land over to farmers who are willing to till the soil; not the millionaires who buy off politicians and the Senator Eastlands who collect annuities without lifting a boll weevil.

Or housing programs which are not designed for investors looking for tax write-offs but for the poor people who need housing.‡

† The General Accounting Office (GAO) reported in 1970 that urban renewal—two decades and seven billion dollars later—has achieved a net loss of 315,000 housing units with 3.5 units destroyed for each new one built. Needless to say, very few low-income tenants who were displaced made their way into the new housing.

‡ On March 29, 1972, Dun & Bradstreet, nine other corporations, and forty individuals (including an officer of D&B and an official of the Federal Housing Authority, FHA) were indicted by the U.S. Government in an alleged multimillion-dollar housing fraud scheme.

The five-hundred-count indictment accused: real estate speculators, brokers, lawyers, appraisers, and bribed FHA employees of conspiring to falsify credit records and appraisals—among other violations. The victimized families were all low-income, particularly black and Puerto Rican.

On the same day Anthony Accetta, the assistant U.S. attorney who pre-

It can begin with economic development programs that are designed not for the white corporate liberals but for those individuals—be they black, tan, white, or red—who lack capital.

All of this is wishful thinking unless one deals with the problem of control. After eight years of the Great Society and what came after, few people can believe but that the answer to the question of who controls a public program also gives the answer to the question of who benefits. All of the programs and policies and proposals of all of the bureaucrats, professors, politicians, and corporate liberals in the nation will have no significant impact on our racial and economic troubles unless those who propose the programs are willing to address the question of control.

Black Capitalism is a species of a GOP form of humbug, but there is more at stake than Republican hypocrisy. The real assumption behind all the game-playing and noise-making (and the Democrats have their own names for it like Concentrated Employment Programs, etc.) is that the race issue in America is "essentially" economic, or socio-economic, or "really" psychological or anything else other than what it really is. It is basically a political problem and therefore susceptible to political solutions. The issues are citizen participation, community control and self-government, and the common role of both parties is to make people forget what is at stake.

Therefore, on both economic and political grounds, the approach represented by community development corporations, co-ops, and similar community-controlled institutions makes a hell of a lot more sense than does the tired old Nixon-Stans model of the single entrepreneur. As an economic institution CDCs can pool the scarce resources and talents of the low-income minority community to achieve larger and more efficient projects: shop-

---

sented the case to the Federal grand jury, said: "I don't see how anyone who is black or Puerto Rican could have faith in the white system after being shaken down like this and then losing his house two months later . . . The low-income Italians I grew up with were the same kind of people as the Puerto Rican and blacks being victimized here—basically hard-working individuals trying to get ahead in a new country."

Investigatory reporters have uncovered scandals in Oakland, Philadelphia, Chicago, St. Louis, Wilmington, Miami, and Berkeley, among other cities (New York *Times,* March 30, 1972, p. 1).

ping centers instead of "mom-and-pop" stores, a manufacturing facility instead of a shoeshine shop, a restaurant chain instead of an exploitive fast food franchise.

Because they are controlled by the people in the minority community, CDCs have the incentive to see to it that the benefits from economic development programs that they sponsor will go to the people of the community, not to one sharp minority businessman, or to a downtown bank or developer, or to massage the social conscience of the Vice-President in charge of Public Relations at some large corporation.

CDCs can offer minority people an institutional way to translate political power into economic power. A CDC can be subsidized like other American corporations. It can receive Government contracts. It can operate as a land developer. It can combine the best techniques of business and management and do it within the context of a policy of sound and sane community development. It can have a humanizing effect on individuals who are being crushed by the inherent brutalities of a technological revolution that is also destroying our air, land, water, wildlife, and civility.

Private business corporations receive favors because of their ability to furnish personnel to Federal agencies to bribe politicians and to contribute money to political campaigns regardless of: their lack of competition, price-rigging, false advertising, inefficiency, mismanagement, waste, pollutant habits, and shoddy products. Jesse Unruh, former speaker of the California House, once said that "money is the mother's milk of politics." And it is through such nourishment that corporations grow. Since CDCs represent poor people, they have no money to spend on political campaigns. But they do have votes, and through the democratic process CDCs can demand economic favors in return.

But while CDCs may make some sense for minorities, they do not suit those who represent corporate America. Theodore Cross calls them "quasi-socialistic"; a Nixon official in the Office of Economic Opportunity complains that they are not consistent with the "Protestant ethic," and Maurice Stans dismisses them as not being in the mainstream of American business. The flavor of a community development corporation is too political for the tastes of the Nixon "liberals." These are the same people who do not bat an eyelash when the Administration announces that it has to suspend investigation of AT&T's annual expenses ($14 billion) and its $50 billion investments in plant and equipment, for want of enough staff positions at the FCC.*

Thus, the "piece of the action" Richard Nixon was selling blacks was not a piece of white corporate America's action. It was a piece the corporations had long since thrown away repackaged in a new label.

And sell it they did. The following quotes are from an article by one Vincent Capozzi, which appeared in the December 1971 issue of *Black Business Digest*. The magazine has a picture of Richard Nixon on the cover and it was bought up in great quantities and distributed by the Maurice Stans's Department of Commerce.

The article is entitled "Jesus Christ, Businessman." It begins by describing Jesus as the entrepreneur of a successful, small carpentry shop. He treated his employees fairly, but his parables show that he knew they often were unappreciative of an employer's generosity. "Of course," says Mr. Capozzi, "Jesus did not have to contend with labor unions as would a present-day employer if he were to behave like the landowner of the parable."

Jesus had his problems with "wholesalers and various middlemen." And "Nazareth was not particularly affluent so his prices, his markup, had to be extremely modest." What about driving the money-changers from the Temple? "Yes," says Mr. Capozzi, "Jesus did his share of haggling; he had to in a world where even his own people exploited their brothers. Yet, we can safely conclude that he was a successful small businessman, and again the Gospel so implies . . . Indeed, directors of today's large corporations would do well to study the techniques of the man who founded the world's largest corporation." Jesus, we learn, "test-marketed" his "new venture" among the Jews. John the Baptist was his "advance man." His preaching was a "full-fledged sales campaign." Jesus served as "Chairman of the Board" of the new corporation and the Last Supper was their "stockholders meeting."

That such tasteless drivel could be handed out to black people as an inspirational text for Richard Nixon's Black Capitalism reveals the contempt which the people running the administration's program had for those they were purporting to help.

---

* See Appendix for AT&T assets, et al.

If there is one lesson that can be clearly drawn from the bizarre quackery of this Administration, it is that no minority or low-income person can rely on benefits from such people. In point of fact, almost every economic gain that racial minorities achieved in this country has been a result of political organizing rather than a result of people in the establishment "getting religion." It was not until three hundred thousand people marched in the streets of Washington that the Kennedy Administration endorsed civil rights legislation. It was the need for black votes that began Lyndon Johnson's War on Poverty. It was riots in the streets that induced businessmen in cities where there were riots to hire a few more blacks in their plants. And it was the lack of any political incentive to deliver benefits to minorities that resulted in the Nixon Administration's doing so little for the blacks.

Black Capitalism offers nothing for the political development of minority people. Moreover, it tends to undermine political development in two important ways. First, it tends to break up political unity. Black Capitalism offers a vision of personal rewards for minority leaders who leave their concern for their community and strike out on their own as entrepreneurs. And in fact in every ghetto community there are those who in the last three years have declared that they have given enough of their life to the cause and now they are going to get "theirs" in black business. Given that there is not all that much to get in black business, the defector often returns to the fold soon enough, but his credibility for leadership is often permanently damaged.

Secondly, Black Capitalism, like any program focused exclusively on minority people, tends to isolate them from other disadvantaged people who in the long run will be their best allies. The political structure of Black Capitalism is an attempted alliance between corporations and blacks. The Wyly committee was the symbol of such an alliance. Well-publicized MESBICs and franchise programs are the substance of it. Although these projects and committees have not produced much for minorities, the visibility of such projects engenders a reaction among whites who also feel themselves to be disadvantaged. People complain to their politicians that blacks are getting advantages that they never had. As a result, the politicians limit the amount of aid that they will give to the blacks. Conversations with people black and white, critics and supporters of the Administration's program constantly referred to the "political realities" which prevented the Administration from doing more for black businesses. Yet these realities were a direct result of the way the program was structured and publicized!

In SBA offices all over the country white applicants have been told that they could not be financed because priorities were being given to blacks. Thus it appeared that marginal white businessmen were being asked to pay for a program to support marginal black businessmen. And as both white and black unemployment increased because of Nixon's economic policies, aid to black businessmen was touted as being the Administration's major antipoverty program. A reaction from lower income whites was inevitable. The Johnson Administration did the same thing. Its much-heralded employment programs to give blacks jobs were paid for by white workers who suffered more unemployment. It is a measure of the power of large corporations that both political parties would risk alienating an important constituency (Democratic workers, Republican small businessmen) rather than ask the powerful corporations to pay for social progress.

Nixon Administration officials claim that Black Capitalism was not viewed as an antipoverty program. But it was funds from the War on Poverty that were used to set up the Office of Minority Enterprise, and to pay for the staff of the Wyly Council. And while the Administration was recommending $40 million for Black Capitalism, it was cutting the budget of the Office of Economic Opportunity by $100 million. And finally, Nixon himself, in his message to Congress of October 13, 1971, claimed that his minority enterprise effort was "the best way to fight poverty." Black Capitalism was paid for not by the corporation men who ran it and advised how to run it, but by the poor of all colors.

As one prominent academic economist put it, "The Democrats always want to put a nickel in the pot and the Republicans always want to take another nickel out." But, it's always the same pot!

The political lesson is clear. Minorities will not achieve equality by eating the discarded scraps from the ideological table of big business. They will achieve it through the use of political power which, because they are minorities, will necessitate alliances with those whites whose objectives are the same: the poor and the working people. They are both being screwed by the same system, in slightly different ways. This alliance, to be sure, is a more difficult road. It requires educating whites as well as working with them. Poor and working-class whites can be racist and suspicious—exploited and kept in ignorance from the same source as blacks. But if this analysis of the motives and performance of corporate liberalism is anywhere near accurate, then there is no other choice.

One incident, in the state of Mississippi in the fall of 1971, suggests that in terms of alliances between black and white people, times may be changing.

The pulp wood cutters of the South are perhaps the most exploited entrepreneurs in the nation. They cut and haul wood for sale to the large pulp and paper corporations—St. Regis Paper, Masonite, International Paper, Scott Paper, etc. They usually work in the lands owned by the corporation, they get their credit through the corporations, they buy all supplies and equipment through the corporations, and they even have to maintain much of the roadways through the corporations' land at their own expense in order to get at the wood.

The following is one description of the life of such an entrepreneur in Mississippi:

> Sitting on the front porch of his home, Leroy talked about the paper-wood business. There was a time, several years ago, when he had his own truck. He had a crew of three or four men, but he didn't do much better than he is doing now.
>
> Having no established credit, he had accepted a dealer's offer to co-sign loans and finance equipment for him. He was to pay the dealer, who in turn paid the bank or finance company. When he cashed in his tickets at a dealer's office, there were deductions for equipment, gas, severance tax, and assorted other necessities which he had financed through the dealer.
>
> By the time he received his check, he had enough to give every man on his crew between $30 and $50 for a week's work. (A week generally means 48–60 hours.) He seldom got that much himself.
>
> He has never seen statements from banks or finance companies at which dealers co-signed loans for him. The dealers seemed to keep deducting. As he put it, "You'd have to be an expert bookkeeper to figure out how they charge you."
>
> When Leroy realized that he'd never make a living by paying most of his earnings on an account every week, he decided to join his

brother's crew. The one dealer to whom Leroy owed the greatest amount sued him. He had tried to persuade Leroy to sign his truck over to the company and keep cutting. But Wilson refused.

Other cutters around South Alabama told Leroy that this same dealer had told other dealers "not to accept any wood from Leroy Wilson." Finally, in an apparent last-ditch effort to keep Wilson on the company's debt book, in a final stab at his freedom, the dealer's attorney told him that he could probably "work off this account gradually provided you put on wood for him [the dealer]."

According to the corporations, Leroy Wilson is an independent businessman. His office is a pulpwood truck; his filing cabinet is his billfold stuffed with settlement sheets; his coffee breaks are irregular—they come when his truck breaks down or his chain saw jumps off its sprocket; his capital is his back; and his profits do not exist.

As he says: "You get what they want to give you, and it ain't a living."[2]

One black cutter is quoted as saying: "It's worse than sharecropping. A sharecropper could at least get a mess of greens or a piece of meat from his Man, but a woodcutter can't get nothing in a woodyard—not even a drink of water."

The average annual earnings of the woodcutters has been about $2,500 per year. And in the summer of 1971 the Masonite Corporation cut back the prices it was paying to the cutters by 25 percent.

The Office of Minority Business Opportunity did not of course interest itself in the plight of these businessmen. The cutters, black and white, joined together in the Gulfcoast Pulpwood Association and called a strike. The strike was long and bitter. The Association members were harassed, threatened, and "red-baited" by the corporations and the local officials.

During the strike Charlie Evers, the black man running for Governor of Mississippi in the fall of 1971, visited the cutters. The only politician who dared. Said one white woodcutter: "I live over the line in Alabama, where I vote for George Wallace. If I lived in Mississippi, I'd vote for Charlie Evers." Evers even went to Washington and badgered Federal officials to permit surplus food to go to strikers' families.

Evers lost the election, as expected. But the woodcutters won the strike. And perhaps for the first time in recent years, these small, independent "businessmen" acted on the premise that the difference between their skins was not as important as the same emptiness in their stomachs.

Black Capitalism? Hardly. But perhaps it is the beginning of something much more important. For at this writing, America is gearing up for a new Presidential campaign. In board rooms and union halls, cocktail parties and political clubs, garden affairs and street corner rallies throughout the nation, the "haves" of America are putting up the funds to bankroll another quadrennial election carnival.

What are all those people paying for? "A piece of the action," of course. When the votes are in and the last blurry-eyed political analyst has read the last computer projection, the game will begin anew. A new administration—or a replay of the last one—will once again sell the American public another acronym. It may be called a PROGRAM TO GET AMERICA MOVING AGAIN or it might be called FREE ENTERPRISE TO ENHANCE SELF-RESPECT, but Law and Order (with fear feeding hate) will still be the underlying issue.

It does not necessarily have to be that way. Perhaps more blacks and whites will do what the pulp wood cutters are trying to do. Perhaps they won't elect another slick huckster to the White House. Perhaps some of those millions of people who have lived through the obscenity of the War on Poverty and the horror of the War in Southeast Asia will finally see through the veils of fog that place blame for their troubles on caricatures of uppity blacks, dumb cops, and lazy bureaucrats as causes, and look beyond to the glass-and-steel-encased corporations. Perhaps some day Americans will demand that these same corporate fortresses of glass and steel open their doors—both to let the rest of us in to see what is going on and to free those trapped inside. Perhaps. But one thing is sure—the star-spangled hustle will not stop of its own accord. It will not stop when it has taken enough because it can never have enough. It will continue to trade on the misery and the frustration of black, brown, yellow, red, and white Americans as it has in the past. For in the America of Richard Nixon and others like him who have sat in the White House, the piece of the action goes to those that put up a piece of the cash.

A buck for a buck—the American way.

APPENDIX

TABLE 1. COMPARISON OF NUMBER OF FIRMS AND BUSINESS RECEIPTS OF MINORITY-OWNED FIRMS TO TOTAL BUSINESS ACTIVITY

Industry division	Firms (1,000)						
		All minorities		Negro		Spanish-speaking	
	Number of all firms[1]	Number of firms	Percent of all firms	Number of firms	Percent of all firms	Number of firms	Percent of all firms
ALL INDUSTRIES, TOTAL...	7,489	322	4.3	163	2.2	100	1.3
Contract construction........	856	30	3.5	16	1.9	10	1.2
Manufactures	401	8	2.0	3	.8	4	1.0
Transportation and other public utilities	359	24	6.7	17	4.7	5	1.4
Wholesale trade	434	5	1.2	1	.2	2	.5
Retail trade	2,046	97	4.7	45	2.2	33	1.6
Finance, insurance, and real estate	1,223	22	1.8	8	.6	8	.7
Selected services...........	1,803	101	5.6	56	3.1	29	1.6
Other industries and not classified	367	35	9.5	17	4.5	9	2.5

Industry division	Receipts (million dollars)						
		All minorities		Negro		Spanish-speaking	
	Receipts of all firms[1]	Receipts	Percent of all receipts	Receipts	Percent of all receipts	Receipts	Percent of all receipts
ALL INDUSTRIES, TOTAL...	1,497,969	10,639	.7	4,474	.3	3,360	.2
Contract construction	92,291	947	1.0	464	.5	300	.3
Manufactures	588,682	650	.1	303	.1	212	(Z)
Transportation and other public utilities	106,040	395	.4	211	.2	115	.1
Wholesale trade	213,196	939	.4	385	.2	275	.1
Retail trade	320,751	5,178	1.6	1,932	.6	1,689	.5
Finance, insurance, and real estate	86,670	539	.6	288	.3	109	.1
Selected services...........	61,858	1,464	2.4	663	1.1	507	.8
Other industries and not classified	28,481	527	1.8	228	.8	153	.5

(Z) Less than .05 percent.
[1] Based on data from IRS statistics of income for 1967.

Source: U.S. Department of Commerce: Bureau of the Census.

TABLE 2. COMPARISON OF AVERAGE RECEIPTS FOR MINORITY-OWNED FIRMS WITH AND WITHOUT PAID EMPLOYEES

Item	Total	Negro	Spanish-speaking
All minority-owned firms:			
Number 1,000	322	163	100
Receipts .... million dollars	10,639	4,474	3,360
Firms with paid employees:			
Number 1,000	90	38	33
Receipts .... million dollars	8,934	3,653	2,814
Receipts per firm $1,000	99	95	86
Firms with no paid employees:			
Number 1,000	232	125	67
Receipts .... million dollars	1,705	821	546
Receipts per firm $1,000	7	7	8

Source: U.S. Department of Commerce: Bureau of the Census.

TABLE 3. METROPOLITAN AREAS WITH LARGEST NUMBERS OF MINORITY-OWNED FIRMS: 1969

Black-owned		Spanish-speaking owned	
City	Number	City	Number
Chicago	8,747	Los Angeles/Long Beach	11,218
Los Angeles/Long Beach	8,318	New York	5,468
Washington, D.C.	7,768	San Antonio	4,117
New York	7,753	Miami	3,447
Philadelphia	6,246	San Francisco/Oakland	3,158

Source: U.S. Department of Commerce: Bureau of the Census.

TABLE 4. TEN MOST IMPORTANT INDUSTRY GROUPS OF MINORITY-OWNED FIRMS RANKED BY RECEIPTS: 1969

Industry group	Rank	Firms (number)	Receipts (million dollars)	Rank	Firms (number)	Receipts (million dollars)	Rank	Firms (number)	Receipts (million dollars)
	All minority-owned firms			Black			Spanish-speaking		
Food stores	1	22,492	1,493	2	11,268	438	1	6,378	373
Automotive dealers and gasoline filling stations	2	12,086	1,181	1	6,380	631	2	4,087	315
Eating and drinking places	3	27,318	953	4	14,125	360	4	7,518	265
Wholesale trade	4	5,479	939	3	1,660	385	3	2,300	274
Miscellaneous retail stores	5	13,527	584	7	6,412	278	6	3,800	125
Special trade contractors	6	22,890	549	6	13,477	284	5	6,683	172
Personal services	7	53,252	532	5	33,906	288	7	10,701	123
Laundry and drycleaning plants	—	9,113	159	—	4,296	74	—	1,122	21
Beauty shops	—	18,589	125	—	13,548	55	—	3,312	45
Barber shops	—	15,118	96	—	9,469	50	—	4,079	33
General building contractors	8	4,164	282	8	2,359	140	8	1,164	68
Trucking and warehousing	9	10,988	229	9	7,252	134	10	2,933	61
Real estate	10	13,140	222	—	—	—	9	3,900	65
Insurance carrier	—	—	—	10	104	133	—	—	—
Agricultural services	—	—	—	—	—	—	—	—	—

READY OR NOT

A *Reality Study*

Carl Davids is an entrepreneur in the classic mold. For ten years he worked for wages at progressively more skilled metal-working jobs. In 1966 he quit his position as a shop foreman and opened his own shop—"CD Products." He had $20,000—three thousand that he had saved, two thousand invested by friends, and fifteen thousand as a loan from the Small Business Administration.

He used his funds prudently and profitably, buying the necessary machinery and equipment, at first hiring only his wife to help him. Orders were heavy since there was a large demand for the lamp bases and parts which CD makes. He got orders, filled them, paid his bills, and met his payroll—which had grown by 1969 to twenty-one full- and part-time employees.

Mr. and Mrs. Davids are still working twelve-hour days and six-day weeks, but CD Products is their own so they deem it worth the effort. An enterprising, hard-working, and ambitious businessman such as Carl Davids would seem marked for ever higher financial rewards and for wholehearted acceptance in the financial community. But CD Products is in Bedford-Stuyvesant—a "high-risk zone"—and Carl Davids is a black man.

Mr. Davids has found working capital so hard to obtain that he can accept orders only from buyers who promise immediate cash—at discount rates. More profitable accounts are sometimes not paid for a month or two; Davids cannot meet his weekly expenses if he must wait that long for payment.

He was rejected for loans at Harlem's black-owned banks. Their funds are low and other borrowers are able to put up more collateral than Davids—though he is willing to accept a lien on his machinery. An official at one of these banks offered Mr. Davids his loan in exchange for 33 percent ownership in CD Products. Mr. Davids refused.

He was also rejected by every "white" bank he approached, despite his CPA-audited records showing his past economic performance, his outstanding character references, and $25,000 *in orders* from reputable department stores and distributors. Even the bank in which he keeps his personal and payroll accounts has turned him down. No banker has ever offered Davids a reason for his refusal.

A Capital Formation volunteer was able to get answers when he pursued the matter. Mr. Davids once co-signed a personal loan for a friend who later defaulted on payment; Davids has consequently been labeled a credit risk. Davids suggested that he could pay the $992 if he got the funds he was trying to raise. No banker has accepted this way of removing Davids' credit-risk brand. After nine months of continued effort, Davids received a $25,000 SBA-guaranteed loan from a Harlem bank. He is still undercapitalized.

Manuel Esposito left his native Puerto Rico after high school graduation. On arriving in New York he found work in a Bronx sheet metal shop, soon becoming a skilled welder. He put this skill to work after hours, doing piecework in a garage to earn extra money.

Esposito's initiative and hard work were noticed by his employer and by several organizations that promote minority-owned businesses. The employer offered to help back him in setting up a spin-off business of his own, and the service organizations helped Esposito get an SBA start-up loan of $20,000.

His former boss had a contract for Air Force missile container assemblies, a portion of which he subcontracted to Esposito to get him started. This subcontract accounted for almost all of the first year's $140,000 gross. Seventeen men, mostly Puerto Ricans, were hired to do the work. Esposito taught all these untrained men to be skilled metal-workers like himself.

But as the Air Force contract neared fulfillment, Esposito found no new contracts to sustain his level of operations. The payroll was cut to five and he had to take a personal loan from his former boss just to keep going at this level.

A volunteer from Capital Formation and a JPM professional agreed to launch a campaign of phone calls and letters to potential customers. They made seventy-six phone calls to twenty-six major corporations, following up with letters to the few corporate presidents and purchasing agents who expressed interest.

Out of all this, four major companies made inspections of Esposito's facilities preliminary to certifying him as a supplier. Bids have been submitted to these four companies, but as one company has indicated —if there are no snags at all—their vendor screening process will take a minimum of a hundred working days before any contract award could be made, and that the long-awaited contract would be only a $500 to $1,000 pilot award to test his performance.

Esposito is trying to keep his reduced staff going by picking up quick piecework in his neighborhood.[1]

[1] JPM Associates, Inc., and Capital Formation.

FOR BUSINESSES AND INVESTORS[1]

	Tax Loss to Government (*millions of dollars*)
Lower tax rate on first $25,000 of annual corporate earnings	$2,000
Deductions for percentage depletion, exploration and development costs	$1,305
Tax credit for investment in machinery and equipment	$ 910
Special treatment of farmers' investments, expenses	$ 820
Deductions for research and development	$ 540
Rapid write-offs of factories, other nonrental buildings	$ 500
Capital gains of corporations	$ 425
"Excess" allowance for bad-debt reserves of financial institutions	$ 380
Special benefits for corporations doing business abroad	$ 350
Rapid depreciation on rental properties	$ 255
Capital-gains treatment on sales of timber	$ 130
Rapid depreciation on rail freight cars	$ 105
Tax exemption for credit-union earnings	$ 40
Fast write-offs for outlays on pollution controls	$ 15
Postponement of taxes on shipping lines	$ 10
Capital-gains treatment on coal and ore royalties	$ 5

Source: House Ways and Means Committee.

The above table represents estimates made by the Treasury or the amounts of taxes lost to Government during the fiscal year ending June 30, 1971. They were singled out as tax subsidies by staff members of the Joint Economic Committee.

[1] U. S. NEWS & WORLD REPORT, December 27, 1971, p. 30.

DIVIDING UP THE NEW TAX CUTS[2]

TAX REDUCTIONS UNDER THE NEW LAW START TAKING EFFECT ON
1971 INCOME, AND WILL BRING GREATER SAVINGS IN FUTURE YEARS.
FOR A LOOK AT THE IMPACT THROUGH 1973—

Tax savings to individuals	*1971*	*1972*	*1973*	*Total, 3 years*
Cuts in income taxes	$1.4 bil.	$3.4 bil.	$1.2 bil.	$6 bil.
End of excise tax on cars and small trucks	$800 mil.	$2.3 bil.	$2.0 bil.	$5.1 bil.
Investment credit for individual businessmen	$300 mil.	$700 mil.	$800 mil.	$1.8 bil.
New depreciation rules for individual businessmen	$200 mil.	$400 mil.	$500 mil.	$1.1 bil.
Tax savings to corporations	*1971*	*1972*	*1973*	*Total, 3 years*
New investment credit	$1.2 bil.	$2.9 bil.	$3.1 bil.	$7.2 bil.
New depreciation rules	$500 mil.	$1.3 bil.	$1.9 bil.	$3.7 bil.
End of excise tax on cars and small trucks	$100 mil.	$300 mil.	$200 mil.	$600 mil.
Tax deferment for domestic international-sales corporations	—	$100 mil.	$200 mil.	$300 mil.

TOTAL TAX CUTS OVER THREE YEARS

1971	*1972*	*1973*	*Total, 3 Years*
$4.5 bil.	$11.4 bil.	$9.9 bil.	$25.8 bil.

Source: House Ways and Means Committee.

[2] Ibid., p. 26.

BELL SYSTEM FINANCIAL CONNECTIONS IN 1965
192 billion dollars worth of interlocking connections

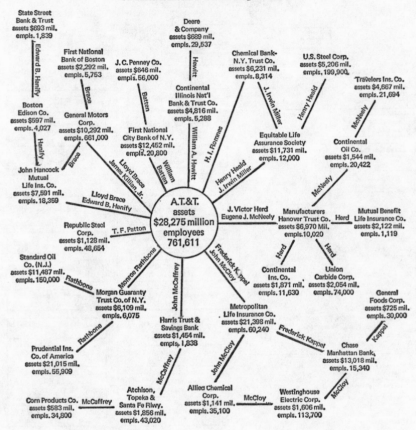

A.T.&T. directors are also directors of many other smaller corporations, banks, and insurance companies.

Sources:
Poor's Register of Directors and Executives, 1965
Standard & Poor's Standard Corp. Descriptions, 1965
Moody's Banks & Finance, 1965
A.T.&T. Annual Report, 1964

BELL SYSTEM STRUCTURE[1]

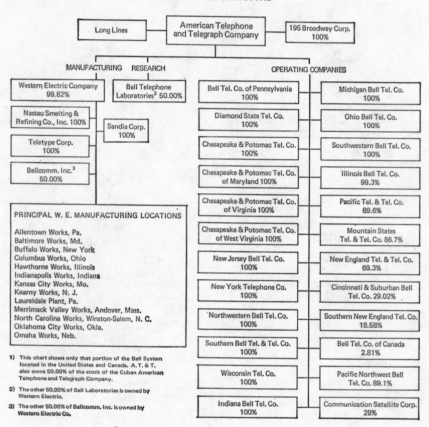

| Long Lines | American Telephone and Telegraph Company | 195 Broadway Corp. 100% |

MANUFACTURING RESEARCH

Western Electric Company 99.82%

Nassau Smelting & Refining Co., Inc. 100%

Teletype Corp. 100%

Bellcomm. Inc.[3] 50.00%

Bell Telephone Laboratories[2] 50.00%

Sandia Corp. 100%

OPERATING COMPANIES

Bell Tel. Co. of Pennsylvania 100%	Michigan Bell Tel. Co. 100%
Diamond State Tel. Co. 100%	Ohio Bell Tel. Co. 100%
Chesapeake & Potomac Tel. Co. 100%	Southwestern Bell Tel. Co. 100%
Chesapeake & Potomac Tel. Co. of Maryland 100%	Illinois Bell Tel. Co. 99.3%
Chesapeake & Potomac Tel. Co. of Virginia 100%	Pacific Tel. & Tel. Co. 89.6%
Chesapeake & Potomac Tel. Co. of West Virginia 100%	Mountain States Tel. & Tel. Co. 86.7%
New Jersey Bell Tel. Co. 100%	New England Tel. & Tel. Co. 69.3%
New York Telephone Co. 100%	Cincinnati & Suburban Bell Tel. Co. 29.02%
Northwestern Bell Tel. Co. 100%	Southern New England Tel. Co. 18.58%
Southern Bell Tel. & Tel. Co. 100%	Bell Tel. Co. of Canada 2.81%
Wisconsin Tel. Co. 100%	Pacific Northwest Bell Tel. Co. 89.1%
Indiana Bell Tel. Co. 100%	Communication Satellite Corp. 29%

PRINCIPAL W. E. MANUFACTURING LOCATIONS

Allentown Works, Pa.
Baltimore Works, Md.
Buffalo Works, New York
Columbus Works, Ohio
Hawthorne Works, Illinois
Indianapolis Works, Indiana
Kansas City Works, Mo.
Kearny Works, N. J.
Laureldale Plant, Pa.
Merrimack Valley Works, Andover, Mass.
North Carolina Works, Winston-Salem, N. C.
Oklahoma City Works, Okla.
Omaha Works, Neb.

1) This chart shows only that portion of the Bell System located in the United States and Canada. A. T. & T. also owns 50.00% of the stock of the Cuban American Telephone and Telegraph Company.

2) The other 50.00% of Bell Laboratories is owned by Western Electric.

3) The other 50.00% of Bellcomm. Inc. is owned by Western Electric Co.

Sources:
A.T.&T. Annual Report, 1964
Western Electric Annual Report, 1964
Moody's Public Utilities, 1965
Standard & Poor's Standard Corp. Descriptions, 1965

THE DOZEN BIGGEST U.S. FOUNDATIONS

Name	Assets
1. Ford Foundation	$2,902,000,000
2. Robert Wood Johnson Foundation	$1,100,000,000
3. Lilly Endowment	$ 778,000,000
4. Rockefeller Foundation	$ 757,000,000
5. Duke Endowment	$ 510,000,000
6. Kresge Foundation	$ 433,000,000
7. W. K. Kellogg Foundation	$ 393,000,000
8. Charles S. Mott Foundation	$ 371,000,000
9. Pew Memorial Trust	$ 367,000,000
10. Alfred P. Sloan Foundation	$ 303,000,000
11. Carnegie Corporation of New York	$ 283,000,000
12. John A. Hartford Foundation	$ 277,000,000

Note: Assets as of 1970, except those of Johnson Foundation, which were announced December 6. Source: Foundation Library Center

REFERENCES

Chapter 1

[1] Harold D. Lasswell, *World Politics and Personal Insecurity* (New York: The Free Press, 1965), p. 3.

[2] For an excellent history of the role business in politics see: Edwin M. Epstein, *The Corporation in American Politics* (Englewood Cliffs, N.J.: Prentice-Hall, 1969).

[3] For further information regarding the military-industrial complex see: Dr. Ralph Lapp, *The Weapons Culture* (Baltimore, Md.: Penguin Books, Inc., 1969).

Chapter 2

[1] Joe McGinniss, *The Selling of the President, 1968* (New York: Trident Press, 1969), p. 68.

[2] Ibid., p. 266–72.

[3] Ibid., p. 120–21.

[4] Andrew Shonfield, *Modern Capitalism* (London: Oxford University Press, 1966), p. 298.

[5] Burton R. Fisher and Stephen B. Withey, *Big Business as the People See It* (Ann Arbor, Mich.: The Survey Research Center Institute for Social Research, University of Michigan, University of Michigan Press, 1951), p. 20.

[6] *Divided We Stand* (San Francisco: Canfield Press, a Department of Harper & Row, 1970).

Chapter 3

[1] Mike Royko, *Boss: Richard J. Daley of Chicago* (New York: Signet, 1971), p. 26.

[2] James Heibrun and Stanislaw Wellisz, "An Economic Program for the Ghetto," *Urban Riots* (New York: Vintage Books, 1968), p. 82.

[3] Lester Thurow, *Poverty and Discrimination* (Washington: Brookings Institution, 1969), p. 158.

Chapter 4

[1] For a detailed description of the bill and its political history see: John McClaughry, "Black Ownership and National Politics," in Haddad and Pugh, ed., *Black Economic Development*, The American Assembly, (Englewood Cliffs, N.J.: Prentice-Hall, 1969).

[2] See Roy Innis, "Separatist Economics: A New Social Contract" in Haddad and Pugh, op. cit., pp. 50–59.

[3] Kenneth B. Clark, *Dark Ghetto* (New York: Harper Torchbook, Harper & Row, 1967), p. 189.

[4] Ibid.

[5] Ibid., pp. 188–89.

[6] E. Franklin Frazier, *Black Bourgeoisie* (New York: Collier Books, The Macmillan Co., 1970), p. 141.

[7] Ibid., p. 145.

Chapter 5

[1] E. B. O'Callaghan, *Documents Relative to the Colonial History of New York*, IV, 510–11 (Signed: Earl of Bellmont, April 27, 1969).

[2] W. G. Sumner, *Folkways* (Boston, 1907), intro., iv.

[3] R. F. Foerster, *Italian Emigration of Our Times* (Cambridge, Mass.: 1938), p. 334; R. S. Baker, "The Negro Struggle for Survival," *North American Magazine* (1907–08), pp. 65, 479.

[4] E. F. Frazier, "A Negro Industrial Group" in *Howard Review*, June 1924, p. 198; Barnes, op. cit., p. 9.

[5] L. H. Butterfield, W. D. Garrett, and M. R. Sprague, eds., *The Adams Papers* (New York: Atheneum, 1964), cited in *Life* Magazine, July 25, 1963, p. 4.

[6] Leon F. Litwack, *North of Slavery: The Negro in the Free States, 1790–1860* (Chicago: University of Chicago Press, 1965).

[7] Leon F. Litwack, "The Emancipation of the Negro Abolitionist" in Martin B. Duberman, ed., *The Antislavery Vanguard* (Princeton, N.J.: Princeton University Press, 1965), pp. 141–43.

[8] J. M. McPherson, *Struggle for Equality* (Princeton, N.J.: Princeton University Press, 1964), p. 233.

[9] Quoted in E. L. Franklin, *The Negro Labor Unionist in New York* (New York: 1936), p. 21.

[10] C. Vann Woodward, "The Political Legacy of Reconstruction," *The Journal of Negro Education*, XXVI (1957), pp. 231–40.

[11] "The Awakening of the Negro," *The Atlantic Monthly*, LXXVII, September 1896, p. 326. Reprinted in *Booker T. Washington*, ed. by E. L. Thornbrough (Englewood Cliffs, N.J.: Spectrum, Prentice-Hall, 1969), p. 44.

[12] Andrew Carnegie, "The Negro in America." An address delivered before the Institute of Edinburgh (Inverness, 1907). Reprinted in Thornbrough, op. cit.

[13] W. E. B. DuBois, "Of Mr. Washington and Others" in *The Soul of Black Folk* (Chicago: 1903). Reprinted in Thornbrough, op. cit.

[14] Michael Zweig, "Black Capitalism and the Ownership of Property in Harlem" (August 1970), Stony Brook Working Papers.

[15] Quoted in Daniel Mitchell, *The Numbers and the Ghetto: An Opportunity for Change* (Cambridge, Mass.: Center for Community Economic Development, April 1970).

[16] Ibid.

[17] Representative William Clay, "Economics of Hustling . . . A Ghetto Blight" in the Boston *Globe*, December 21, 1971, p. 25.

[18] Andrew Hacker, "Introduction: Corporate America" in Andrew Hacker, ed., *The Corporation Take-Over* (New York: Harper & Row, 1964), pp. 7–8.

Chapter 6

[1] U.S. Congress, House. Select Committee on Small Business, Subcommittee Chairman's Report, *Tax Exempt: Foundations and Charitable Trusts.* 90th Cong. 2nd Sess. March 26, 1968, p. 2.

[2] Jules Cohn, *The Conscience of the Corporations* (Baltimore, Md.: The John Hopkins Press, 1971).

[3] R. A. Wright, "Beyond the Profits: Business Readies for a Social Role," in the New York *Times,* July 3, 1961: 1, Sect. 3.

[4] U.S. Office of Economic Opportunity, "Private Enterprise and the Office of Economic Opportunity" (Staff Paper, March 1965).

[5] New York *Times,* February 3, 1969.

[6] Andrew Hacker, "Introduction" in Andrew Hacker, ed., *The Corporation Take-Over* (New York: Harper & Row, 1964), pp. 3–5.

[7] Quoted by Robert Theobald, *Free Men and Free Markets* (New York: Clarkson N. Potter, 1963), pp. 36–37.

[8] Source: Life Insurance Institute of America, 1969.

[9] *Ready or Not,* by JPM Associates, Inc., and Capital Formation (1969), p. 7.

[10] For additional discussion of this point, see Earl F. Cheit, "Why Managers Cultivate Social Responsibility," *California Management Review,* VII, No. 1 (Fall 1964), pp. 3–22.

[11] An interview with Joseph P. Lyford, "The Establishment and All That," *The Center Magazine,* September 1968.

[12] Murray Kempton, "Land of Dreams," New York *Post,* May 14, 1967.

[13] Eugene P. Foley, *The Achieving Ghetto* (Washington, D.C.: The National Press, Inc., 1968).

[14] Jerry Carroll, *Big Mickey Mouse Law Suit*, San Francisco *Chronicle*, January 8, 1972, p. 4.

[15] Roger Rapoport, "Disney's War Against the Wilderness," *Ramparts*, November 1971.

[16] Rapoport, op. cit.

[17] Section 202A, Title II, Economic Opportunity Act of 1964.

[18] Ibid.

[19] Economic Opportunity Act, op. cit.

[20] The Congressional Record, Washington, August 2, 1968, Vol. 114, No. 137.

[21] The Congressional Record, loc. cit.

Chapter 9

[1] For more detailed descriptions of the characteristics of CDCs see *CDCs: New Hope for the Inner City*, Report of the Twentieth Century Fund Task Force on Community Development Corporations, The Twentieth Century Fund, New York, 1971, and "Profiles in Community-Based Economic Development," The Center for Community Economic Development, Cambridge, Mass., January 1971.

[2] Theodore Cross, *Black Capitalism* (New York: Atheneum, 1969), p. 15.

Chapter 10

[1] Rosenbloom and Shank, "Let's Write Off Mesbics," in *Harvard Business Review*, September–October 1970, p. 94.

[2] James K. Brown, "Arcata Investment Company: The Prototype Mesbic" in *Conference Board Record*, April 1970, p. 58.

[3] "The Impact of Franchising on Small Business." Hearing before the Subcommittee on Rural and Economic Development of the Select Committee on Small Business, U.S. Senate 91st Congress. Part 1. Page 259.

[4] "Stans Offers Pipedreams to Minorities," by Jack Anderson, Washington *Post*, July 13, 1970.

[5] Office of Minority Enterprise, "Accomplishments in Minority Business Development, 1969 to Date," mimeo, October 4, 1971, p. 3.

[6] Department of Commerce, Office of Minority Enterprise, "MESBIC Report—Summer of 1971," unpublished document, p. 2.

[7] Michael Harrington, *The Other America; Poverty in the United States* (New York: Macmillan, 1962).

[8] *Equal Opportunity in Farm Programs: An Appraisal of Services rendered by Agencies of the U.S. Department of Agriculture.* U.S. Commission of Civil Rights (1965).

9 In *Human Resources Development in the Rural South,* Center for the Study of Human Resources, The University of Texas, Austin, September 30, 1971.

Chapter 11

1 (*The Washington Monthly,* Vol. II, No. 10, December 1970, p. 18.)

2 *Wall Street Journal,* Monroe, W. Karwin, "Best Laid Plans . . ." December 24, 1970, p. 1.

3 Harold D. Lasswell, *Power and Personality* (New York: Compass Books, The Viking Press).

4 *Wall Street Journal,* op. cit.

5 (Phillip W. Moore, "What's Good for the Country Is Good for G.M.," *The Washington Monthly,* p. 13.)

6 *Business and Society,* Vol. 2, No. 15 (January 27, 1970), p. 2.

7 *Barron's National Business & Financial Weekly,* May 18, 1970.

8 *Business and Society,* loc. cit.

9 Quoted in the New York *Times,* January 11, 1970.

10 James Rowe, The Washington *Post,* July 12, 1971.

11 Ibid.

12 *Urban Read-Out,* November 16, 1971, p. 2.

13 *Business and Society,* Vol. 4, No. 9 (December 7, 1971).

14 Quoted in *Newsweek,* October 4, 1971.

15 The New York *Times,* January 9, 1972, p. 8.

16 For an incisive analysis see: Nat Goldfinger, "The Fast Write-Off Tax Gimmick," *The Federationist,* Vol. 78, No. 6.

17 Nick Kotz, *Let Them Eat Promises* (Garden City, N.Y.: Anchor Books, Doubleday & Company, Inc., 1971), pp. 198–200.

18 The New York *Times,* March 14, 1971. (Three days after his death.)

Chapter 12

1 "Shine Boy Wasn't the First Mistake" by Jonathan Cottin in *The Village Voice,* November 4, 1971.

2 *Anger in the Southern Pines,* Gulfcoast Pulpwood Association, Forest Home, Alabama, undated.